Prentice Hall

Algebra

Practice and Problem Solving Workbook

PEARSON

Boston, Massachusetts • Chandler, Arizona • Glenview, Illinois • Upper Saddle River, New Jersey

ISBN-13: 978-0-7854-7037-3
ISBN-10: 0-7854-7037-9
1 2 3 4 5 6 7 8 9 10   V084   13 12 11 10 09

Contents

Chapter 6

Chapter 7

Contents

Contents

Contents

1-1 Think About a Plan

Patterns and Expressions

Use the graph shown.

a. Identify a pattern of the graph by making a table of the inputs and outputs.

b. What are the outputs for inputs 6, 7, and 8?

1. What are the ordered pairs of the points in the graph?

_____

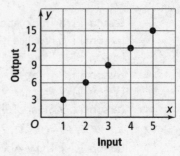

2. Complete the table of the input and output values shown in the ordered pairs.

Input	Output
1	
2	
3	
4	
5	

3. Complete the process column with the process that takes each input value and gives the corresponding output value.

Input	Process Column	Output
1	1( )	
2	2( )	
3	3( )	
4	4( )	
5	5( )	

4. output = _____

5. Complete the process column for inputs 6, 7, and 8. Then find the outputs for inputs 6, 7, and 8.

Input	Process Column	Output
6	6( )	
7	7( )	
8	8( )	

6. The outputs for inputs 6, 7, and 8 are _____

1-1 Practice

Form K

Patterns and Expressions

Describe each pattern using words. Draw the next figure in each pattern.

1.

2.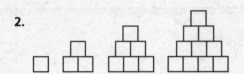

3.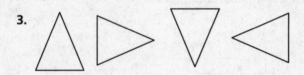

Make a table with a process column to represent the pattern. Write an expression for the number of circles in the *n*th figure. The table has been started for you.

4.

Figure Number (Input)	Process Column	Number of Circles (Output)
1	1(2)	2
2	2(2)	4
3	3(2)	
4		
■	■	■
n		

1-1 Practice (continued)

Patterns and Expressions

Form K

The graph shows the number of cups of flour needed for baking cookies.

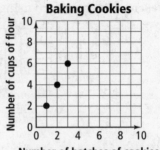

Baking Cookies

5. How many cups of flour are needed for baking 4 batches of cookies?

6. How many cups of flour are needed for baking 30 batches of cookies?

7. How many cups of flour are needed for baking *n* batches of cookies?

Identify a pattern by making a table. Include a process column.

Hint: To start, list the points on the graph. Make a table of input and output values shown in the ordered pairs. Use the process column to figure out the pattern.

8.

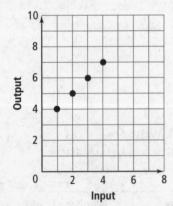

9.

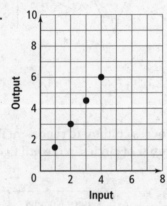

Identify the pattern and find the next three numbers in the pattern.

10. 1, 4, 16, 64, . . .

11. 3, 6, 12, 24, . . .

1-1 | Standardized Test Prep

Patterns and Expressions

Multiple Choice

For Exercises 1–5, choose the correct letter.

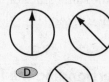

1. What is the next figure in the pattern at the right?

    A   B   C   D

2. Which is the next number in the table?

   F 14   H 15

   G 16   I 20

Input	Output
1	1
2	3
3	6
4	10
5	■

3. How many toothpicks would be in the tenth figure?

    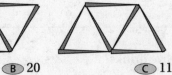

   A 21   B 20   C 11   D 23

4. What is the next number in the pattern?   2, 7, 12, 17, . . .

   F 21   G 22   H 23   I 27

5. What is the next number in the pattern?   1, −1, 2, −2, 3, . . .

   A −3   B 0   C 3   D 4

Short Response

6. Ramon has 25 books in his library. Each month, he adds 3 new books to his collection. How many books will Ramon have after 12 months?

1-2

Think About a Plan

Properties of Real Numbers

Five friends each ordered a sandwich and a drink at a restaurant. Each sandwich costs the same amount, and each drink costs the same amount. What are two ways to compute the bill? What property of real numbers is illustrated by the two methods?

Understanding the Problem

1. There are ☐ sandwiches and ☐ drinks on the bill.

2. What is the problem asking you to determine?

_____

_____

Planning the Solution

3. How can you represent the cost of five sandwiches?

_____

4. How can you represent the cost of five drinks?

_____

5. How can you represent the cost of the items ordered by one friend?

_____

Getting an Answer

6. Write an expression that represents the cost of five drinks and the cost of five sandwiches.

_____

7. Write an expression that represents the cost of the items ordered by five friends.

_____

8. What property of real numbers tells you that these two expressions are equal? Explain.

_____

1-2 Practice   *Form K*
Properties of Real Numbers

Classify each variable according to the set of numbers that best describes its values.

1. the number of students in your class
   To start, make a list of some numbers that could describe the number of students in your class.

2. the area of the circle A found by using the formula $A = \pi r^2$
   To start, make a list of some numbers that could describe the area of a circle.

3. the elevation e of various land points in the United States measured to the nearest foot
   To start, make a list of some numbers that could describe elevation levels.

Graph each number on a number line.

4. $5\frac{1}{2}$ 5. -4

6. 2.25 7. $-6\frac{1}{3}$

8. $\sqrt{8}$
   To start, use a calculator to approximate the square root.

Compare the two numbers. Use < or >.

9. $\sqrt{50}$ and 8.8 10. 5 and $\sqrt{23}$

11. 6.2 and $\sqrt{40}$ 12. $-\sqrt{3}$ and -3

1-2 Practice (continued)   *Form K*
Properties of Real Numbers

Name the property of real numbers illustrated by each equation.

13. $\frac{2}{3} \cdot \frac{3}{2} = 1$

14. $6(2 + x) = 6 \cdot 2 + 6 \cdot x$

15. $2 \cdot 20 = 20 \cdot 2$

16. $8 + (-8) = 0$

17. $2(0.5 \cdot 4) = (2 \cdot 0.5) \cdot 4$

18. $-11 + 5 = 5 + (-11)$

Estimate the numbers graphed at the labeled points.

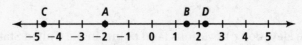

19. point A

20. point B

21. point C

22. point D

To find the length of the side b of the square base of a rectangular prism, use the formula $b = \sqrt{\frac{V}{h}}$, where V is the volume of the prism and h is the height. Which set of numbers best describes the value of b for the given values of V and h?

23. $V = 100, h = 1$

24. $V = 100, h = 10$

Write the numbers in increasing order.

25. $\frac{5}{6}, \sqrt{28}, -\frac{5}{2}, -0.8, 1$

26. $\frac{2}{3}, -4, \sqrt{32}, \sqrt{13}, -0.4$

1-2 Standardized Test Prep
Properties of Real Numbers

Multiple Choice

For Exercises 1–5, choose the correct letter.

1. Which letter on the graph corresponds to $\sqrt{5}$?

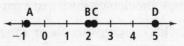

2. Which letter on the graph corresponds to -1.5?

What property of real numbers is illustrated by the equation?

3. $-6 + (6 + 5) = (-6 + 6) + 5$

    A Identity Property of Addition   C Commutative Property of Addition

    B Inverse Property of Addition   D Associative Property of Addition

4. $2(-4 + x) = 2(-4) + 2 \cdot x$

    F Associative Property of Multiplication   H Associative Property of Addition

    G Distributive Property   I Closure Property of Multiplication

5. Which of the following shows the numbers 13, 1.3, $1\frac{2}{7}$, -4, and $-\sqrt{10}$ in order from greatest to least?

    A 13, 1.3, $1\frac{2}{7}$, -4, $-\sqrt{10}$ C 13, $1\frac{2}{7}$, 1.3, $-\sqrt{10}$, -4

    B 13, 1.3, $1\frac{2}{7}$, $-\sqrt{10}$, -4 D -4, $-\sqrt{10}$, $1\frac{2}{7}$, 1.3, 13

Short Response

Geometry The length c of the hypotenuse of a right triangle with legs having lengths a and b is found by using the formula $c = \sqrt{a^2 + b^2}$. Which set of numbers best describes the value of c for the given values of a and b?

6. $a = 3, b = 4$

7. $a = \frac{1}{3}, b = \frac{1}{4}$

8. $a = \sqrt{3}, b = \sqrt{4}$

1-3 Think About a Plan

Algebraic Expressions

Write an algebraic expression to model the situation.

The freshman class will be selling carnations as a class project. What is the class's income after it pays the florist a flat fee of $200 and sells x carnations for $2 each?

1. What does the variable represent?

   _____

2. How will the class's income change for each carnation sold?

   _____

3. Will paying the florist increase or decrease their income? By how much?

   _____

4. Will the expression include both the income for each carnation and the florist's fee? Explain.

   _____

   _____

5. Write the expression in words.

   The   income   is   [   ]   and   [   ]   times   [   ] .

6. Write the expression using symbols.

   income   =   [   ]   [   ]   [   ]   [   ]   [   ]

7. Check your expression by substituting 300 for the number of carnations. Does your answer make sense? Explain.

   _____

   _____

8. The algebraic expression [   ] models the freshman class income.

1-3 Practice

Form K

Algebraic Expressions

Write an algebraic expression that models each word phrase.

1. six less than the number r

To start, relate what you know.   "Less than" means subtraction.
Describe what you need to find.   Begin with the number r and subtract 6.

2. twelve more than the number b

3. five times the sum of 3 and the number m

Write an algebraic expression that models each situation.

4. Alexis has $250 in her savings account and deposits $20 each week for w weeks.

5. You have 30 gallons of gas and you use 5 gallons per day for d days.

Evaluate each expression for the given values of the variables.

6. $-2a + 5b + 6a - 2b + a$; $a = -3$ and $b = 2$

To start, substitute the value
for each variable. $-2(-3) + 5(2) + 6(-3) - 2(2) + (-3)$

7. $y(3 - x) + x^2$; $x = 2$ and $y = 12$

8. $3(4e - 2f) + 2(e + 8f)$; $e = -3$ and $f = 10$

The expression $6s^2$ represents the surface area of a cube with edges of length s. What is the surface area of a cube with each edge length?

9. 4 centimeters   **10.** 2.5 feet

Lesson 1-3

1-3 **Practice** (continued)

Algebraic Expressions

Write an algebraic expression to model the total score in each situation.
Then evaluate the expression to find the total score.

11. In the first half, there were fifteen two-point shots, ten three-point shots and
5 one-point free throws.

To start, define your variables. Let $w =$ the number of two-point shots,
$r =$ the number of three-point shots, and $f =$ the number of one-point free throws.

12. In the first quarter, there were two touchdowns and 1 extra point kick.

Hint: A touchdown is worth 6 points. An extra point kick is worth 1 point.

Simplify by combining like terms.

13. $10b - b$

14. $12 + 8s - 3s$

15. $3a + 2b + 6a$

16. $5m + 2n + 6m + 4n$

17. $8r - (3s - 5r)$

18. $2.5y - 4y$

The expression $19.95 + 0.05x$ models a household's monthly Internet charges,
where x represents the number of online minutes during the month. What are
the monthly charges for each number of online minutes?

19. 65 minutes

20. 128 minutes

Evaluate each expression for the given value of the variable.

21. $3a + (2a + 6)$; $a = 2$

22. $x - 5(x + 2)$; $x = -5$

23. $-r + (3r^2 + 1)$; $r = 4$

24. $x^2 - 5(3x - 12)$; $x = 10$

1-3 Standardized Test Prep
Algebraic Expressions

Multiple Choice

For Exercises 1–3, choose the correct letter.

1. The expression $2\pi(rh + r^2)$ represents the total surface area of a cylinder with height h and radius r. What is the surface area of a cylinder with height 6 centimeters and radius 2 centimeters?

   (A) 16π cm^2 (C) 32π cm^2

   (B) 28π cm^2 (D) 96π cm^2

2. Which expression best represents the simplified form of $3(m - 3) + m(5 - m) - m^2$?

   (F) $-2m^2 + 8m - 9$ (H) $-2m^2 - 2m - 9$

   (G) $8m - 9$ (I) $-2m - 9$

3. The price of a discount airline ticket starts at $150 and increases by $30 each week. Which algebraic expression models this situation?

   (A) $30 + 150w$ (C) $30 - 150w$

   (B) $150 - 30w$ (D) $150 + 30w$

Extended Response

4. Members of a club are selling calendars as a fundraiser. The club pays $100 for a box of wall and desk calendars. They sell wall calendars for $12 and desk calendars for $8.

   a. Write an algebraic expression to model the club's profit from selling w wall calendars and d desk calendars. Explain in words or show work for how you determined the expression

   b. What is the club's profit from selling 9 wall calendars and 7 desk calendars? Show your work.

1-4

Think About a Plan

Solving Equations

Geometry The measure of the supplement of an angle is 20° more than three times the measure of the original angle. Find the measures of the angles.

Know

1. The sum of the measures of the two angles is ☐ .

2. What do you know about the supplemental angle?

_____

Need

3. To solve the problem, I need to define:

_____

_____

Plan

4. What equation can you use to find the measure of the original angle?

5. Solve the equation.

6. What are the measures of the angles?

7. Are the solutions reasonable? Explain.

_____

_____

1-4 Practice

Solving Equations

Form K

Solve each equation.

1. $5x + 4 = 2x + 10$
To start, subtract $2x$ from each side.

2. $10w - 3 = 8w + 5$
To start, subtract $8w$ from each side.

3. $4(d - 3) = 2d$

4. $s + 2 - 3s - 16 = 0$

Solve each equation. Check your answer.

5. $9(z - 3) = 12z$

6. $7y + 5 = 6y + 11$

7. $5w + 8 - 12w = 16 - 15w$

8. $3(x + 1) = 2(x + 11)$

Write an equation to solve each problem.

9. Lisa and Beth have babysitting jobs. Lisa earns \$30 per week and Beth earns \$25 per week. How many weeks will it take for them to earn a total of \$275?

To start, record what you know.	Lisa earns \$30 per week.
	Beth earns \$25 per week.
	Total earned: \$275
Describe what you need to find.	an equation to find the number of weeks it takes to earn \$275 together

10. The angles of a triangle are in the ratio 2 : 12 : 16. The sum of all the angles in a triangle must equal 180 degrees. What is the degree measure of each angle of the triangle? Let $x =$ the common factor.

11. What two consecutive numbers have a sum of 53?

Determine whether the equation is *always*, *sometimes*, or *never* true.

12. $3(2x - 4) = 6(x - 2)$

13. $4(x + 3) = 2(2x + 1)$

1-4 · Practice (continued) · Form K

Solving Equations

Solve each formula for the indicated variable.

14. $A = \frac{1}{2}bh$, for b

15. $P = 2w + 2l$, for w

16. $A = \frac{1}{2}h(b_1 + b_2)$, for h

17. $S = 2\pi rh + 2\pi r^2$, for h

Solve each equation for y.

18. $ry - sy = t$

19. $\frac{3}{7}(y + 2) = g$

20. $\frac{y}{m} + 3 = n$

21. $\frac{3y - 1}{2} = z$

Solve each equation.

22. $(x - 3) - 2 = 6 - 2(x + 1)$

23. $4(a + 2) - 2a = 10 + 3(a - 3)$

24. $2(2c + 1) - c = -13$

25. $8u + 2(u - 10) = 0$

26. The first half of a play is 35 minutes longer than the second half of the play. If the entire play is 155 minutes long, how long is the first half of the play? Write an equation to solve the problem.

Name _____ Class _____ Date _____

1-4 | Standardized Test Prep
Solving Equations

Gridded Response

Solve each exercise and enter your answer in the grid provided.

1. A bookstore owner estimates that her weekly profits p can be described by the equation $p = 8b - 560$, where b is the number of books sold that week. Last week the store's profit was \$720. What is the number of books sold?

2. What is the value of m in the equation $0.6m - 0.2 = 3.7$?

3. Three consecutive even integers have a sum of 168. What is the value of the largest integer?

4. If $6(x - 3) - 2(x - 2) = 11$, what is the value of x?

5. Your long distance service provider charges you \$.06 per minute plus a monthly access fee of \$4.95. For referring a friend, you receive a \$10 service credit this month. If your long-distance bill is \$7.85, how many long-distance minutes did you use?

Answers _____

1. 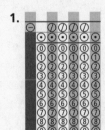 2. 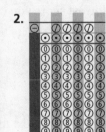 3. 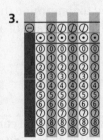 4. 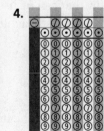 5.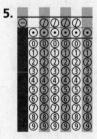

Lesson 1-4

1-5 Think About a Plan

Solving Inequalities

Your math test scores are 68, 78, 90, and 91. What is the lowest score you can earn on the next test and still achieve an average of at least 85?

Understanding the Problem

1. What information do you need to find an average of scores? How do you find an average?

   _____

   _____

2. How many scores should you include in the average? _____

3. You want to achieve an average that is [   ] or [   ] what score?

   _____

Planning the Solution

4. Assign a variable, x.

   _____

5. Write an expression for the sum of all of the scores, including the next test.

   _____

6. Write an expression for the average of all of the scores.

   _____

7. Write an inequality that can be used to determine the lowest score you can earn on the next test and still achieve an average of at least 85.

   _____

Getting an Answer

8. Solve your inequality to find the lowest score you can earn on the next test and still achieve an average of at least 85. What score do you need to earn?

1-5 Practice   *Form K*

Solving Inequalities

Write the inequality that represents the sentence.

1. Five less than a number is at least −28.

2. The product of a number and four is at most −10.

3. Six more than a quotient of a number and three is greater than 14.

Solve each inequality. Graph the solution.

4. $5a - 10 > 5$

To start, add 10 to each side.

5. $25 - 2y \geq 33$

6. $-2(n + 2) + 6 \leq 16$

7. $2(7a + 1) > 2a - 10$

Solve the following problem by writing an inequality.

8. The width of a rectangle is 4 cm less than the length. The perimeter is at most 48 cm. What are the restrictions on the dimensions of the rectangle?

To start, record what you know.   width: length − 4

perimeter: at most 48 cm

Describe what you need to find.   restrictions on the width and length of the rectangle

Is the inequality *always*, *sometimes*, or *never* true?

9. $5(x - 2) \geq 2x + 1$

10. $2x + 8 \leq 2(x + 1)$

11. $6x + 1 < 3(2x - 4)$

12. $2(3x + 3) > 2(3x + 1)$

1-5 Practice (continued)

Solving Inequalities

Solve each compound inequality. Graph the solution.

13. $2x > -4$ and $4x < 12$

To start, simplify each inequality. $x > -2$ and $x < 3$

Remember, "and" means that a solution makes BOTH inequalities true.

14. $3x \geq -12$ and $5x \leq 5$

15. $6x > 6$ and $9x \leq 45$

Solve each compound inequality. Graph the solution.

16. $3x < -9$ or $8x > -8$

To start, simplify each inequality. $x < -3$ or $x > -1$

Remember, "or" means that a solution makes EITHER inequality true.

17. $7x \leq -28$ or $2x > -2$

18. $3x > 3$ or $5x < 2x - 3$

Write an inequality to represent each sentence.

19. The average of Shondra's test scores in Physics is between 88 and 93.

20. The Morgans are buying a new house. They want to buy either a house more the 75 years old or a house less than 10 years old.

1-5 Standardized Test Prep

Solving Inequalities

Multiple Choice

For Exercises 1–5, choose the correct letter.

1. What is the solution of $4t - (3 + t) \le t + 7$?

   (A) $t \le \frac{5}{2}$ (B) $t \le 5$ (C) $t \le 2$ (D) $t \le 1$

2. What is the solution of $-17 - 2r < 3(r + 1)$?

   (F) $r > 4$ (G) $r > -20$ (H) $r < -4$ (I) $r > -4$

3. Which graph best represents the solution of $\frac{3}{4}(m + 4) > m + 3$?

   (A)   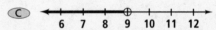   (C)

   (B)   (D) 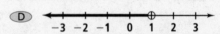

4. What is the solution of the compound inequality $4x < -8$ or $9x > 18$?

   (F) $x < 2$ or $x > -2$ (H) $x > 2$

   (G) $x < -2$ (I) $x < -2$ or $x > 2$

5. What is the solution of the compound inequality $-2x \le 6$ and $-3x > -27$?

   (A) $x \le -3$ and $x > 9$ (C) $x \ge -3$ and $x < 9$

   (B) $x \ge 3$ and $x < -9$ (D) $x \le 3$ and $x > -9$

Short Response

6. **Geometry** The lengths of the sides of a triangle are in the ratio $3 : 4 : 5$. Describe the length of the longest side if the perimeter is not more than 72 in.

7. Between 8.5% and 9.4% of the city's population uses the municipal transit system daily. According to the latest census, the city's population is 785,000. How many people use the transit system daily?

1-6 Think About a Plan

Absolute Value Equations and Inequalities

Write an absolute value inequality to represent the situation.

Cooking Suppose you used an oven thermometer while baking and discovered that the oven temperature varied between $+5$ and -5 degrees from the setting. If your oven is set to 350°, let t be the actual temperature.

1. How do you have to think to solve this problem?

_____

_____

_____

2. Write a compound inequality that represents the actual oven temperature t.

3. It often helps to draw a picture. Graph this compound inequality on a number line.

4. What is the definition of tolerance?

_____

_____

_____

5. What is the tolerance of the oven? _____

6. Use the tolerance to write an inequality without absolute values.

7. Rewrite the inequality as an absolute value inequality.

1-6

Practice

Form K

Absolute Value Equations and Inequalities

Solve each equation. Check your answers. Graph the solution.

1. $|-2x| = 12$

2. $|7y| = 28$

Solve each equation. Check your answers.

3. $|t + 7| = 1$

To start, rewrite the absolute value
equation as two equations.

$t + 7 = 1$ or $t + 7 = -1$

4. $4|z + 1| = 24$

5. $|2w + 1| = 5$

6. $|2x - 2| = 4$

7. $|5 - 2y| + 3 = 8$

Solve each equation. Check for extraneous solutions.

8. $|2z - 9| = z - 3$

To start, rewrite as two equations.

$2z - 9 = z - 3$ or $2z - 9 = -(z - 3)$

9. $|x + 6| = 2x - 3$

10. $|2t - 5| = 3t - 10$

11. $2|4y + 1| = 4y + 10$

12. $|w + 1| - 5 = 2w$

Write an absolute value equation to describe each graph.

13.

14.

Is the absolute value equation *always*, *sometimes*, or *never* true? Explain.

15. $|w| = -2$

16. $|z| + 1 = z + 1$

1-6   Practice (continued)   Form K
Absolute Value Equations and Inequalities

Solve each inequality. Graph the solution.

17. $2|x + 5| \leq 8$

To start, divide each side by 2. $|x + 5| \leq 4$

$x + 5$ is greater than or equal to -4 and less than or equal to 4. $-4 \leq x + 5 \leq 4$

18. $|x + 1| - 3 \leq 1$ **19.** $|2z + 2| - 1 > 3$

20. $2|w + 3| - 1 < 1$ **21.** $|y - 3| + 2 \geq 4$

22. $|2t + 2| + 5 \leq 9$ **23.** $|2s + 1| > 3$

Write each compound inequality as an absolute value inequality.

24. $1.2 \leq a \leq 2.4$

To start, find the tolerance. $\dfrac{2.4 - 1.2}{2} = \dfrac{1.2}{2} = 0.6$

25. $-2 < x < 4$ **26.** $1 \leq m \leq 2$

27. $20 \leq y \leq 30$ **28.** $-3 < t < 17$

Write an absolute value inequality to represent each situation.

29. In order to enter the kiddie rides at the amusement park, a child must be between the ages of 4 and 10. Let a represent the age of a child who may go on the kiddie rides.

30. The outdoor temperature ranged between 42°F and 60°F in a 24-hour period. Let t represent the temperature during this time period.

1-6 Standardized Test Prep

Absolute Value Equations and Inequalities

Multiple Choice

For Exercises 1–5, choose the correct letter.

1. What is the solution of $|5t - 3| = 8$?

   Ⓐ $t = 8$ or $t = -8$

   Ⓑ $t = 1$ or $t = -\frac{11}{5}$

   Ⓒ $t = \frac{11}{5}$ or $t = -1$

   Ⓓ $t = \frac{8}{5}$ or $t = -\frac{8}{3}$

2. What is the solution of $|3z - 2| \leq 8$?

   Ⓕ $-2 \leq z \leq \frac{10}{3}$

   Ⓖ $-\frac{10}{3} \leq z \leq 2$

   Ⓗ $z \leq -2$ or $z \geq \frac{10}{3}$

   Ⓘ $z \leq -\frac{10}{3}$ or $z \geq 2$

3. What is the solution of $\frac{1}{2}|2x + 3| - 1 > 1$?

   Ⓐ $-\frac{7}{2} < x < \frac{1}{2}$

   Ⓑ $x < -\frac{7}{2}$ or $x > \frac{1}{2}$

   Ⓒ $x > \frac{7}{2}$ or $x < -\frac{1}{2}$

   Ⓓ $x < \frac{1}{2}$ or $x > -\frac{7}{2}$

4. Which absolute value inequality is equivalent to the compound inequality $23 \leq T \leq 45$?

   Ⓕ $|T - 11| \leq 34$ Ⓖ $|T - 45| \leq 22$ Ⓗ $|T - 24| \leq 1$ Ⓘ $|T - 34| \leq 11$

5. Which is the correct graph for the solution of $|2b + 1| - 3 \leq 2$?

   Ⓐ

   Ⓑ

   Ⓒ

   Ⓓ

Short Response

6. An employee's monthly earnings at an electronics store are based on a salary plus commissions on her sales. Her earnings can range from $2500 to $3200, depending on her commission. Write a compound inequality to describe E, the amount of her monthly earnings. Then rewrite your inequality as an absolute value inequality.

2-1

Think About a Plan

Relations and Functions

Geometry Suppose you have a box with a 4×4-in. square base and variable height h. The surface area of this box is a function of its height. Write a function to represent the surface area. Evaluate the function for $h = 6.5$ in.

Understanding the Problem

1. The width of the box is ☐ inches. The length of the box is ☐ inches. The height of the box is ☐ inches.

2. What is the problem asking you to determine?

   _____

   _____

Planning the Solution

3. What is the area of the top of the box? What is the area of the bottom of the box?

4. What is the total area of the top and the bottom of the box?

5. What is the area of each side of the box?

6. What is the total area of the sides of the box?

Getting an Answer

7. Write a function to represent the surface area of the box.

8. Evaluate your function for $h = 6.5$ inches.

2-1 Practice

Form K

Relations and Functions

A motion detector tracks an egg as it drops from 10 ft above the ground. The table shows the height at various times.

1. Represent the data using each of the following:
   a. a mapping diagram
   b. ordered pairs
   c. a graph on the coordinate plane

Time (seconds)	Height (feet)
0.0	10
0.1	9.8
0.2	9.4
0.3	8.6
0.4	7.4

2. What are the domain and range of this relation?

Determine whether each relation is a function.

3.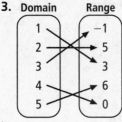

4. $\{(-4, 1), (-3, 5), (-1, 0), (6, 2), (9, 5)\}$

Use the vertical-line test to determine whether each graph represents a function.

5.

6.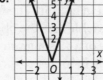

7.

Lesson 2-1

2-1

Practice (continued)

Relations and Functions

Evaluate each function for the given value of *x*.

8. $f(x) = 4x + 1$ for $x = 3$ **9.** $f(x) = 2x - 11$ for $x = 5$ **10.** $f(x) = \frac{6x + 3}{7}$ for $x = 3$

11. $f(x) = \frac{5}{2}x + 8$ for $x = 4$ **12.** $f(x) = 7x - \frac{1}{4}$ for $x = \frac{3}{4}$ **13.** $f(x) = -2x + 5$ for $x = 6$

14. Open-Ended Write a function rule that produces an output of 7 for an input of 1.5.

15. A cable company charges a monthly fee of $24.50 for cable service. There is an additional monthly fee of $3 for each premium channel. George has cable service with 4 premium channels. Write and evaluate a function to find the monthly cost of George's cable service.

16. Mr. Reynolds is a car salesman. He makes a salary of $55,000 a year. He also earns a commission of $\frac{1}{12}$ of his total sales for the year. This year, Mr. Reynolds has a sales total of $295,200. Write and evaluate a function to find Mr. Reynolds's total earnings for the year.

17. Kinetic energy is the energy of an object in motion. The formula $K = \frac{1}{2}mv^2$ is used to calculate kinetic energy. The variable m is the object's mass, and v is its velocity. Calculate the kinetic energy of a 45 kilogram object traveling at 3 meters per second. Your answer will be in Joules.

2-1 Standardized Test Prep

Relations and Functions

Multiple Choice

For Exercises 1–4, choose the correct letter.

1. Which relations are functions?

   I.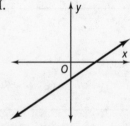

   II.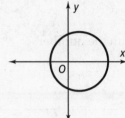

   III.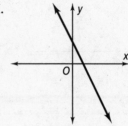

   IV.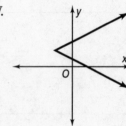

   (A) II and III   (B) I and II   (C) III and IV   (D) I and IV

2. Which point could not be part of a function that includes $(3, -1)$, $(4, 2)$, $(5, 4)$, $(-2, 0)$, and $(8, -3)$?

   (F) $(6, -7)$ (G) $(3, -2)$ (H) $(7, 4)$ (I) $(2, 2)$

3. For the function $f(x) = -4x - 3$, which of the following is $f(-2)$?

   (A) -11 (B) -2 (C) 5 (D) 11

4. What is the domain of the relation given by the ordered pairs?
   $(2, -1), (-4, 1), (-2, -1), (3, -3), (2, 3)$

   (F) $\{-3, -2, 1, 3\}$ (G) $\{-4, -2, 2, 3\}$ (H) $\{-3, -1, 1, 3\}$ (I) $\{-4, -1, 1, 3\}$

Short Response

5. A phone store employee earns a salary of $450 per week plus 10% commission on her weekly sales.
   a. What function rule models the employee's weekly earnings?
   b. If the employee earned $570 in a week, what was the amount of her sales for that week?

2-2

Think About a Plan

Direct Variation

Sports The number of rotations of a bicycle wheel varies directly with the number of pedal strokes. Suppose that in the bicycle's lowest gear, 6 pedal strokes move the cyclist about 357 in. In the same gear, how many pedal strokes are needed to move 100 ft?

Know

1. The number of _____ varies directly with the number

   of _____.

2. _____

   _____

Need

3. To solve the problem I need to:

   _____

   _____

   _____

Plan

4. Write an equation of direct variation to model the situation. Find the constant of variation.

5. Substitute for one variable and the constant of variation in the equation of direct variation.

6. What does the solution mean?

   _____

7. Is the solution reasonable? Explain.

   _____

   _____

Name _____ Class _____ Date _____

2-2 Practice
Form K

Direct Variation

For each function, determine whether y varies directly with x. If so, find the constant of variation and write the function rule. To start, write ratios of output to input.

1.

x	y
3	-9
4	-12
5	-15

$$-\frac{9}{3}, -\frac{12}{4}, -\frac{15}{5}$$

2.

x	y
2	6
5	10
10	30

3.

x	y
-4	-8
1	2
3	6

Determine whether y varies directly with x. If so, find the constant of the variation.

4. $y = 5x$

5. $3y = 4x + 6$

6. $y = \frac{7}{x}$

For Exercises 7–10, y varies directly with x.

7. If $y = -2$ when $x = 1$, find x when $y = 4$.

8. If $y = 4$ when $x = 5$, find y when $x = 10$.

9. If $y = 12$ when $x = 36$, find x when $y = 7$.

10. If $y = 121$ when $x = 11$, find y when $x = 5$.

11. The length of an object's shadow varies directly with the height of the object.
A 15 ft tree casts a 60 ft shadow.
  a. Write a function rule and determine the constant of variation.
  b. What length shadow would a 7 ft tree cast?
  c. What height tree would cast a 90 ft long shadow?

Lesson 2-2

2-2 Practice (continued)

Direct Variation

Write and graph a direct variation that passes through each point.

12. $(6, 2)$

13. $(-1, 5)$

14. $(-4, -8)$

For each function, determine whether y varies directly with x. If so, find the constant of variation and write the function rule. To start, write ratios of output to input.

15.

x	y
-8	12
-2	3
4	-6

$-\dfrac{12}{8}, -\dfrac{3}{2}, -\dfrac{6}{4}$

16.

x	y
-1	-4
-10	-40
-15	-60

17.

x	y
6	3
8	4
10	6

18. Error Analysis Suppose y varies directly with x. If $y = 10$ when $x = 5$, what is x when $y = 16$? You say that $x = 32$ and your friend says $x = 8$. Who is correct? What mistake was made?

19. Suppose you drive a car 392 mi on a tank of gas. The tank holds 14 gallons. The number of miles traveled varies directly with the number of gallons of gas you use.

   a. Write an equation that relates miles traveled to gallons of gas used. Let $x =$ the number of gallons of gas used and $y =$ the number of miles driven.

   b. Last year you drove 11,700 mi. Approximately how many gallons of gas did you use?

2-2 Standardized Test Prep

Direct Variation

Multiple Choice

For Exercises 1–5, choose the correct letter.

1. If y varies directly with x and y is 18 when x is 6, which of the following represents this situation?

   Ⓐ $y = 24x$ Ⓑ $y = 3x$ Ⓒ $y = 12x$ Ⓓ $y = \frac{1}{3}x$

2. Which function best represents the relationship between the quantities in the table?

x	y
6	4
12	8
21	14
30	20

   Ⓕ $x = \frac{2}{3}y - 2$ Ⓖ $x = \frac{2}{3}y + 2$ Ⓗ $y = \frac{2}{3}x$ Ⓘ $y = \frac{3}{2}x$

3. If y varies directly with x and y is 9 when x is 5, what is x when y is -1?

   Ⓐ -1 Ⓑ $-\frac{5}{9}$ Ⓒ 1 Ⓓ $\frac{5}{9}$

4. Which equation of direct variation has $(24, -8)$ as a solution?

   Ⓕ $y = \frac{1}{3}x$ Ⓖ $y = -3x$ Ⓗ $y = 3x$ Ⓘ $y = -\frac{1}{3}x$

5. Which equation does NOT represent a direct variation?

   Ⓐ $y - 4x = 0$ Ⓑ $\frac{y}{x} = \frac{3}{4}$ Ⓒ $y - 4 = \frac{1}{4}x$ Ⓓ $4y = -\frac{1}{4}x$

Short Response

6. You can download a 5 MB file in 2 seconds. The time t it takes to download a file varies directly with the size s of the file. Write an equation of direct variation to represent the situation. How long will it take you to download a 3 MB file?

Lesson 2-2

2-3 Think About a Plan

Linear Functions and Slope-Intercept Form

The equation $d = 4 - \frac{1}{15}t$ represents your distance from home d for each minute of your walk t.

a. If you graphed this equation, what would the slope represent? Explain.

b. Are you walking towards or away from your home? Explain.

1. What does d represent?

_____

2. What does t represent?

_____

3. Is the equation in slope-intercept form? If not, write the equation in slope-intercept form.

_____

4. What units make sense for the slope? Explain.

_____

_____

_____

5. What does the slope represent? Explain.

_____

_____

_____

6. Is your distance from home increasing or decreasing?

_____

2-3 Practice   *Form K*

Slope-Intercept Form

Find the slope of the line through each pair of points. To start, substitute (x_1, y_1) and (x_2, y_2) into the slope formula.

1. $(1, 6)$ and $(8, -1)$ **2.** $(-5, -7)$ and $(0, 10)$ **3.** $(-2, 1)$ and $(8, -3)$

$m = \dfrac{y_2 - y_1}{x_2 - x_1} = \dfrac{-1 - 6}{8 - 1}$

Write an equation for each line.

4. $m = 4$ and the y-intercept is 3   **5.** $m = \dfrac{7}{2}$ and the y-intercept is -5

6. 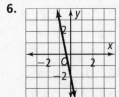   **7.**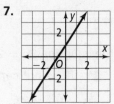

Write each equation in slope-intercept form. Then find the slope and y-intercept of each line. To start, isolate the y-term on one side of the equation.

8. $8y + 3x = 24$ **9.** $-5y + 2 = -7x$ **10.** $-4 - 2y = 10x$

   $8y = -3x + 24$

Graph each equation.

11. $y = 3x - 1$ **12.** $y = -\dfrac{1}{2}x + 4$ **13.** $y = -x + 3$

Lesson 2-3

2-3

Practice (continued)

Form K

Slope-Intercept Form

14. The equation $y - 4x = 15$ models the number of pages y you read in x minutes.

    a. Write this equation in slope-intercept form.

    b. If you graph this equation, what would the slope represent?

    c. Reasoning In this situation, what does the point $(1, 19)$ represent?

Graph each equation. Find the slope and y-intercept.

15. $5y + 4x = 1$ **16.** $x = 3y + 6$ **17.** $\frac{x}{4} + \frac{y}{8} = \frac{3}{16}$

18. Multiple Choice For the equation $3x - 2y = 12$, which has value -6?

    Ⓐ the x-intercept   Ⓑ the y-intercept   Ⓒ the slope   Ⓓ the origin

19. Error Analysis For the graph at the right, a classmate said the slope is $-\frac{1}{4}$. What mistake did she make? What is the correct slope?

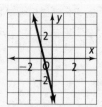

20. Writing Explain how the graph of a line with a negative slope differs from the graph of a line with a positive slope.

2-3 Standardized Test Prep

Linear Functions and Slope-Intercept Form

Multiple Choice

For Exercises 1–5, choose the correct letter.

1. For the linear equation $5x - y = 2$, which of the following has a value of 5?

   Ⓐ the slope   Ⓑ the x-intercept   Ⓒ the y-intercept   Ⓓ the origin

2. What is true about the line that passes through the points $(3, -7)$ and $(3, 2)$?

   Ⓕ It is horizontal.   Ⓗ It is vertical.

   Ⓖ It rises from left to right.   Ⓘ It falls from left to right.

3. What is the slope-intercept form of $3x + 2y = 1$?

   Ⓐ $y = \frac{3}{2}x - \frac{1}{2}$ Ⓑ $y = -\frac{3}{2}x + \frac{1}{2}$ Ⓒ $y = -\frac{2}{3}x + \frac{1}{2}$ Ⓓ $y = \frac{2}{3}x - \frac{1}{2}$

4. What is the y-intercept of the graph of $5x - 9y = 45$?

   Ⓕ -9 Ⓖ 9 Ⓗ -5 Ⓘ 5

5. Which of the following is a graph of $4x = -\frac{1}{2}y - 1$?

   Ⓐ 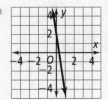   Ⓑ 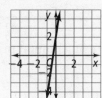   Ⓒ 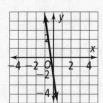   Ⓓ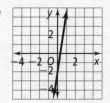

Short Response

Write the equation in slope-intercept form. What are the slope and the y-intercept?

6. $\frac{1}{2}x + \frac{3}{2}y - 1 = 0$

2-4 Think About a Plan

More About Linear Equations

a. Write the point-slope form of the line that passes through $A(-3, 12)$ and $B(9, -4)$. Use point A in the equation.

b. Write the point-slope form of the same line using point B in the equation.

c. Rewrite each equation in standard form. What do you notice?

1. What is the point-slope form of an equation of a line?

   _____

2. What is the standard form of an equation of a line?

   _____

3. What is the slope formula? Use the slope formula to find m.

   _____

4. Use point A to write the point-slope form. $x_1 = \boxed{}$ $y_1 = \boxed{}$

   _____

5. Write the point-slope form of the equation using point A in standard form.

   _____

6. Use point B to write the point-slope form. $x_1 = \boxed{}$ $y_1 = \boxed{}$

   _____

7. Write the point-slope form of the equation using point B in standard form.

   _____

8. Compare the standard form of the equation using point A with the standard form of the equation using point B.

   _____

2-4 Practice

More About Linear Equations

Form K

Write an equation of each line.

1. slope 6; through $(0, 4)$

2. slope $\frac{2}{3}$; through $(-3, 7)$

3. slope -5; through $(9, -1)$

4. slope 0; through $(-3, -5)$

Write in point-slope form an equation of the line through each pair of points. To start, substitute values for (x_1, y_1) and (x_2, y_2) into the slope formula.

5. $(2, 7)$ and $(-4, 1)$

$m = \dfrac{y_2 - y_1}{x_2 - x_1} = \dfrac{1 - 7}{-4 - 2}$

6. $(-5, 0)$ and $(3, 3)$

7. $\left(\dfrac{3}{4}, \dfrac{5}{2}\right)$ and $\left(-\dfrac{7}{8}, \dfrac{3}{2}\right)$

Write an equation of each line in standard form with integer coefficients. To start, multiply each side by the least common denominator of all fractional coefficients.

8. $y = \dfrac{3}{5}x - 4$

$5(y) = 5\left(\dfrac{3}{5}x - 4\right)$

9. $y = -\dfrac{4}{3}x + \dfrac{5}{6}$

10. $y = -x + 8$

11. Reasoning The line $y + 4 = \dfrac{3}{4}(x - 8)$ contains point $(a, 2)$. Find a. Show your work.

2-4 Practice (continued)

More About Linear Equations

Form K

Find the intercepts and graph each line.

12. $4x + 5y = 20$ **13.** $-2x + y = 6$ **14.** $6x - 8y = 24$

15. Rosa must read 20 pages of a book for English class. It will take Rosa about 50 minutes to complete her reading. Draw a graph and write an equation to represent the situation.

16. According to the information in Exercise 15, how long will it take Rosa to read 30 pages?

Write an equation in slope-intercept form for each line.

17. the line parallel to $y = 4x - 1$ through $(2, 7)$

18. the line perpendicular to $y = -\frac{1}{3}x + 5$ through $(6, 3)$

Name _____ Class _____ Date _____

2-4 Standardized Test Prep

More About Linear Equations

Multiple Choice

For Exercises 1–5, choose the correct letter.

1. For the linear equation $x - 2y = 10$, which of the following has value 10?

   Ⓐ the slope   Ⓑ the x-intercept   Ⓒ the y-intercept   Ⓓ the origin

2. Which represents the slope of a line that is parallel to a line with a slope of -2?

   Ⓕ $-\frac{1}{2}$ Ⓖ $\frac{1}{2}$ Ⓗ -2 Ⓘ 2

3. Which equation represents a line through $(-2, 1)$ that is perpendicular to $y = -5x + 2$?

   Ⓐ $y = \frac{1}{5}x + \frac{7}{5}$ Ⓑ $y = -5x - 9$ Ⓒ $y = -\frac{1}{5}x - \frac{7}{5}$ Ⓓ $y = 5x + 9$

4. Which equation represents a line through $(-1, 1)$ with a slope of $\frac{2}{3}$?

   Ⓕ $y - 1 = \frac{2}{3}(x + 1)$ Ⓗ $y - 1 = \frac{2}{3}(x - 1)$

   Ⓖ $y + 1 = \frac{2}{3}(x - 1)$ Ⓘ $y + 1 = \frac{2}{3}(x + 1)$

5. Which of the following equations is shown in the graph?

   Ⓐ $y + 2 = -\frac{1}{2}(x + 2)$ Ⓒ $y - 3 = -\frac{1}{2}(x - 6)$

   Ⓑ $y + 3 = -\frac{1}{2}(x + 6)$ Ⓓ $y - 2 = -\frac{1}{2}(x - 2)$

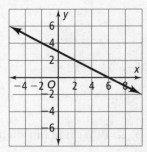

Short Response

6. The line $y = \frac{5}{9}x + 6$ is graphed on a coordinate plane. A second line is drawn on the same plane with a slope of $-\frac{5}{9}$ and y-intercept $(0, -6)$. Write the equation of the second line. Describe the relationship between these two graphs.

41

2-5 Think About a Plan
Using Linear Models

Data Analysis The table shows population and licensed driver statistics from a recent year.

a. Make a scatter plot.

b. Draw a trend line.

c. The population of Michigan was approximately 10 million that year. About how many licensed drivers lived in Michigan that year?

d. **Writing** Is the correlation between population and number of licensed drivers strong or weak? Explain.

Licensed Drivers

State	Population (millions)	Number of Drivers (millions)
Arkansas	2.7	1.9
Illinois	12.4	7.7
Kansas	2.7	1.8
Massachusetts	6.4	4.4
Pennsylvania	12.3	8.3
Texas	20.9	12.8

Know

1. The independent variable should be _____.

2. Points to plot: _____

Need

3. To solve the problems, I need to _____

_____

_____

Plan

4. Make the scatter plot.

5. Draw a trend line on the scatter plot.

6. How do you find the equation of the trend line? Write the equation.

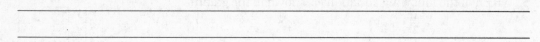

7. About how many licensed drivers lived in Michigan that year? _____

8. What is correlation? Is the correlation between population and licensed drivers strong or weak? Explain.

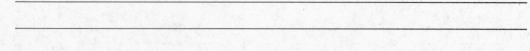

_____

2-5 Practice   *Form K*

Using Linear Models

Make a scatter plot and describe the correlation. To start, plot the points.

1. (1, 2), (2, 4), (3, 7), (4, 6), (5, 9)   **2.** (1, 9), (2, 8), (3, 4), (6, 3), (8, 5)

Write the equation of a trend line, if possible.

3. (2, 1), (4, 5), (5, 4), (6, 6), (8, 8)

4. To begin, make a scatter plot and let $x = 0$ correspond to 1950.

Life Expectancy for People Born in Various Years							
Year	1950	1960	1970	1980	1990	2000	2002
Life Expectancy	68.2	69.7	70.8	73.7	75.4	76.9	77.3

SOURCE: National Center for Health Statistics

5. The table below shows the average daily energy requirements for male children and adolescents.

Daily Energy Requirements for Males							
Age (years)	1	2	5	8	11	14	17
Energy needed (calories)	1100	1300	1800	2200	2500	2800	3000

SOURCE: *Go Figure: The Numbers You Need for Everyday Life*

a. Use a calculator to find the line of best fit.

b. Use your linear model to predict how many calories a 19-year old needs per day.

c. Use your linear model to predict the age of a male who needs 2300 calories per day.

d. Reasoning Do you think this model also applies to adult males? Explain.

2-5

Practice (continued)   Form K

Using Linear Models

6. A woman is considering buying a car. She researches prices for various years of the same model of car. The table below shows the data from her research.

Car Prices by Model Year					
Model Year	2000	2001	2002	2003	2004
Prices	$5784	$6810	$8237	$9660	$10,948

a. Use a calculator to find the line of best fit. Let x = the number of years since 2000.

b. Use your linear model to predict how much a 2007 model should cost.

c. **Error Analysis** She predicts that a 2005 model costs $9800. Does this seem reasonable? Why or why not?

Consider each situation and predict the type of correlation you might find. Do you think that changes in the first quantity caused the changes in the second quantity?

7. a person's weight and the size of clothing they wear

8. the number of rooms in a person's home and the number of books a person owns

9. the length of time a candle has been burning and the height of the candle

For each situation, find a linear model and use it to make a prediction.

10. A 2-mi cab ride costs $5.25. A 5-mi cab ride costs $10.50. How much does a 3.8-mi cab ride cost?

11. There are 55 blades of grass in 1 in.^{2} of lawn. There are 230 blades of grass in 4 in.^{2} of the same lawn. How many blades of grass are in 3 in.^{2} of lawn?

12. An empty 5-gal water jug weighs 0.75 lb. With 3 c of water inside, the jug weighs 2.25 lb. Predict the weight of the jug with 5 c of water inside.

2-5

Standardized Test Prep

Using Linear Models

Gridded Response

Solve each exercise and enter your answer in the grid provided.

Use the table and the scatter plot for Exercises 1–4.

U.S. Health Expenditures Drug and Other Medical Nondurables

Year	Expenditures (billions of dollars)
1995	8.9
1996	9.4
1997	10.0
1998	10.6

Source: *The World Almanac and Book of Facts, 2001*

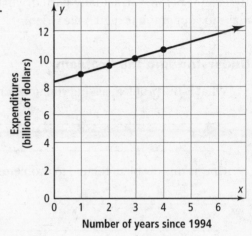

Number of years since 1994

1. What is the *y*-intercept of the trend line if the trend line has slope 0.6, rounded to the nearest tenth?

2. During what year did the U.S. spend $10 billion in health expenditures?

3. Using the points for 1995 and 1997, what is the slope of the trend line?

4. If the trend continued, about how many billion dollars would the U.S. have spent on health expenditures in the year 2001, rounded to the nearest tenth?

Answers

1.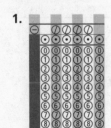
2.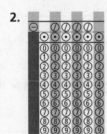
3.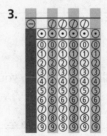
4.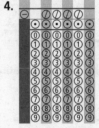

Lesson 2-5

2-6

Think About a Plan

Families of Functions

Suppose you are playing with a yo-yo during a school talent show. You make a graph of the yo-yo's distance from the auditorium floor during the show. If someone started to take a video of your yo-yo routine when you were introduced, 10 seconds before you actually started, what transformation would you have to make to your graph to match the video?

Understanding the Problem

1. What is the problem asking you to determine?

   _____

   _____

2. How is this problem related to problems about parent functions?

   _____

   _____

Planning the Solution

3. What quantity is represented by the independent axis in your graph? _____

4. What quantity is represented by the dependent axis in your graph?

   _____

5. If you graph the routine that you perform, what is represented on the independent axis in your graph? The dependent axis?

   _____

6. If you graph the routine that you see on the video, what is represented on the independent axis in your graph? The dependent axis?

   _____

Getting an Answer

7. What transformation would you make to your graph to match a graph of the video?

   _____

2-6 Practice

Families of Functions

Form K

How is each function related to its parent function? Graph the function by translating the parent function.

1. $y = x + 5$

2. $y = (x + 5)^2$

3. $y = x - 2.5$

4. $y = \left(x - \frac{1}{2}\right)^2$

Make a table of values for $f(x) = x$ after each given translation.

5. 8 units down

x	y	y = x − 8
−2	−2	
−1	−1	
0	0	
1	1	
2	2	

6. 4 units up

x	y	y = x + 4
−2	−2	
−1	−1	
0	0	
1	1	
2	2	

7. 7 units down

x	y	y = x − 7
−2	−2	
−1	−1	
0	0	
1	1	
2	2	

Write an equation for each horizontal translation of $f(x) = x^2$.

8. 3.7 units right

9. $\frac{1}{4}$ units left

10. 5 units right

47

2-6   **Practice** (continued)   *Form K*

Families of Functions

Describe the transformation that changes the parent function $f(x) = 4x$ to $g(x)$.

11. $g(x) = 0.15(4x)$ **12.** $g(x) = -4x$ **13.** $g(x) = 6(4x)$

Write an equation for each transformation of $f(x) = 6x - 2$.

14. a vertical compression by a factor of $\frac{1}{3}$ and a reflection in the y-axis

15. a vertical stretch by a factor of 7 and a vertical translation up 5 units

16. a vertical stretch by a factor of 1.5 and a reflection in the y-axis

17. Writing Explain how to tell the difference between a stretch and a compression without graphing.

Graph each pair of functions on the same coordinate plane. Describe the transformation that changes $f(x)$ to $g(x)$.

18. $f(x) = 2x + 1$ **19.** $f(x) = x + 3$
$\quad\,\,$ $g(x) = 2x + 4$ $\quad\,\,$ $g(x) = -x + 1$

2-6 Standardized Test Prep

Families of Functions

Multiple Choice

For Exercises 1–4, choose the correct letter.

1. Which of the following is the graph of $y = -3x - 6$ reflected in the y-axis and vertically compressed by a factor of $\frac{1}{3}$?

A 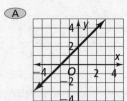 B 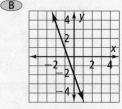 C 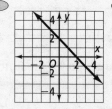 D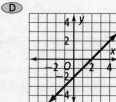

2. The graph of $y = x + 4$ is translated 3 units down. Which point is on the new graph?

   F $(-2, 5)$ G $(0, 8)$ H $(1, 5)$ I $(-1, 0)$

3. The graph of $y = f(x)$ is reflected in the x-axis and translated 3 units right. Which is the equation of the new graph?

   A $y = -f(x + 3)$ B $y = f(-x + 3)$ C $y = -f(x - 3)$ D $y = f(-x - 3)$

4. Which equation represents the vertical translation of $y = f(x)$ up 5 units?

   F $y = f(x) - 5$ G $y = f(x - 5)$ H $y = f(x) + 5$ I $y = f(x + 5)$

5. Which equation represents the horizontal translation of $y = 3x - 2$ to the left $\frac{2}{3}$ units?

   A $y = 3x$ B $y = 3x + \frac{8}{3}$ C $y = 3x + \frac{4}{3}$ D $y = 3x - \frac{8}{3}$

Short Response

6. How will a vertical compression of the parent function $y = x$ change the graph of the function? Write a new equation that represents this transformation.

2-7 Think About a Plan

Absolute Value Functions and Graphs

Graph $y = 4|x - 3| + 1$. List the vertex and the x- and y-intercepts, if any.

Understanding the Problem

1. What is the problem asking you to determine?

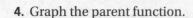
_____

2. What is the parent function for the function $y = 4|x - 3| + 1$? _____

Planning the Solution

3. What do you know about the function $y = 4|x - 3| + 1$?

_____

_____

4. Graph the parent function.

5. What transformations do you need to apply to the parent function to graph this function?

_____

_____

Getting an Answer

6. What is the vertex of the function? _____

7. What are the x- and y-intercepts of the function?

_____

8. Graph the function.

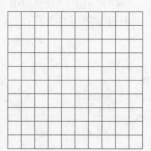

2-7 Practice

Absolute Value Functions and Graphs

Form K

Make a table of values for each equation. Then graph the equation.

1. $y = |x| + 4$

2. $y = |x| - 2$

3. $y = |x + 2|$

4. $y = |x + 1| - 3$

Graph each function. Then describe the transformation from the parent function $f(x) = |x|$.

5. $y = 5|x|$

6. $y = -\frac{1}{3}|x|$

7. $y = 3|x|$

Without graphing, identify the vertex, axis of symmetry, and transformations from the parent function $f(x) = |x|$.

8. $y = 2|x + 1|$

9. $y = |x - 2| + 3$

10. $y = -\frac{1}{2}|x| - 2$

2-7 **Practice** (continued)   *Form K*

Absolute Value Functions and Graphs

Write an absolute value equation for each graph.

11.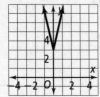

12.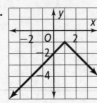

13.

14. Error Analysis For the graph to the right, you said the absolute
value equation is $y = |x + 2| - 5$. Your friend said the equation is
$y = |x - 2| + 5$. Which one of you is correct? What mistake did
the other person make?

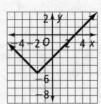

Graph each absolute value equation.

15. $y = |2x - 1| + 4$ **16.** $y = -3|x + 4| - 2$ **17.** $y = \left|\frac{2}{3}x + 1\right| - 3$

18. Writing Explain how to find the vertex of $y = |3x - 6|$.

2-7 Standardized Test Prep

Absolute Value Functions and Graphs

Multiple Choice

For Exercises 1–3, choose the correct letter.

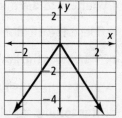

1. Which equation has the graph shown at the right?

   Ⓐ $y = -\frac{1}{2}|x|$ Ⓒ $y = \frac{1}{2}|x|$

   Ⓑ $y = 2|x|$ Ⓓ $y = -2|x|$

2. Which statement about the graph of the function $y = -\frac{1}{3}|x + 2| - 5$ is true?

   Ⓕ the vertex is at $(2, -5)$ Ⓗ the vertex is at $(-2, 5)$

   Ⓖ the vertex is at $(2, 5)$ Ⓘ the vertex is at $(-2, -5)$

3. The graph of which equation is the graph of $f(x) = |x|$ reflected in the x-axis, translated 2 units left, vertically compressed by a factor of $\frac{1}{3}$, and translated down 4 units?

   Ⓐ $y = 3|x - 2| + 4$ Ⓒ $y = -3|x + 2| + 4$

   Ⓑ $y = -\frac{1}{3}|x + 2| + 4$ Ⓓ $y = -\frac{1}{3}|x - 2| + 4$

Extended Response

4. Determine the parent function of $y = -|x + 4| - 1$. Describe the graph of $y = -|x + 4| - 1$ as three transformations of the parent function. Then graph the parent function and each translation.

2-8 Think About a Plan
Two-Variable Inequalities

The graph at the right relates the amount of gas in the tank of your car to the distance you can drive.

Miles Traveled

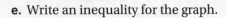

a. Describe the domain for this situation.

b. Why does the graph stop?

c. Why is only the first quadrant shown?

d. **Reasoning** Would every point in the solution region be a solution?

e. Write an inequality for the graph.

f. What does the coefficient of *x* represent?

1. What is the domain of a function? _____

2. What is the domain for this situation?

_____

3. What is the upper bound of the domain in this situation? _____

4. Why does the graph stop?

_____

5. What do you know about the *x*- and *y*-values of points in the first quadrant?

_____

6. Why is only the first quadrant shown?

_____

7. Would every point in the solution region be a solution? Explain.

_____

_____

8. Write an equation for the boundary line in the graph. _____

9. Write an inequality for the graph. _____

10. What does the coefficient of *x* represent? _____

2-8 Practice

Form K

Two-Variable Inequalities

Graph each inequality. To start, graph the boundary line.

1. $y < x + 4$ **2.** $y \geq -3x - 1$ **3.** $y - 2 < 5x$

4. You want to buy some CDs that cost $10 each and some DVDs that cost
$15 each. You have $45 to spend.

  a. Write an inequality to represent the situation, where x is the number of CDs
you buy and y is the number of DVDs.

  b. Graph the inequality.

  c. Reasoning Why did the graph in b only include quadrant I?

  d. Reasoning Can you buy 3 CDs and 2 DVDs? Explain.

Graph each absolute value inequality. To start, graph the boundary line.

5. $y \geq |2x - 1|$ **6.** $y - 7 \leq |x + 2|$ **7.** $y + 5 < |3x|$

8. Open-Ended Write an absolute value inequality for which the boundary is
dashed and the shaded region is above the boundary.

Lesson 2-8

2-8 Practice (continued) Form K
Two-Variable Inequalities

Write an inequality for each graph. The equation for the boundary line is given.

9. $y = 2x + 5$

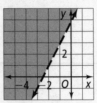

10. $y = |x + 4| - 3$

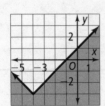

11. $y = -|x - 2|$

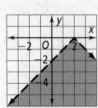

Graph each inequality on a coordinate plane.

12. $-3x + 4y > 6$

13. $-2y - 8 \geq 6x$

14. $y + |x| \geq 4$

15. The graph at the right relates the number of hours you spend sleeping to the number of hours you spend on the computer each weekend.

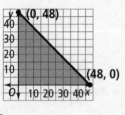

   a. Describe the domain for this situation.
   b. Write an inequality for the graph.
   c. What is the least amount of time you can spend sleeping? What is the most amount of time you can spend on the computer?
   d. **Reasoning** Why does this graph only go to 48 on both the *x*-and *y*-axes?

2-8 Standardized Test Prep

Two-Variable Inequalities

Multiple Choice

For Exercises 1–4, choose the correct letter.

1. Which graph best represents the solution of the inequality $-6x - 2y \leq 4$?

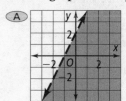 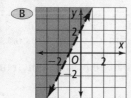 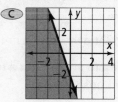 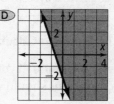

2. Which ordered pair is a solution of $2x - 2y > 8$?

   F $(-2, 0)$ G $(2, -4)$ H $(0, -4)$ I $(4, 1)$

3. Which ordered pair is not a solution of $y \geq \frac{1}{2}\left|x + 2\right|$?

   A $(-2, 0)$ B $(-1, -2)$ C $(0, 2)$ D $(2, 2)$

4. The graph of which absolute value inequality has its vertex at $(1, 5)$?

   F $y > |x - 1| + 5$ H $y > -|x + 1| - 5$

   G $y > |x + 1| - 5$ I $y > -5|x - 1|$

Short Response

5. **Transportation** The high school band is expecting to take at least 120 students to a regional band competition. The school rents some passenger vans that can transport 8 students. Other students, in groups of 4, will need to ride in personal vehicles driven by parents.
   a. Write an inequality that shows all the possible combinations of vans and cars that could be used to drive students to the competition.
   b. Explain in words or show work for how you determined the inequality.

Lesson 2-8

3-1 Think About a Plan

Solving Systems Using Tables and Graphs

Sports You can choose between two tennis courts at two university campuses to learn how to play tennis. One campus charges $25 per hour. The other campus charges $20 per hour plus a one-time registration fee of $10.

a. Write a system of equations to represent the cost c for h hours of court use at each campus.

b. Graphing Calculator Find the number of hours for which the costs are the same.

c. Reasoning If you want to practice for a total of 10 hours, which university campus should you choose? Explain.

1. What is an equation that represents the cost c for h hours of court use for the first campus?

_____

2. What is an equation that represents the cost c for h hours of court use for the second campus?

_____

3. What is one method you can use to find the number of hours for which the costs are the same?

_____

4. What is another method you can use to find the number of hours for which the costs are the same?

_____
_____

5. Use one of your methods to find the number of hours for which the costs are the same.

_____

6. What happens to the cost at the two campuses after you have practiced for the number of hours you found in Exercise 5?

_____
_____

7. If you want to practice for a total of 10 hours, which university campus should you choose? Explain.

_____
_____
_____

3-1 Practice

Form K

Solving Systems Using Tables and Graphs

Solve each system by graphing or using a table. Check your answers.

1. $\begin{cases} y = 2x + 4 \\ y = -5x - 3 \end{cases}$

2. $\begin{cases} x - y = 2 \\ y = -x \end{cases}$

3. $\begin{cases} y = -2x - 2 \\ 2y = x + 6 \end{cases}$

Write and solve a system of equations for each situation. Check your answers.

4. Each morning you do a combination of aerobics, which burns about 12 calories per minute, and stretching, which burns about 4 calories per minute. Your goal is to burn 416 calories during a 60-minute workout. How long should you spend on each type of exercise to burn the 416 calories?

5. Suppose 28 members of your class went on a rafting trip. Class members could either rent canoes for $16 each or rent kayaks for $19 each. The class spent a total $469. How many people rented canoes and how many people rented kayaks?

For Exercise 6, use your graphing calculator to find a linear model for the set of data. In what year will the two quantities be equal?

6.

Winning Times for the Olympic 100-Meter Butterfly										
Year	1972	1976	1980	1984	1988	1992	1996	2000	2004	2008
Male Times (s)	54.27	54.35	54.92	53.08	53.00	53.32	52.27	52.00	51.25	50.58
Female Times (s)	63.34	60.13	60.42	59.26	59.00	58.62	59.13	56.61	57.72	56.73

Source: www.infoplease.com

3-1 **Practice** (continued)   Form K

Solving Systems Using Tables and Graphs

Without graphing, does each system have zero, one, or infinitely many solutions? To start, rewrite each equation in slope-intercept form.

7. $\begin{cases} 4y + 8 = 12x \\ y - 5 = 3x \end{cases}$ 8. $\begin{cases} 6y - 3x = 12 \\ 2y = x + 4 \end{cases}$ 9. $\begin{cases} \frac{1}{5}y = x - \frac{1}{5} \\ x = 11 - y \end{cases}$

$\begin{cases} y = 3x - 2 \\ y = 3x + 5 \end{cases}$

Graph and solve each system.

10. $\begin{cases} y = -2x + 9 \\ 2y = -x + 6 \end{cases}$ 11. $\begin{cases} y = 3x - 8 \\ y = x - 8 \end{cases}$ 12. $\begin{cases} y + 5 = 4x \\ 2y = 8x + 2 \end{cases}$

13. Your business needs to ship a package to another store. Company A charges $2.50 per pound plus a $20 service charge. Company B charges $4.50 per pound without any service charge.
    a. At what weight does it cost the same for both companies?
    b. If your package weighs 14 pounds, which shipping company should your business use?

14. **Reasoning** Is it possible for a linear system with infinitely many solutions to contain two lines with different *y*-intercepts?

3-1 Standardized Test Prep

Solving Systems Using Tables and Graphs

Multiple Choice

For Exercises 1–4, choose the correct letter.

1. Which system of equations is inconsistent?

   Ⓐ $\begin{cases} x + y = 4 \\ x - y = 3 \end{cases}$ 　　Ⓒ $\begin{cases} 6x + 3y = 12 \\ 2y = -4x + 4 \end{cases}$

   Ⓑ $\begin{cases} 2y - x = 5 \\ 4y = 2x + 10 \end{cases}$ 　　Ⓓ $\begin{cases} -3x + y = 4 \\ 2y = -6x + 8 \end{cases}$

2. Which ordered pair of numbers is the solution of the system? $\begin{cases} 2x + 3y = 12 \\ 2x - y = 4 \end{cases}$

   Ⓕ $(2, 3)$ 　　Ⓖ $(3, 2)$ 　　Ⓗ $(1, -2)$ 　　Ⓘ $(-3, 6)$

3. Which of the following graphs shows the solution of the system?
   $\begin{cases} x + y = -4 \\ 2x - 2y = -8 \end{cases}$

   Ⓐ 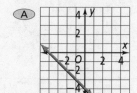 　Ⓑ 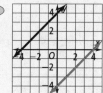 　Ⓒ 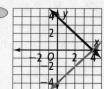 　Ⓓ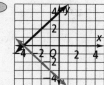

4. You and your friend are both knitting scarves for charity. You knit 8 rows each minute and already have knitted 10 rows. Your friend knits 5 rows each minute and has already knitted 19 rows. When will you both have knitted the same number of rows?

   Ⓕ 2.6 minutes 　Ⓖ 3 minutes 　Ⓗ 9.7 minutes 　Ⓘ 34 minutes

Short Response

5. The sides of an angle are two lines whose equations are $4x + y = 12$ and $y = 3x - 2$. An angle has its vertex at the point where the lines meet. Use a graph to determine the coordinates of the vertex. What are the coordinates of the vertex?

3-2

Think About a Plan

Solving Systems Algebraically

Chemistry A scientist wants to make 6 milliliters of a 30% sulfuric acid solution. The solution is to be made from a combination of a 20% sulfuric acid solution and a 50% sulfuric acid solution. How many milliliters of each solution must be combined to make the 30% solution?

Know

1. The scientist will begin with [   ] % and [   ] % solutions.

2. The scientist wants to make [   ] ml of 30% solution.

Need

3. To solve the problem you need to define:

_____

_____

Plan

4. What are two equations you can write to model the situation?

_____

5. Which method should you use to solve the system of equations? Explain.

_____

_____

6. Solve the system of equations.

_____

7. How can you interpret the solutions in the context of the problem?

_____

8. Do your solutions check? Explain.

_____

_____

3-2 Practice

Form K

Solving Systems Algebraically

Solve each system by substitution. Check your answers. To start, solve one equation for y and substitute into the other equation.

1. $\begin{cases} 4x + 3y = 9 \\ 2x - y = 7 \end{cases}$
$y = 2x - 7$
$4x + 3(2x - 7) = 9$

2. $\begin{cases} 3x - y = 0 \\ 5x + 2y = -44 \end{cases}$

3. $\begin{cases} x - 4y = 1 \\ x + 2y = 13 \end{cases}$

4. Your internet provider offers two different plans. One plan costs $.02 per email plus a $9 monthly service charge. The other plan costs $.05 per email with no service charge.
   a. Write a system of equations to model the cost of the two internet plans.
   b. For how many email messages will both plans cost the same?
   c. If you send and receive about 500 email messages per month, which plan should you use?

5. A boat can travel 24 mi in 3 h when traveling with the current. When traveling against the same current, the boat can travel only 16 mi in 4 h. Find the rate of the current and the rate of the boat in still water.

6. **Writing** Explain how you would solve the system $\begin{cases} 2x + y = 10 \\ y = x + 4 \end{cases}$ using substitution.

Lesson 3-2

3-2 Practice (continued) — Form K

Solving Systems Algebraically

7. Error Analysis You and your friend are solving the system $\begin{cases} y = 7x + 5 \\ 3y = 21x + 15 \end{cases}$.

You say there are infinitely many solutions and your friend says the solution is $\left(-\frac{5}{7}, 0\right)$. Which of you is correct? What mistake was made?

Solve each system by elimination. Check your answers.

8. $\begin{cases} 2x - 2y = 4 \\ -2x + 3y = 6 \end{cases}$

$y = 10$

9. $\begin{cases} 2x + 4y = 18 \\ x - 4y = 6 \end{cases}$

10. $\begin{cases} -3x + 5y = 16 \\ 3x + y = 8 \end{cases}$

11. $\begin{cases} x + 3y = 8 \\ 4x - 2y = 4 \end{cases}$

12. $\begin{cases} 3x - y = 2 \\ 6x + 2y = 16 \end{cases}$

13. $\begin{cases} 4x - 5y = 6 \\ 2x - 2y = 4 \end{cases}$

14. Writing Explain how you would solve the system $\begin{cases} 4x + 2y = 16 \\ 2x + 5y = 10 \end{cases}$ using elimination.

15. Open-Ended Write a system of equations in which one equation could be multiplied by −2 and the other equation could be multiplied by 3 in order to solve the system using elimination.

3-2

Standardized Test Prep

Solving Systems Algebraically

Multiple Choice

For Exercises 1−4, choose the correct letter.

Use the system of equations for Exercises 1 and 2. $\begin{cases} 4x - 10y = -3 \\ 12x + 5y = 12 \end{cases}$

1. What is the value of x in the solution?

Ⓐ $-\frac{9}{7}$ Ⓑ $-\frac{15}{28}$ Ⓒ $\frac{3}{5}$ Ⓓ $\frac{3}{4}$

2. What is the value of y in the solution?

Ⓕ $\frac{3}{35}$ Ⓖ $\frac{3}{5}$ Ⓗ $\frac{3}{4}$ Ⓘ $\frac{24}{35}$

3. Which of the following systems of equations has the solution $(4, -1)$?

Ⓐ $\begin{cases} 3x - 2y = 14 \\ 2x + 2y = 6 \end{cases}$ Ⓒ $\begin{cases} -2x + 4y = 6 \\ -3x + 6y = 8 \end{cases}$

Ⓑ $\begin{cases} 3x - y = 0 \\ 4x + 3y = 26 \end{cases}$ Ⓓ $\begin{cases} 4x + 9y = 1 \\ 4x + 6y = -2 \end{cases}$

4. At a bookstore, used hardcover books sell for $8 each and used softcover books sell for $2 each. You purchase 36 used books and spend $144. How many softcover books do you buy?

Ⓕ 9   Ⓖ 12   Ⓗ 18   Ⓘ 24

Extended Response

5. A local cell phone company offers two different calling plans. In the first plan, you pay a monthly fee of $30 and $.35 per minute. In the second plan you pay a monthly fee of $99 and $.05 per minute.

   a. Write a system of equations showing the two calling plans.

   b. When is it better to use the first calling plan?

   c. When is it better to use the second calling plan?

   d. How much does it cost when the calling plans are equal?

Lesson 3-2

3-3 Think About a Plan

Systems of Inequalities

College Admissions An entrance exam has two sections, a verbal section and a mathematics section. You can score a maximum of 1600 points. For admission, the school of your choice requires a math score of at least 600. Write a system of inequalities to model scores that meet the school's requirements. Then solve the system by graphing.

Know

1. The sum of the verbal score and the mathematics score must be

   _____

2. Each of the scores must be _____

3. _____

Need

4. To solve the problem, you need to find _____

   _____.

Plan

5. What system of inequalities models this situation?

   _____

   _____

6. Graph your system of inequalities on the grid at the right.

7. How do you know which region in your graph represents
   the solution?

   _____

   _____

   _____

3-3 Practice

Form K

Systems of Inequalities

Find all whole number solutions of each system using a table. To start, make a table of values for x and y that satisfy the first inequality.

1. $\begin{cases} y + x \leq 8 \\ y - 1 > 2x \end{cases}$

2. $\begin{cases} y - 2x \leq -2 \\ y \leq -x + 5 \end{cases}$

3. $\begin{cases} -y + x \geq -4 \\ 3y < -9x + 3 \end{cases}$

Solve each system of inequalities by graphing. To start, graph the first inequality.

4. $\begin{cases} y \leq 2x + 2 \\ y < -x + 1 \end{cases}$

5. $\begin{cases} -x - y \leq 2 \\ y - 2x > 1 \end{cases}$

6. $\begin{cases} y \geq x - 3 \\ 2y < x + 6 \end{cases}$

7. You want to bake at least 6 loaves of bread for a bake sale. You want at least twice as many loaves of banana bread as nut bread. Write and graph a system of inequalities to model the situation.

3-3

Practice (continued)

Systems of Inequalities

Form K

8. Writing Explain how you would test whether $(-5, 9)$ is a solution of the system $\begin{cases} y > 6x + 2 \\ y \le -3x + 1 \end{cases}$.

9. An exam has two sections: a multiple choice section and an essay. You can score a maximum of 100 points. To pass the test, you must get at least 65 points on the essay. Write a system of inequalities to model passing scores. Then graph the system.

10. For your rock collection display, you want to have at most 25 samples. You want to have at least 3 times as many sedimentary samples as metamorphic samples. Write and graph a system of inequalities to model the situation.

Solve each system of inequalities by graphing.

11. $\begin{cases} x - y \le 5 \\ x \ge 0 \\ y \ge 0 \end{cases}$

12. $\begin{cases} 5x - 2y > 6 \\ x \ge 0 \\ y \ge 0 \end{cases}$

13. $\begin{cases} y < 3x + 4 \\ x \ge 1 \\ y \ge 0 \end{cases}$

3-3 Standardized Test Prep

Systems of Inequalities

Multiple Choice

For Exercises 1–4, choose the correct letter.

1. Which system of inequalities is shown in the graph?

   (A) $\begin{cases} y \le -2x + 2 \\ y > x - 4 \end{cases}$

   (B) $\begin{cases} y > -2x + 2 \\ y \le x - 4 \end{cases}$

   (C) $\begin{cases} y \ge -2x + 2 \\ y < x - 4 \end{cases}$

   (D) $\begin{cases} y < -2x + 2 \\ y \ge x - 4 \end{cases}$

   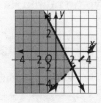

2. Which of the following graphs shows the solution of the system of inequalities? $\begin{cases} y \ge -2x + 2 \\ y \le |3x| \end{cases}$

   (F) 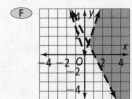   (G) 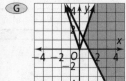   (H) 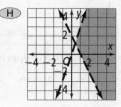   (I)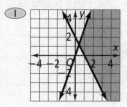

3. Which point lies in the solution set for the system? $\begin{cases} y < 5x - 1 \\ y \ge 7 - 3x \end{cases}$

   (A) $(-5, 1)$ (B) $(2, -3)$ (C) $(4, 4)$ (D) $(1, 6)$

4. How many of the ordered pairs in the data table provided are solutions of the system? $\begin{cases} x + y \le 4 \\ x \ge 1 \end{cases}$

   (F) 6   (H) 9
   (G) 10   (I) 15

x	y
0	4, 3, 2, 1, 0
1	3, 2, 1, 0
2	2, 1, 0
3	1, 0
4	0

Short Response

5. Is $(4, -2)$ a solution of the system? $\begin{cases} x + y > 2 \\ 2x - y < 1 \end{cases}$

   Explain how you made your determination.

Lesson 3-3

3-4   Think About a Plan

Linear Programming

Cooking   Baking a tray of corn muffins takes 4 cups of milk and 3 cups of wheat flour. Baking a tray of bran muffins takes 2 cups of milk and 3 cups of wheat flour. A baker has 16 cups of milk and 15 cups of wheat flour. He makes $3 profit per tray of corn muffins and $2 profit per tray of bran muffins. How many trays of each type of muffin should the baker make to maximize his profit?

Understanding the Problem

1. Organize the information in a table.

	Corn Muffin Trays, x	Bran Muffin Trays, y	Total
Milk (cups)			
Flour (cups)			
Profit			

2. What are the constraints and the objective function?

Constraints: _____   Objective Function: _____

Planning the Solution

3. Graph the constraints on the grid at the right.

4. Label the vertices of the feasible region on your graph.

Getting an Answer

5. What is the value of the objective function at each vertex?

_____

6. At which vertex is the objective function maximized?

_____

7. How can you interpret the solution in the context of the problem?

_____

_____

3-4

Practice
Linear Programming

Graph each system of constraints. Name all vertices. Then find the values of x and y that maximize or minimize the objective function.

1. $\begin{cases} y \le -x + 3 \\ y \le -\frac{1}{2}x + 2 \\ x \ge 0, y \ge 0 \end{cases}$

Maximum for
$P = -4x + 3y$

2. $\begin{cases} y \le -x + 4 \\ y \le -\frac{1}{3}x + 2 \\ x \ge 0, y \ge 0 \end{cases}$

Minimum for
$P = 2x + 3y$

3. $\begin{cases} y \le \frac{1}{2}x + 2 \\ y \le -x + 8 \\ x \ge 2, y \ge 1 \end{cases}$

Maximum for
$P = x - 4y$

4. Teams chosen from 30 forest rangers and 16 trainees are planting trees. An experienced team consisting of two rangers can plant 500 trees per week. A training team consisting of one ranger and two trainees can plant 200 trees per week.

	Experienced Teams	Training Teams	Total
Number of Teams	x	y	$x + y$
Number of Rangers	$2x$	y	30
Number of Trainees	0	$2y$	16
Number of Trees Planted	$500x$	$200y$	$500x + 200y$

a. Write an objective function and constraints for a linear program that models the problem.

b. How many of each type of team should be formed to maximize the number of trees planted? How many trainees are used in this solution? How many trees are planted in a week?

3-4 **Practice** (continued)
Linear Programming

Graph each system of constraints. Name all vertices. Then find the values of x
and y that maximize or minimize the objective function. Find the maximum or
minimum value.

5. $\begin{cases} y \le -3x + 7 \\ 2y + x \le 9 \\ x \ge 0, y \ge 0 \end{cases}$

6. $\begin{cases} y - 5 \le 4x \\ y + x \le 10 \\ x \ge 0, y \ge 3 \end{cases}$

7. $\begin{cases} 3y \le -x + 9 \\ y + 2x \le 8 \\ x \ge 0, y \ge 0 \end{cases}$

Minimum for
$P = 2x + y$

Maximum for
$P = 7x - 5y$

Maximum for
$P = 4x + y$

8. **Reasoning** Why are $x \ge 0$ and $y \ge 0$ part of the constraints in many linear
programs?

9. **Error Analysis** Your friend says the graph to the right can
be used to determine the maximum for $P = 2x + 3y$ with the
constraints $\begin{cases} 2y + x \le 5 \\ y - 12 \le -4x. \\ x \ge 0, y \ge 0 \end{cases}$ What mistake did your friend make?

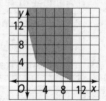

3-4 Standardized Test Prep

Linear Programming

Multiple Choice

For Exercises 1–4, choose the correct letter.

1. The vertices of a feasible region are $(0, 0)$, $(0, 2)$, $(5, 2)$, and $(4, 0)$. For which objective function is the maximum cost C found at the vertex $(4, 0)$?

   Ⓐ $C = -2x + 3y$ Ⓑ $C = 2x + 7y$ Ⓒ $C = 4x - 3y$ Ⓓ $C = 5x + 3y$

2. A feasible region has vertices at $(0, 0)$, $(3, 0)$, $\left(\frac{3}{2}, \frac{7}{2}\right)$, and $(0, 3)$. What are the maximum and minimum values for the objective function $P = 6x + 8y$?

   Ⓕ minimum $(0, 0) = 0$ Ⓗ minimum $(0, 0) = 14$

      maximum $\left(\frac{3}{2}, \frac{7}{2}\right) = 37$ maximum $\left(\frac{3}{2}, \frac{7}{2}\right) = 17$

   Ⓖ minimum $(0, 0) = 0$ Ⓘ minimum $(0, 0) = 0$

      maximum $(3, 0) = 24$ maximum $(0, 3) = 30$

3. Which values of x and y minimize N for the objective function $N = 2x + y$?

   Constraints $\begin{cases} x + y \geq 8 \\ x + 2y \geq 14 \\ x \geq 0, y \geq 0 \end{cases}$

   Ⓐ $(0, 0)$ Ⓑ $(0, 7)$ Ⓒ $(2, 6)$ Ⓓ $(8, 0)$

4. Which of the following systems has the vertices $(0, 5)$, $(1, 4)$, $(3, 0)$, and $(0, 0)$?

   Ⓕ $\begin{cases} x + y \geq 5 \\ 2x + y \geq 6 \\ x \geq 0, y \geq 0 \end{cases}$ Ⓖ $\begin{cases} x + y \leq 5 \\ 2x + y \leq 6 \\ x \geq 0, y \geq 0 \end{cases}$ Ⓗ $\begin{cases} x + y \leq 5 \\ x + 2y \leq 6 \\ x \geq 0, y \geq 0 \end{cases}$ Ⓘ $\begin{cases} x + y \leq 5 \\ 2x + 2y \leq 6 \\ x \geq 0, y \geq 0 \end{cases}$

Short Response

5. The figure at the right shows the feasible region for a system of constraints. This system includes $x \geq 0$ and $y \geq 0$. What are the remaining constraints? Show your work.

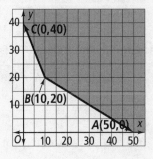

3-5

Think About a Plan

Systems With Three Variables

Sports A stadium has 49,000 seats. Seats sell for $25 in Section A, $20 in Section B, and $15 in Section C. The number of seats in Section A equals the total number of seats in Sections B and C. Suppose the stadium takes in $1,052,000 from each sold-out event. How many seats does each section hold?

Understanding the Problem

1. Define a variable for each unknown in this problem.

   Let $x =$ _____

   Let $y =$ _____

   Let $z =$ _____

2. What system of equations represents this situation?

   _____

   _____

   _____

Planning the Solution

3. Can you write a simpler equivalent equation for one of the equations in your system? If so, write the equivalent equation.

   _____

4. What method of solving looks easier for this problem? Explain.

   _____

   _____

Getting an Answer

5. Solve the system of equations.

   _____

6. How can you interpret the solution in the context of the problem?

   _____

   _____

3-5 Practice

Form K

Systems With Three Variables

Solve each system by elimination. Check your answers. To start, pair the equations to eliminate one variable and add.

1. $\begin{cases} x + 2y + z = 10 \\ 2x - y + 3z = -5 \\ 2x - 3y - 5z = 27 \end{cases}$

2. $\begin{cases} 2a + b + c = 9 \\ a + 2b + c = 8 \\ a + b + 2c = 11 \end{cases}$

$$-2(x + 2y + z) = (-2 \cdot 10)$$
$$\underline{+ \; 2x - y + 3z = -5}$$
$$-5y + \; z = -25$$

Solve each system by substitution. Check your answers.

3. $\begin{cases} 2x + y + z = 14 \\ -x - 3y + 2z = -2 \\ 4x - 6y + 3z = -5 \end{cases}$

4. $\begin{cases} 3x + 2y - z = 12 \\ -4x + y - 2z = 4 \\ x - 3y + z = -4 \end{cases}$

$$y = -2x - z + 14$$
$$-x - 3(-2x - z + 14) + 2z = -2$$
$$-x + 6x + 3z - 42 + 2z = -2$$
$$5x + 5z = 40$$
$$x + z = 8$$

5. You have 17 coins in pennies, nickels, and dimes in your pocket. The value of the coins is $0.47. There are four times the number of pennies as nickels. How many of each type of coin do you have?

6. **Writing** When you solve a system of equations, explain how you can determine if your solution is correct.

3-5 Practice (continued)   *Form K*
Systems With Three Variables

Solve each system using any method.

7. $\begin{cases} 4x - y + z = 0 \\ -2x + 2y + 3z = 3 \\ -x + 3y - 2z = -19 \end{cases}$

8. $\begin{cases} x + 2y + z = -20 \\ -2x + y - z = -5 \\ 5x + 2y - z = 16 \end{cases}$

9. $\begin{cases} 3x + 2y + 2z = 13 \\ 2x + y - z = -5 \\ x - 3y + z = -16 \end{cases}$

10. For a party, you are cooking a large amount of stew that has meat, potatoes, and carrots. The meat costs $6 per pound, the potatoes cost $3 per pound, and the carrots cost $1 per pound. You spend $48.50 on 13.5 pounds of food. You buy twice as many carrots as potatoes.
    a. Write a system of three equations that represent how much food you bought.
    b. How much of each ingredient did you buy?

11. **Multiple Choice** What is the value of z in the solution of the system?

    $\begin{cases} 3x - 4y + 2z = 20 \\ x + y - z = -4 \\ 6x - y + 2z = 23 \end{cases}$

    Ⓐ 2

    Ⓑ −1

    Ⓒ 5

    Ⓓ −5

3-5 Standardized Test Prep

Systems With Three Variables

Gridded Response

Solve each exercise and enter your answer in the grid provided.

1. A change machine contains nickels, dimes, and quarters. There are 75 coins in the machine, and the value of the coins is $7.25. There are 5 times as many nickels as dimes. How many quarters are in the machine?

2. The sum of three numbers is 23. The first number is equal to twice the second number minus 7. The third number is equal to one more than the sum of the first and second numbers. What is the first number?

3. A fish's tail weighs 9 lb. Its head weighs as much as its tail plus half its body. Its body weighs as much as its head and tail. How many pounds does the fish weigh?

4. You are training for a triathlon. In your training routine each week, you bike 5 times as far as you run and you run 4 times as far as you swim. One week you trained a total of 200 miles. How many miles did you swim that week?

5. Three multiplied by the first number is equal to the second number plus 4. The second number is equal to one plus two multiplied by the third number. The third number is one less than the first number. What is the sum of all three numbers?

Answers

1.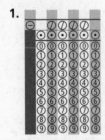
2.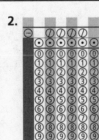
3.
4.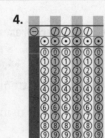
5.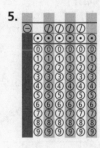

3-6

Think About a Plan

Solving Systems Using Matrices

Paint A hardware store mixes paints in a ratio of two parts red to six parts yellow to make two gallons of pumpkin orange. A ratio of five parts red to three parts yellow makes two gallons of pepper red. A gallon of pumpkin orange sells for $25, and a gallon of pepper red sells for $28. Find the cost of 1 quart of red paint and the cost of 1 quart of yellow paint.

Know

1. There are ☐ quarts in 1 gallon.

2. ☐ qt red + ☐ qt yellow = ☐ qt pumpkin orange

   ☐ qt red + ☐ qt yellow = ☐ qt pepper red

3. ☐ quarts of pumpkin orange cost ☐ .

   ☐ quarts of pepper red cost ☐ .

Need

4. To solve the problem you need to define:

   _____

5. To solve the problem you need to find:

   _____

Plan

6. What system of equations represents this situation?

   _____

7. How can you represent the system of equations with a matrix?

8. Solve the system of equations using the matrix.

   _____

9. How can you interpret the solutions in the context of the problem?

   _____

3-6

Practice

Solving Systems Using Matrices

Form K

Identify the indicated element.

$$A = \begin{bmatrix} 4 & -2 & 2 \\ 1 & 4 & 1 \\ 0 & 5 & -7 \end{bmatrix}$$

1. a_{21}
row 2, column 1

2. a_{13}

3. a_{32}

4. a_{33}

Write a matrix to represent each system.

5. $\begin{cases} 2x + y = 8 \\ x - 3y = -3 \end{cases}$

6. $\begin{cases} -4x + y = -3 \\ 2x + y = 0 \end{cases}$

7. $\begin{cases} 3x + 2y - 2z = 9 \\ 5x + y - 3z = -7 \\ x + 4y + 3z = 5 \end{cases}$

Write the system of equations represented by each matrix.

8. $\begin{bmatrix} -1 & 2 & | & 5 \\ 4 & 3 & | & -1 \end{bmatrix}$

9. $\begin{bmatrix} 1 & 6 & | & 7 \\ 2 & 4 & | & -2 \end{bmatrix}$

10. $\begin{bmatrix} -1 & 5 & -4 & | & 0 \\ 3 & 4 & 1 & | & -1 \\ -3 & 6 & -7 & | & 2 \end{bmatrix}$

Lesson 3-6

3-6   **Practice** (continued)   *Form K*

Solving Systems Using Matrices

11. Error Analysis Your classmate says that in the matrix to the right, a_{23} is 6. What mistake did your classmate make? What is the correct answer?

$$A = \begin{bmatrix} 3 & -1 & 4 \\ 1 & 5 & -2 \\ 2 & 6 & -3 \end{bmatrix}$$

Solve the system of equations using a matrix.

12. $\begin{cases} x - 2y = -10 \\ -2x - 3y = -1 \end{cases}$

$$\begin{bmatrix} 1 & -2 & | & -10 \\ -2 & -3 & | & -1 \end{bmatrix}$$

13. $\begin{cases} -3x - y = -1 \\ 4x + y = 3 \end{cases}$

14. $\begin{cases} 2x + 5y = -11 \\ -x + y = 2 \end{cases}$

15. You work at a fruit stand that sells apples for $2 per pound, oranges for $5 per pound, and bananas for $3 per pound. Yesterday you sold 60 pounds of fruit and made $180. You sold 10 more pounds of apples than bananas.
   a. Write a matrix to show the system of equations for this situation.
   b. How many pounds of each kind of fruit did you sell yesterday?
   c. What kind of fruit did you sell the most?

16. Open-Ended Write a matrix for a system of two equations that does not have a solution.

17. Writing Explain how to write the system $\begin{cases} 5x + 2y = 3 \\ 4x = 7 \end{cases}$ as a matrix.

3-6 Standardized Test Prep

Solving Systems Using Matrices

Multiple Choice

For Exercises 1–3, choose the correct letter.

1. Which system of equations is equivalent to $\begin{bmatrix} 4 & -1 & 2 & | & 6 \\ 3 & 0 & 4 & | & 2 \\ 1 & 5 & 3 & | & 7 \end{bmatrix}$?

   (A) $\begin{cases} 4x + y + 2z = 6 \\ 3x + 4z = 2 \\ z + 5y + 3z = 7 \end{cases}$

   (C) $\begin{cases} 4x + y + 2z = 6 \\ 3x + y + 4z = 2 \\ z + 5y + 3z = 7 \end{cases}$

   (B) $\begin{cases} 4x - y + 2z = 6 \\ 3x + 4z = 2 \\ z + 5y + 3z = 7 \end{cases}$

   (D) $\begin{cases} 4x - y + 2z = 6 \\ 3x + y + 4z = 2 \\ z + 5y + 3z = 7 \end{cases}$

2. What is the solution of the system represented by the matrix $\begin{bmatrix} 2 & 3 & -1 & | & 2 \\ -3 & -4 & 2 & | & -2 \\ 1 & 2 & -1 & | & 3 \end{bmatrix}$?

   (F) $(1, 3, 4)$ (G) $(4, -3, 1)$ (H) $(-4, 3, -1)$ (I) $(3, -4, -1)$

3. How many elements are in a 2×3 matrix?
   (A) 2   (B) 4   (C) 5   (D) 6

Short Response

4. A clothing store is having a sale. A pair of jeans costs \$15 and a shirt costs \$8. You spend \$131 and buy a total of 12 items. Using a matrix, how many pairs of jeans and shirts do you buy? Show your work.

Lesson 3-6

4-1 Think About a Plan

Quadratic Functions and Transformations

Write a quadratic function to represent the areas of all rectangles with a perimeter of 36 ft. Graph the function and describe the rectangle that has the largest area.

1. Write an equation that represents the area of a rectangle with a perimeter of 36 ft. Let x = width and y = length.

2. Solve your equation for y.

3. Write a quadratic function for the area of the rectangle.

$$A = \boxed{} \cdot \boxed{}$$

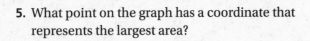

$$= \boxed{} \cdot \left(\boxed{} \right)$$

$$= \boxed{}$$

4. Graph the quadratic function you wrote.

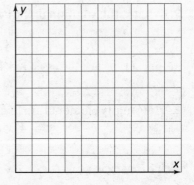

5. What point on the graph has a coordinate that represents the largest area?

6. How can you find the coordinates of this point? What are the coordinates?

_____

_____

7. Describe the rectangle that has the largest area. What is its area?

_____

_____

4-1

Practice

Form K

Quadratic Functions and Transformations

Graph each function.

1. $y = 4x^2$

2. $f(x) = -3x^2$

3. $y = -\frac{1}{2}x^2$

Graph each function. How is each graph a translation of $f(x) = x^2$?

4. $f(x) = x^2 + 4$

5. $f(x) = (x + 3)^2$

6. $f(x) = x^2 - 2$

7. $f(x) = (x - 5)^2$

8. $f(x) = x^2 + 6$

9. $f(x) = (x + 1)^2$

What are the vertex, the axis of symmetry, the maximum or minimum value, the domain, and the range of each function?

10. $f(x) = 2(x - 4)^2 + 3$

11. $f(x) = -(x + 3)^2 - 2.5$

12. $f(x) = -2(x - 6)^2$

Lesson 4-1

4-1

Practice (continued)   *Form K*

Quadratic Functions and Transformations

What is the graph of each function? Identify the axis of symmetry.

13. $f(x) = 6(x - 1)^2 - 4$ **14.** $f(x) = -(x + 5)^2 + 2$ **15.** $f(x) = (x + 2)^2 - 7$

What quadratic function models each graph?

16.   **17.**   **18.**

19. Error Analysis A classmate said that the vertex of $y = -5(x + 2)^2 - 6$ is $(2, 6)$. What mistake did your classmate make? What is the correct vertex?

20. Open-Ended Write a quadratic function that has a maximum value.

Write the equation of each parabola in vertex form.

21. vertex $(-3, 7)$, point $(-2, -5)$ **22.** vertex $(4, 0)$, point $(-6, -3)$

23. vertex $(-2, -5)$, point $(-6, 0)$ **24.** vertex $(1, 3)$, point $(2, 5)$

4-1 Standardized Test Prep

Quadratic Functions and Transformations

Multiple Choice

For Exercises 1–4, choose the correct letter.

1. What is the vertex of the function $y = 3(x - 7)^2 + 4$?

   Ⓐ $(-7, -4)$ Ⓑ $(-7, 4)$ Ⓒ $(7, -4)$ Ⓓ $(7, 4)$

2. Which is the graph of the function $f(x) = -2(x + 3)^2 + 5$?

   Ⓕ 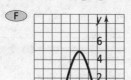   Ⓖ 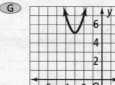   Ⓗ 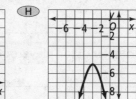   Ⓘ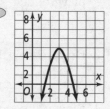

3. Which of the following best describes how to transform $y = x^2$ to the graph of $y = 4(x - 2.5)^2 - 3$?

   Ⓐ Translate 2.5 units left, stretch by a factor of 4, translate 3 units down.

   Ⓑ Translate 3 units right and 2.5 units down, stretch by a factor of 4.

   Ⓒ Translate 2.5 units right, stretch by a factor of 4, translate 3 units down.

   Ⓓ Stretch by a factor of 4, translate 2.5 units left and 3 units down.

4. What is the equation of the parabola with vertex $(-4, 6)$ passing through the point $(-2, -2)$?

   Ⓕ $y = -2(x + 4)^2 - 6$ Ⓗ $y = 2(x + 4)^2 + 6$

   Ⓖ $y = 2(x - 4)^2 - 6$ Ⓘ $y = -2(x + 4)^2 + 6$

Short Response

5. A baseball is hit so that its height above ground is given by the equation $h = -16t^2 + 96t + 4$, where h is the height in feet and t is the time in seconds after it is hit. Show your work.

   a. How long does it take the baseball to reach its highest point?

   b. How high will it go?

Lesson 4-1

4-2

Think About a Plan

Standard Form of a Quadratic Function

Landscaping A town is planning a playground. It wants to fence in a rectangular space using an existing wall. What is the greatest area it can fence in using 100 ft of donated fencing?

Understanding the Problem

1. Write an expression for the width of the playground. Let *l* be the length of the playground.

   _____

2. Do you know the perimeter of the playground? Explain?

   _____

3. What is the problem asking you to determine?

   _____

   _____

Planning the Solution

4. Write a quadratic equation to model the area of the playground.

   _____

5. What information can you get from the equation to find the maximum area? Explain.

   _____

   _____

Getting an Answer

6. What is the value of *l* that produces the maximum area?

7. What is the greatest area the town can fence in using 100 ft of fencing?

4-2 Practice

Form K

Standard Form of a Quadratic Function

What are the vertex, the axis of symmetry, the maximum or minimum value, and the range of each parabola?

1. $y = -x^2 + 2x - 5$ **2.** $y = -2x^2 - 8x + 3$ **3.** $y = 4x^2 - 2x + 1$

What is the graph of each function?

4. $y = -x^2 - 6x - 11$ **5.** $y = 5x^2 + 10x + 8$ **6.** $y = \frac{1}{2}x^2 - 3x + \frac{11}{2}$

7. $y = -2x^2 + 4x + 3$ **8.** $y = x^2 + 4x + 2$ **9.** $y = -6x^2 - 12x + 5$

Sketch each parabola using the given information.

10. vertex $(-2, 1)$, y-intercept 4

11. vertex $(3, -5)$, point $(4, 1)$

12. vertex $(-1, -7)$, point $(-5, 1)$

Lesson 4-2

4-2 **Practice** (continued)   *Form K*

Standard Form of a Quadratic Function

What is the vertex form of the following quadratic functions?

13. $y = 4x^2 + 16x + 19$ **14.** $y = -x^2 + 2x + 4$ **15.** $y = \frac{1}{2}x^2 - 6x + 15$

16. $y = -3x^2 - 18x - 29$ **17.** $y = 2x^2 + 4x + 9$ **18.** $y = \frac{2}{3}x^2 - \frac{8}{3}x + \frac{5}{3}$

19. Reasoning When is it better to have the quadratic function in vertex form instead of standard form?

20. The Gateway Arch in St. Louis was built in 1965. It is the tallest monument in the United States. The arch can be modeled with the function $y = -0.00635x^2 + 4x$, where x and y are in feet.
  a. How high above the ground is the tallest point of the arch?
  b. How far apart are the legs of the arch at their bases?

21. The height of a batted ball is modeled by the function $h = -0.01x^2 + 1.22x + 3$, where x is the horizontal distance in feet from the point of impact with the bat, and h is the height of the ball in feet.
  a. What is the maximum height that the ball will reach?
  b. At what distance from the batter will the ball hit the ground?

4-2 Standardized Test Prep

Standard Form of a Quadratic Function

Multiple Choice

For Exercises 1–6, choose the correct letter.

1. What is the vertex of the parabola $y = x^2 + 8x + 5$?

   Ⓐ $(4, -11)$ Ⓑ $(-4, -11)$ Ⓒ $(-4, 5)$ Ⓓ $(4, 5)$

2. What is the maximum value of the function $y = -3x^2 + 12x - 8$?

   Ⓕ 4   Ⓗ 8

   Ⓖ -8 Ⓘ 2

3. Which function has the graph shown at the right?

   Ⓐ $y = -2x^2 - 5x + 1$ Ⓒ $y = -2x^2 - 5x - 1$

   Ⓑ $y = 2x^2 + 5x - 1$ Ⓓ $y = -2x^2 + 5x - 1$

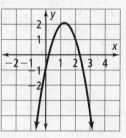

4. What is the vertex form of the function $y = 3x^2 - 12x + 17$?

   Ⓕ $y = 3(x - 2)^2 + 5$ Ⓗ $y = 3(x - 2)^2 + 11$

   Ⓖ $y = 3(x - 2)^2 + 17$ Ⓘ $y = 3(x + 2)^2 + 5$

5. What is the equation of the parabola with vertex $(3, -20)$ and that passes through the point $(7, 12)$?

   Ⓐ $y = 2x^2 + 12x - 2$ Ⓒ $y = -2x^2 + 12x - 38$

   Ⓑ $y = 2x^2 - 12x - 2$ Ⓓ $y = 2x^2 - 12x + 38$

6. For the function $y = -5x^2 - 10x + c$, the vertex is $(-1, 8)$. What is c?

   Ⓕ -13 Ⓖ -3 Ⓗ 3   Ⓘ 13

Short Response

7. To increase revenue, a county wants to increase park fees. The overall income will go up, but there will be expenses involved in collecting the fees. For a $p\%$ increase in the fees, this cost C will be $C = 0.6p^2 - 7.2p + 48$, in thousands of dollars. What percent increase will minimize the cost to the county? Show your work.

4-3

Think About a Plan

Modeling With Quadratic Functions

a. Postal Rates Find a quadratic model for the data. Use 1981 as year 0.

Price of First-Class Stamp								
Year	1981	1991	1995	1999	2001	2006	2007	2008
Price (cents)	18	29	32	33	34	39	41	42

b. Describe a reasonable domain and range for your model. (*Hint*: This is a discrete, real situation.)

c. Estimation Estimate when first-class postage was 37 cents.

d. Use your model to predict when first-class postage will be 50 cents. Explain why your prediction may not be valid.

1. How can you find the *x*-coordinates of the data points?

_____

2. What calculator function finds a quadratic model for data? _____

3. Find a quadratic model for the data. $y = \boxed{} x^2 + \boxed{} x + \boxed{}$

4. What does the domain of your model represent? What set of numbers would be a reasonable domain?

_____

5. What does the range of your model represent? What set of numbers would be a reasonable domain?

_____

6. How can you find the *x*-value that produces a given *y*-value?

_____

_____

7. Estimate the year when first-class postage was 37 cents. $\boxed{}$

8. Predict the year when first-class postage will be 50 cents. $\boxed{}$

9. Why might your prediction not be valid?

_____

_____

4-3 Practice   Form K

Modeling With Quadratic Functions

Find an equation in standard form of the parabola passing through the points. To start, substitute the (x, y) values into $y = ax^2 + bx + c$ to write a system of equations.

1. $(2, -20), (-2, -4), (0, -8)$ **2.** $(1, -3), (2, 0), (3, 9)$

3. $(3, -1), (2, -5), (4, -5)$ **4.** $(-4, 3), (-6, 7), (-1, 12)$

5. $(2, 1), (1, -1), (4, -7)$ **6.** $(-1, 2), (-2, 7), (0, 7)$

7. A player hits a tennis ball across the court and records the height of the ball at different times, as shown in the table.
   a. Find a quadratic model for the data.
   b. Use the model to estimate the height of the ball at 4 seconds.
   c. What is the ball's maximum height?

Time (s)	Height (ft)
0	5.5
1	6.0
2	5.5
3	4.0

8. Reasoning Explain why the quadratic model only works up to 4.5 seconds — that height measurements made after 4.5 seconds are not valid. (Remember this is a discrete, real situation.)

9. The table at the right shows the height of the tides measured at the Santa Monica Municipal Pier in California. Hours are measured from 0.00 at midnight.
   a. Find a quadratic model for this data using quadratic regression.
   b. Use the model to predict the lowest tide height.
   c. When does the lowest tide occur?

Time	Tide Height (ft)
0.33	3.9
3.30	2.7
11.11	4.6

Source: www.tidesandcurrents.noaa.gov

Lesson 4-3

4-3

Practice (continued)   Form K

Modeling With Quadratic Functions

10. The table at the right shows average retail gasoline prices.
    a. Find a quadratic model for the data using 1976 as year 0, 1986 as year 10, 1996 as year 20, and 2005 as year 29.
    b. Use the model to estimate the average retail gasoline price in 2000.

Year	Price per gallon (cents)
1976	61.4
1986	92.7
1996	141.3
2005	208.0

Source: U.S. Dept. of Energy

Determine whether a quadratic model exists for each set of values. If so, write the model.

11. $f(0) = 5, f(-4) = 13, f(2) = 7$

12. $f(1) = 1, f(-3) = -19, f(-1) = -9$

13. $f(0) = 0, f(1) = 2, f(2) = 4$

14. $f(-5) = 3, f(-2) = 6, f(0) = -2$

15. The table at the right shows in thousands how many people in the U.S. subscribe to a cellular telephone.
    a. Find a quadratic model for the data. Let x = the number of years since 1985.
    b. Use the model to estimate the number of subscribers in 1995.
    c. Describe a reasonable domain and range for this situation.

Year	U.S Cellular Telephone Subscribership (in thousands)
1985	340
1990	5283
2000	109,478
2004	182,140

Source: CTIA Semi-Annual Wireless Industry

16. **Error Analysis** In Exercise 15 part (c), your friend said that the range was equal to all real numbers. Why is this incorrect?

17. **Reasoning** Explain how you know your answer to Exercise 15 part (b) is reasonable.

4-3 Standardized Test Prep

Modeling With Quadratic Functions

Multiple Choice

For Exercises 1–5, choose the correct letter.

1. Which parabola passes through the points $(1, -2)$, $(4, 1)$, and $(5, -2)$?

   Ⓐ $y = -x^2 + x - 3$ Ⓒ $y = x^2 - 4x + 1$

   Ⓑ $y = -x^2 + 6x - 7$ Ⓓ $y = x^2 - 4x - 1$

2. Which parabola passes through the points in the table at the right?

   Ⓕ $y = -x^2 - x + 2$ Ⓗ $y = 2x^2 - 4x - 4$

   Ⓖ $y = \frac{1}{2}x^2 - \frac{5}{2}x - 1$ Ⓘ $y = x^2 - 3x - 2$

x	$f(x)$
-1	2
2	-4
4	2

3. A baseball coach records the height at every second of a ball thrown in the air. Some of the data appears in the table below.

Time (s)	0	1	3
Height (ft)	0	64	96

   Which equation is a quadratic model for the data?

   Ⓐ $h = -16t^2 + 80t$ Ⓒ $h = -32t^2 + 80t$

   Ⓑ $h = -48t^2 + 112t$ Ⓓ $h = -16t^2 + 64t$

4. Use the table in Exercise 3. What is the height of the ball at 2.5 s?

   Ⓕ 80 ft   Ⓗ 100 ft

   Ⓖ 88 ft   Ⓘ 112 ft

5. Which of the following sets of values cannot be modeled with a quadratic function?

   Ⓐ $(2, 3), (0, -1), (3, 2)$ Ⓒ $(2, -7), (-1, 5), (3, -11)$

   Ⓑ $f(2) = 7, f(-1) = -2, f(0) = 3$ Ⓓ $f(2) = -6, f(0) = -2, f(-1) = 3$

Short Response

6. The accountant for a small company studied the amount spent on advertising and the company's profit for several years. He made the table below. What is a quadratic model for the data? Show your work.

Advertising (Hundreds of Dollars)	1	2	3
Profit (Dollars)	269	386	501

4-4 Think About a Plan

Factoring Quadratic Expressions

Agriculture The area in square feet of a rectangular field is $x^2 - 120x + 3500$. The width, in feet, is $x - 50$. What is the length, in feet?

Know

1. The area of the field equals the [   ] times the [   ].

2. The area of the field is _____ ft^2.

3. The width of the field is [   ] ft.

Need

4. To solve the problem I need to:

_____

_____ .

Plan

5. One factor is [   ].

6. What is the coefficient of the first term of the other factor? _____

   How do you know?

_____

7. What is the sign of the second term of the other factor? [   ]

   How do you know?

_____

8. The product of 50 and [   ] is 3500.

9. The sum of 50 and [   ] is 120.

10. The other factor is [   ].

11. What is the length of the rectangular field, in feet?

4-4 Practice

Form K

Factoring Quadratic Expressions

Factor each expression.

1. $x^2 + 4x - 5$

2. $x^2 + 13x + 42$

3. $-x^2 - x + 12$

4. $x^2 - 8x + 16$

5. $-x^2 + 16x - 55$

6. $x^2 + 2x - 48$

7. $-y^2 + 17y - 72$

8. $x^2 + 7x + 12$

9. $x^2 - 8x + 12$

Find the GCF of each expression. Then factor the expression.

10. $3x^2 + 15x + 12$

11. $-9y^2 + 6y$

12. $6x^2 + 12x - 48$

13. $-3x^2 - 3x + 60$

14. $2x^2 - 10x$

15. $7x^2 - 14x - 56$

16. $10x^2 + 100x$

17. $9x^2 - 36x + 27$

18. $-5xy^2 - 30xy - 25x$

19. **Writing** When you factor a quadratic expression, explain what it means when $c < 0$ and $b > 0$.

20. **Error Analysis** You factored $-x^2 + 10x - 24$ as $-(x - 6)(x - 4)$. Your friend factored it as $(x + 12)(x - 2)$. Which of you is correct? What mistake was made?

21. **Multiple Choice** What is the factored form of $-14a^2 + 42ab$?

   Ⓐ $a(-14a + 42b)$

   Ⓒ $7(-2a^2 + 6ab)$

   Ⓑ $-2a(7a - 21b)$

   Ⓓ $-14a(a - 3b)$

22. **Reasoning** The area of a carpet is $(x^2 - 11x + 28)$ ft^2. What are the length and the width of the carpet?

Lesson 4-4

4-4

Practice (continued)   *Form K*

Factoring Quadratic Expressions

Factor each expression.

23. $2x^2 + 7x + 6$ **24.** $3x^2 - 14x - 24$ **25.** $5x^2 - 22x + 21$

26. $4x^2 + 18x + 8$ **27.** $2x^2 - 8x + 6$ **28.** $6x^2 + 13x - 28$

29. $4x^2 - 4x + 1$ **30.** $x^2 + 6x + 9$ **31.** $4x^2 - 16$

32. $9x^2 - 4$ **33.** $16x^2 - 40x + 25$ **34.** $x^2 - 25$

35. $9x^2 - 36x + 36$ **36.** $25x^2 - 9$ **37.** $4x^2 + 24x + 36$

38. Error Analysis Which of the following examples is factored correctly? Explain.

Example 1
$4x^2 - 49$
$(2x)^2 - 7^2$
$(2x - 7)(2x + 7)$

Example 2
$4x^2 - 49$
$(2x)^2 - 7^2$
$(2x - 7)(2x - 7)$

39. You can represent the area of a square tabletop with the expression $16x^2 + 24x + 9$. What is the side length of the tabletop in terms of x?

4-4

Standardized Test Prep

Factoring Quadratic Expressions

Multiple Choice

For Exercises 1–6, choose the correct letter.

1. What is the complete factorization of $2x^2 + x - 15$?

   A $(x - 5)(2x + 3)$ **C** $(x - 3)(2x + 5)$

   B $(x + 3)(2x - 5)$ **D** $(x + 5)(2x - 3)$

2. What is the complete factorization of $-x^2 + 3x + 28$?

   F $(x - 4)(x - 7)$ **H** $-(x + 4)(x + 7)$

   G $-(x - 4)(x + 7)$ **I** $-(x - 7)(x + 4)$

3. What is the complete factorization of $6x^2 + 9x - 6$?

   A $3(2x - 1)(x + 2)$ **C** $3(x - 2)(2x + 1)$

   B $(3x + 2)(2x - 3)$ **D** $3(x - 2)(2x - 1)$

4. What is the complete factorization of $16x^2 - 56x + 49$?

   F $(4x - 7)(4x + 7)$ **H** $(4x + 7)^2$

   G $(4x - 7)^2$ **I** $16(x - 7)^2$

5. What is the complete factorization of $5x^2 - 20$?

   A $(5x - 4)(x + 5)$ **C** $5(x + 2)(x - 2)$

   B $5(x + 4)(x - 4)$ **D** $5(x - 2)^2$

6. What is the complete factorization of $x^2 - 14x + 24$?

   F $(x - 8)(x - 3)$ **H** $(x + 2)(x - 12)$

   G $(x - 4)(x - 6)$ **I** $(x - 12)(x - 2)$

Short Response

7. The area in square meters of a rectangular parking lot is $x^2 - 95x + 2100$. The width in meters is $x - 60$. What is the length of the parking lot in meters? Show your work.

Lesson 4-4

4-5 Think About a Plan

Quadratic Equations

Landscaping Suppose you have an outdoor pool measuring 25 ft by 10 ft. You want to add a cement walkway around the pool. If the walkway will be 1 ft thick and you have 304 ft^3 of cement, how wide should the walkway be?

Understanding the Problem

1. Draw a diagram of the pool and the walkway. Let $x =$ the width of the walkway in feet.

2. If you lay the pieces of walkway end to end, what is the total length of the walkway?

3. What is the thickness of the walkway?

4. What is the problem asking you to determine?

   _____

Planning the Solution

5. Write a quadratic equation to model the volume of the walkway.

6. What method can you use to find the solutions of your quadratic equation?

   _____

   _____

   _____

Getting an Answer

7. How many solutions of your quadratic equation do you need to find? Explain.

   _____

8. How wide should the walkway be?

4-5 Practice

Form K

Quadratic Equations

Solve each equation by factoring. Check your answers. To start, factor the quadratic expression.

1. $x^2 - x - 30 = 0$

2. $x^2 - 10x = -21$

3. $x^2 = -10x - 9$

4. $x^2 - 5x = 0$

5. $10x - 24 = x^2$

6. $x^2 = -12x$

Solve each equation using tables. Give each answer to at most two decimal places. To start, enter the equation as Y1. Make a table and look for where the y-values change sign.

7. $x^2 + x = 12$

8. $10x^2 + 26x + 16 = 0$

9. $2x^2 + 11x = 6$

10. $2x^2 - 13x + 18 = 0$

11. $2x^2 = 10x$

12. $0.5x^2 - 8 = 0$

Write a quadratic equation with the given solutions.

13. 4 and −5

14. −6 and 0

15. 3 and 8

16. Writing Explain when you would prefer to use factoring to solve a quadratic equation and when you would prefer to use tables.

17. A parabolic jogging path intersects both ends of a street. The path has the equation $x^2 - 25x = 0$. If one end of the street is considered to be $x = 0$ and the street lies on the x-axis, where else does the path intersect the street?

Lesson 4-5

4-5 Practice (continued)   Form K
Quadratic Equations

Solve each equation by graphing. Give each answer to at most two decimal places.

18. $2x^2 - x - 10 = 0$ **19.** $6x^2 - 13x = 28$ **20.** $4x^2 + 27x = 12$

21. $4x^2 - 5x - 26 = 0$ **22.** $6x^2 - 23x = 18$ **23.** $4x^2 - 9x + 5 = 0$

24. The students in Mr. Wilson's Physics class are making golf ball catapults. The flight of group A's ball is modeled by the equation $y = -0.014x^2 + 0.68x$, where x is the ball's distance from the catapult. The units are in feet.
  a. How far did the ball fly?
  b. How high above the ground did the ball fly?
  c. What is a reasonable domain and range for this function?

25. A rectangular pool is 20 ft wide and 50 ft long. The pool is surrounded by a walkway. The walkway is the same width all the way around the pool. The total area of the walkway is 456 square ft. How wide is the walkway?

26. Reasoning The equation used to solve Exercise 25 has two solutions. Why is only one solution used to answer the question?

4-5 Standardized Test Prep

Quadratic Equations

Gridded Response

Solve each exercise and enter your answer in the grid provided.

1. What is the positive solution of the equation $x^2 = 2x + 35$? Solve by factoring.

2. What is the positive solution of the equation $5x^2 + 2x - 16 = 0$? Solve by factoring.

3. What is the positive solution of the equation $x^2 - 3x = 1$? Solve by using a table or by graphing. If necessary, round your answer to the nearest hundredth.

4. What is the positive solution of the equation $3x^2 - 5x - 7 = 0$? Solve by using a table or by graphing. If necessary, round your answer to the nearest hundredth.

5. What is the positive solution of the equation $\frac{1}{2}x^2 - 3x = 5$? Solve by using a table or by graphing. If necessary, round your answer to the nearest hundredth.

Answers

1.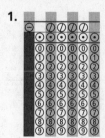
2.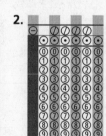
3.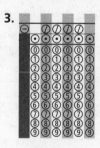
4.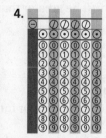
5.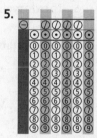

4-6 Think About a Plan

Completing the Square

Geometry The table shows some possible dimensions of rectangles with a perimeter of 100 units. Copy and complete the table.

Width	Length	Area
1	49	49
2	48	
3		
4		
5		

  a. Plot the points (width, area). Find a model for the data set.
  b. What is another point in the data set? Use it to verify your model.
  c. What is a reasonable domain for this function? Explain.
  d. Find the maximum possible area. What are its dimensions?
  e. Find an equation for area in terms of width without using the table. Do you get the same equation as in part (a)? Explain.

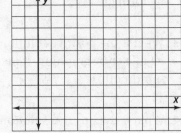

1. What points should you plot? Plot the points on the graph.

  _____

2. Use your graphing calculator to find a model for the data set. [_____]

3. What is another point in the data set? Use it to verify your model.

  _____

4. What does the domain of your function represent?

  _____

5. The domain must be greater than _____ and less than _____.

6. A reasonable domain is:

  _____

7. Write the vertex form of your function.

8. The maximum possible area is [_____].
   The dimensions of this rectangle are [_____] by [_____].

9. If the width of the rectangle is x, then the length is [_____].

   Area = [_____] times [_____] = [_____] · [_____] = [_____]

10. Is the equation in Exercise 9 the same as your model in Exercise 2? Explain.

  _____

4-6 Practice

Form K

Completing the Square

Solve each equation by finding square roots. To start, remember to isolate x^2.

1. $x^2 - 9 = 0$
$x^2 = 9$

2. $x^2 + 4 = 20$
$x^2 = 16$

3. $x^2 + 15 = 16$
$x^2 = 1$

4. $2x^2 - 64 = 0$

5. $4x^2 - 100 = 0$

6. $5x^2 - 25 = 0$

7. You are painting a large wall mural. The wall length is 3 times the height. The area of the wall is 300 ft².
  a. What are the dimensions of the wall?
  b. If each can of paint covers 22 ft², will 12 cans be enough to cover the wall?

8. The lengths of the sides of a carpet have the ratio of 4.4 to 1. The area of the carpet is 1154.7 ft². What are the dimensions of the carpet?

9. A packing box is 4 ft deep. One side of the box is 1.5 times longer than the other. The volume of the box is 24 ft³. What are the dimensions of the box?

Solve each equation. To start, factor the perfect square trinomial.

10. $x^2 - 14x + 49 = 81$
$(x - 7)^2 = 81$

11. $x^2 + 6x + 9 = 1$
$(x + 3)^2 = 1$

12. $9x^2 - 12x + 4 = 49$
$(3x - 2)^2 = 49$

13. $4x^2 + 36x + 81 = 16$

14. $x^2 + 2x + 1 = 36$

15. $x^2 - 16x + 64 = 9$

Lesson 4-6

4-6 Practice (continued) Form K

Completing the Square

Complete the following squares.

16. $x^2 + 8x + \boxed{}$

$\left(\frac{8}{2}\right)^2 = 4^2 = 16$

17. $x^2 + 20x + \boxed{}$

$\left(\frac{10}{2}\right)^2 =$

18. $x^2 - 14x + \boxed{}$

19. $x^2 - 24x + \boxed{}$

20. $x^2 + 34x + \boxed{}$

21. $x^2 - 46x + \boxed{}$

Solve the following equations by completing the square.

22. $x^2 - 8x - 5 = 0$

$x^2 - 8x = 5$

$x^2 - 8x + 16 = 5 + 16$

$(x - 4)^2 = 21$

$x - 4 = \pm\sqrt{21}$

$x = \boxed{}$

23. $x^2 + 12x + 9 = 0$

$x^2 + 12x = -9$

$x^2 + 12x + 36 = -9 + 36$

24. $x^2 - 10x = -11$

25. $2x^2 + 11x - 23 = -x + 3$ **26.** $x^2 - 18x + 64 = 0$

27. $3x^2 - 42x + 78 = 0$

Write the following equations in vertex form.

28. $y = x^2 + 10x - 9$

29. $y = x^2 - 18x + 13$

30. $y = x^2 + 32x - 8$

4-6 Standardized Test Prep
Completing the Square

Multiple Choice

For Exercises 1–6, choose the correct letter.

1. What are the solutions of the equation $36x^2 - 12x + 1 = 4$?

   (A) 4, 8   (B) $-\dfrac{1}{6}, \dfrac{1}{6}$ (C) $-\dfrac{1}{2}, \dfrac{1}{6}$ (D) $-\dfrac{1}{6}, \dfrac{1}{2}$

2. What are the solutions of the equation $2x^2 + 16x + 28 = 0$?

   (F) $-4 \pm \sqrt{30}$ (G) $-4 \pm \sqrt{2}$ (H) $4 \pm \sqrt{2}$ (I) $4 \pm \sqrt{30}$

3. Which value completes the square for $x^2 - 3x$?

   (A) $\dfrac{9}{4}$ (B) $\dfrac{3}{2}$ (C) 9   (D) $-\dfrac{9}{4}$

4. Which value for k would make the left side of $x^2 + kx + \dfrac{49}{64} = 0$ a perfect square trinomial?

   (F) 7   (G) $\dfrac{7}{2}$ (H) $\dfrac{7}{4}$ (I) $\dfrac{7}{8}$

5. What are the solutions of the equation $x^2 = 8x - 1$?

   (A) $-4 \pm \sqrt{17}$ (B) $-4 \pm \sqrt{15}$ (C) $4 \pm \sqrt{15}$ (D) $4 \pm \sqrt{17}$

6. Which equation is the vertex form of $y = -3x^2 + 12x - 7$?

   (F) $y = -3(x - 2)^2 - 5$ (H) $y = -3(x + 2)^2 - 5$

   (G) $y = -3(x - 2)^2 + 5$ (I) $y = -3(x + 2)^2 + 5$

Short Response

7. The equation $p = -x^2 + 8x + 5$ gives the price p, in dollars, for a product when x million units are produced.

   a. What are the solutions of the equation $-x^2 + 8x + 5 = 0$?

   b. What is the positive solution to part (a) rounded to two decimal places? What does this solution mean in terms of this problem?

$\dfrac{4\text{-}7}{}$ **Think About a Plan**

The Quadratic Formula

Sports A diver dives from a 10 m springboard. The equation $f(t) = -4.9t^2 + 4t + 10$ models her height above the pool at time t. At what time does she enter the water?

Understanding the Problem

1. What does the function represent?

   _____

2. What is the problem asking you to determine?

   _____

3. Do you need to use the height of the springboard to solve the problem? Explain.

   _____

   _____

Planning the Solution

4. What are three possible methods for solving this problem?

   _____

5. If a solution exists, which method will give an exact solution? Explain.

   _____

   _____

Getting an Answer

6. Is there more than one reasonable solution to the problem? Explain.

   _____

   _____

7. At what time does the diver enter the water?

   _____

4-7 Practice

Form K

The Quadratic Formula

Solve each equation using the Quadratic Formula. To start, find the values of *a*, *b*, and *c*. Substitute those values into the Quadratic Formula. When necessary round real solutions to the nearest hundredth.

1. $x^2 - 4x + 3 = 0$
$a = 1, b = -4, c = 3$

$$\frac{-(-4) \pm \sqrt{(-4)^2 - (4)(1)(3)}}{2(1)}$$

2. $2x^2 + 3x - 4 = 0$
$a = 2, b = 3, c = -4$

$$\frac{-(3) \pm \sqrt{(3)^2 - (4)(2)(-4)}}{2(2)}$$

3. $8x^2 - 2x - 5 = 0$
$a = 8, b = -2, c = -5$

$$\frac{-(-2) \pm \sqrt{(-2)^2 - (4)(8)(-5)}}{2(8)}$$

4. $x^2 + 3x = 3$

5. $4x^2 + 3 = 9x$

6. $2x - 5 = -x^2$

7. Your school sells yearbooks every spring. The total profit *p* made depends on the amount *x* the school charges for each yearbook. The profit is modeled by the equation $p = -2x^2 + 70x + 520$. What is the smallest amount in dollars the school can charge for a yearbook and make a profit of at least $1000?

To start, substitute 1000 for *p* in the equation. $1000 = -2x^2 + 70x + 520$
Then, write the equation in standard form. $2x^2 - 70x + 480 = 0$

8. Engineers can use the formula $d = 0.05s^2 + 1.1s$ to estimate the minimum stopping distance *d* in feet for a vehicle traveling *s* miles per hour.
   a. If a car can stop after 65 feet, what is the fastest it could have been traveling when the driver put on the brakes?
   b. **Reasoning** Explain how you knew which of the two solutions from the Quadratic Formula to use. (*Hint:* Remember this is a real situation.)

9. Reasoning Explain why a quadratic equation has no real solutions if the discriminant is less than zero.

Lesson 4-7

4-7

Practice (continued)   Form K

The Quadratic Formula

Evaluate the discriminant for each equation. Determine the number of real solutions.

10. $-12x^2 + 5x + 2 = 0$
$(5)^2 - 4(-12)(2)$

11. $x^2 - x + 6 = 0$
$(-1)^2 - 4(1)(6)$

12. $2x - 5 = -x^2$
$(2)^2 - 4(1)(-5)$

13. $4x^2 + 7 = 9x$

14. $x^2 - 4x = -4$

15. $3x + 6 = -6x^2$

Solve each equation using any method. When necessary, round real solutions to the nearest hundredth.

16. $7x^2 + 3x = 12$

$7x^2 + 3x - 12 = 0$

$$\frac{-3 \pm \sqrt{(3)^2 - 4(7)(-12)}}{2(7)}$$

17. $x^2 + 6x - 7 = 0$

$(x + 7)(x - 1) = 0$

18. $5x = -3x^2 + 2$

$-3x^2 - 5x + 2 = 0$

$$\frac{5 \pm \sqrt{(5)^2 - 4(-3)(2)}}{2(-3)}$$

19. $-12x + 7 = 5 - 2x^2$

20. $9x^2 - 6x - 4 = -5$

21. $2x - 24 = -x^2$

Without graphing, determine how many x-intercepts each function has.

22. $y = 2x^2 - 3x + 5$
$(3)^2 - 4(2)(5)$

23. $y = 2x^2 - 4x + 1$
$(-4)^2 - 4(2)(1)$

24. $y = x^2 + 3x + 3$
$(3)^2 - 4(1)(3)$

25. $y = 9x^2 - 12x + 7$

26. $y = -5x^2 + 8x - 3$

27. $y = x^2 + 16x + 64$

4-7

Standardized Test Prep

The Quadratic Formula

Multiple Choice

For Exercises 1–6, choose the correct letter.

1. What is the solution of $3x^2 + 2x - 5 = 0$? Use the Quadratic Formula.

  Ⓐ $-\frac{5}{3}, 1$ Ⓑ $-1, \frac{5}{3}$ Ⓒ $-\frac{1}{3}, 5$ Ⓓ $-5, \frac{1}{3}$

2. What is the solution of $2x^2 - 8x + 3 = 0$? Use the Quadratic Formula.

  Ⓕ $\dfrac{-4 \pm \sqrt{22}}{2}$ Ⓖ $\dfrac{-4 \pm \sqrt{10}}{2}$ Ⓗ $\dfrac{4 \pm \sqrt{10}}{2}$ Ⓘ $\dfrac{4 \pm \sqrt{22}}{2}$

3. What is the solution of $x^2 - 5x = 5$? Use the Quadratic Formula.

  Ⓐ $-5, 1$ Ⓑ $-1, 5$ Ⓒ $\dfrac{5 \pm \sqrt{5}}{2}$ Ⓓ $\dfrac{5 \pm 3\sqrt{5}}{2}$

4. What is the solution of $x^2 = 6x - 3$? Use the Quadratic Formula.

  Ⓕ $-3 \pm \sqrt{6}$ Ⓖ -3 Ⓗ 3 Ⓘ $3 \pm \sqrt{6}$

5. What is the discriminant of the equation $3x^2 - 7x + 1 = 0$?

  Ⓐ 61 Ⓑ 37 Ⓒ $\sqrt{37}$ Ⓓ -19

6. What is the discriminant of the equation $4x^2 + 28x + 49 = 0$?

  Ⓕ -5472 Ⓖ -756 Ⓗ 0 Ⓘ 1568

Extended Response

7. The equation $d = n^2 - 12n + 43$ models the number of defective items d produced in a manufacturing process when there are n workers in a restricted area. Use the discriminant to answer the following questions. Show your work.

  a. Will the number of defective items ever be 10?

  b. Will the number of defective items ever be 7?

  c. Will the number of defective items ever be 5?

Lesson 4-7

4-8

Think About a Plan

Complex Numbers

A student wrote the numbers 1, 5, 1 + 3i, and 4 + 3i to represent the vertices of a quadrilateral in the complex number plane. What type of quadrilateral has these vertices?

Know

1. The vertices of the quadrilateral are:

   _____ .

2. You can write the vertices in the form $a + bi$ as:

   _____ .

Need

3. To solve the problem I need to:

   _____ .

Plan

4. How do you find the coordinates that represent each complex number?

   _____

   _____

5. What are the points you need to graph?

   _____

6. Graph your points in the complex plane. Connect the points with straight lines to form a quadrilateral.

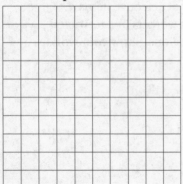

7. What type of quadrilateral did you draw? Explain how you know.

   _____

   _____

4-8

Practice

Complex Numbers

Form K

Simplify each number by using the imaginary number *i*.

1. $\sqrt{-100}$ **2.** $\sqrt{-2}$ **3.** $\sqrt{-48}$ **4.** $\sqrt{-36}$

$\sqrt{-1 \cdot 100}$

$\sqrt{-1} \cdot \sqrt{100}$

Plot each complex number and find its absolute value.

5. $5i$ **6.** $3 + 2i$ **7.** $7 - 1i$ **8.** $-4 + 9i$

Simplify each expression.

9. $(9 + 6i) + (2 - i)$ **10.** $(-12i) - (3 + 3i)$ **11.** $(-2i)(5 + 4i)$

$(9 + 2) + (6i - i)$

Write each quotient as a complex number.

12. $\dfrac{5 + 4i}{7i}$ **13.** $\dfrac{-1 + 5i}{3 - 2i}$ **14.** $\dfrac{2 - 6i}{2 - 3i}$

$\dfrac{5 + 4i}{7i}\left(\dfrac{-7i}{-7i}\right)$

4-8   **Practice** (continued)   *Form K*
Complex Numbers

Solve each equation.

15. $2x^2 + 50 = 0$

$2x^2 = -50$

$x^2 = -25$

$x = \pm 5i$

16. $3x^2 + 13 = -2$

$3x^2 = -15$

17. $x^2 + 49 = 0$

18. $9x^2 + 1 = 0$

19. $5x^2 = -81$

20. $x^2 + 27 = -9$

Find all solutions to each quadratic equation.

21. $2x^2 - 3x + 7 = 0$

$x = \dfrac{3 \pm \sqrt{(-3)^2 - 4(2)(7)}}{2(2)}$

$x = \dfrac{3 \pm \sqrt{9 - 56}}{4}$

$x = \dfrac{3 \pm \sqrt{-47}}{4}$

$x = \dfrac{3}{4} \pm \dfrac{\sqrt{47}}{4}i$

22. $4x^2 - 5x + 6 = 0$

$x = \dfrac{5 \pm \sqrt{(-5)^2 - 4(4)(6)}}{2(4)}$

23. $x(x - 3) + 3 = 0$

24. Error Analysis Robert solved the equation $2x^2 + 16 = 0$. His solution was $x = \pm\sqrt{-8}\,i$. What errors did Robert make? What is the correct solution?

Name _____ Class _____ Date _____

4-8 Standardized Test Prep

Complex Numbers

Multiple Choice

For Exercises 1–8, choose the correct letter.

1. What is the simplified form of $(-8 + 5i) + (3 - 2i)$?

   Ⓐ $-14 + 31i$ Ⓑ $-5 + 3i$ Ⓒ $-11 + 7i$ Ⓓ $5 - 3i$

2. What is the simplified form of $(11 - 6i) - (-4 + 12i)$?

   Ⓕ $7 + 6i$ Ⓖ $7 - 18i$ Ⓗ $15 + 6i$ Ⓘ $15 - 18i$

3. What is the simplified form of $(5 + \sqrt{-36}) - (-4 - \sqrt{-49})$?

   Ⓐ $9 - 13i$ Ⓑ $9 + 85i$ Ⓒ $1 - i$ Ⓓ $9 + 13i$

4. What is the simplified form of $(-5i)(-3i)$?

   Ⓕ $-15i$ Ⓖ -15 Ⓗ 15 Ⓘ $15i$

5. What is the simplified form of $(-3 + 2i)(1 - 4i)$?

   Ⓐ $-2 - 2i$ Ⓑ $-11 - 10i$ Ⓒ $5 + 14i$ Ⓓ $-3 - 8i$

6. What is the simplified form of $(8 - 3i)^2$?

   Ⓕ 73 Ⓖ $16 - 6i$ Ⓗ $55 - 48i$ Ⓘ $55 + 48i$

7. What is $\dfrac{5 + 3i}{4 - 2i}$ written as a complex number?

   Ⓐ $\dfrac{7}{10} + \dfrac{11}{10}i$ Ⓑ $\dfrac{13}{10} + \dfrac{1}{10}i$ Ⓒ $\dfrac{5}{4} - \dfrac{3}{2}i$ Ⓓ $\dfrac{7}{10} - \dfrac{11}{10}i$

8. What are the solutions of $5x^2 + 180 = 0$?

   Ⓕ $\pm 6i$ Ⓖ ± 6 Ⓗ ± 36 Ⓘ $\pm 36i$

Short Response

9. What are the solutions of $2x^2 + 3x + 6 = 0$? Show your work.

Lesson 4-8

5-1 | Think About a Plan

Polynomial Functions

Packaging Design The diagram at the right shows a cologne bottle that consists of a cylindrical base and a hemispherical top.

    a. Write an expression for the cylinder's volume.

    b. Write an expression for the volume of the hemispherical top.

    c. Write a polynomial to represent the total volume.

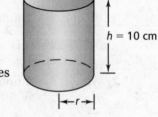

$h = 10$ cm

$\leftarrow r \rightarrow$

1. What is the formula for the volume of a cylinder? Define any variables you use in your formula.

$V_c = \boxed{}$, where r is _____ and h is _____.

2. Write an expression for the volume of the cylinder using the information in the diagram.

$V_c = \boxed{}$

3. What is the formula for the volume of a sphere? Define any variables you use in your formula.

$V_h = \boxed{}$

4. Write an expression for the volume of the hemisphere.

$V_h = \boxed{}$

5. How can you find the total volume of the bottle?

_____ .

6. Write a polynomial expression to represent the total volume of the bottle.

$V = \boxed{} + \boxed{}$

7. Is the polynomial expression you wrote in simplest form? Explain.

_____

_____ .

5-1   **Practice**   *Form K*

Polynomial Functions

Write each polynomial in standard form. Then classify it by degree and by number of terms.

1. $4x^3 - 3 + 2x^2$

To start, write the terms of the polynomial
with their degrees in descending order. $4x^3 + 2x^2 - 3$

2. $8 - x^5 + 9x^2 - 2x$ **3.** $6x + 2x^4 - 2$

4. $-6x^3$ **5.** $3 + 24x^2$

Determine the end behavior of the graph of each polynomial function.

6. $y = 5x^3 - 2x^2 + 1$ **7.** $y = 5 - x + 4x^2$ **8.** $y = x - x^2 + 10$

9. $y = 3x^2 + 9 - x^3$ **10.** $y = 8x^2 - 4x^4 + 5x^7 - 2$ **11.** $y = 20 - x^5$

12. $y = 1 + 2x + 4x^3 - 8x^4$ **13.** $y = 15 - 5x^6 + 2x - 22x^3$ **14.** $y = 3x + 10 + 8x^4 - x^2$

Describe the shape of the graph of each cubic function by determining the end behavior and number of turning points.

x	y
−2	−12
−1	−3
0	0
1	3
2	12

15. $y = x^3 + 2x$

To start, make a table of values to help
you sketch the middle part of the graph.

16. $y = -3x^3 + 4x^2 - 1$ **17.** $y = 4x^3 + 2x^2 - x$

Determine the degree of the polynomial function with the given data.

18.

x	y
−3	−43
−2	−10
−1	1
0	2
1	5
2	22
3	65

19.

x	y
−3	65
−2	5
−1	−5
0	−1
1	5
2	25
3	95

5-1 Practice (continued)   Form K

Polynomial Functions

Determine the sign of the leading coefficient and the degree of the polynomial function for each graph.

20.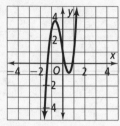

21.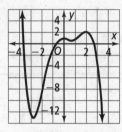

22.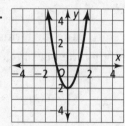

23. **Error Analysis** A student claims the function $y = -2x^3 + 5x - 7$ is a 3rd degree polynomial with ending behavior of down and up. Describe the error the student made. What is wrong with this statement?

24. **The table to the right shows data representing a polynomial function.**
    a. What is the degree of the polynomial function?
    b. What are the second differences of the y-values?
    c. What are the differences when they are constant?

x	y
−3	98
−2	20
−1	6
0	2
1	2
2	48
3	230

Classify each polynomial by degree and by number of terms. Simplify first if necessary.

25. $3x^5 - 6x^2 - 5 + x^2$

26. $a - 2a + 3a^2$

27. $(5x^2 + 2x - 8) + (5x^2 - 4x)$

28. $c^3(5 - c^2)$

29. $(5s^3 - 2s^2) - (s^4 + 1)$

30. $x(3x)(x + 2)$

31. $(2s - 1)(3s + 3)$

32. 5

33. **Open-Ended** Write a fourth-degree polynomial function. Make a table of values and a graph.

5-1 Standardized Test Prep

Polynomial Functions

Multiple Choice

For Exercises 1–7, choose the correct letter.

1. Which expression is a binomial?

   (A) $2x$ (B) $\frac{x}{2}$ (C) $3x^2 + 2x + 4$ (D) $x - 9$

2. Which polynomial function has an end behavior of up and down?

   (F) $-6x^7 + 4x^2 - 3$ (H) $6x^7 - 4x^2 + 3$

   (G) $-7x^6 + 3x - 2$ (I) $7x^6 - 3x + 2$

3. What is the degree of the polynomial $5x + 4x^2 + 3x^3 - 5x$?

   (A) 1   (B) 2   (C) 3   (D) 4

4. What is the degree of the polynomial represented by the data in the table at the right?

   (F) 2   (G) 3   (H) 4   (I) 5

x	y
−3	77
−2	24
−1	1
0	−4
1	−3
2	−8
3	−31

5. For the table of values at the right, if the *n*th differences are constant, what is the constant value?

   (A) −12   (B) −5   (C) 1   (D) 6

6. What is the standard form of the polynomial $9x^2 + 5x + 27 + 2x^3$?

   (F) $27 + 5x + 9x^2 + 2x^3$ (H) $9x^2 + 5x + 27 + 2x^3$

   (G) $9x^2 + 5x + 2x^3 + 27$ (I) $2x^3 + 9x^2 + 5x + 27$

7. What is the number of terms in the polynomial $(2a - 5)(a^2 - 1)$?

   (A) 2   (B) 3   (C) 4   (D) 5

Short Response

8. Simplify $(9x^3 - 4x + 2) - (x^3 + 3x^2 + 1)$. Then name the polynomial by degree and the number of terms.

Lesson 5-1

5-2 Think About a Plan

Polynomials, Linear Factors, and Zeros

Measurement The volume in cubic feet of a CD holder can be expressed as $V(x) = -x^3 - x^2 + 6x$, or, when factored, as the product of its three dimensions. The depth is expressed as $2 - x$. Assume that the height is greater than the width.

    a. Factor the polynomial to find linear expressions for the height and the width.
    b. Graph the function. Find the x-intercepts. What do they represent?
    c. What is a realistic domain for the function?
    d. What is the maximum volume of the CD holder?

1. What do you know about the factors of the polynomial?

_____.

2. Factor the polynomial.

$$V(x) = -x^3 - x^2 + 6x = \left(\boxed{} \right)\left(\boxed{} \right)\left(\boxed{} \right)$$

3. What are the height and width of the CD holder? How do you know which factor is the height and which factor is the width?

_____

_____.

4. Graph the function on a graphing calculator. How can you find the x-intercepts?

_____.

5. What are the x-intercepts? What do they represent?

_____.

6. What are the limits of each of the factors? What is a realistic domain for the function? Explain.

_____

_____

_____.

7. How can you find the maximum volume of the CD holder?

_____

_____.

8. What is the maximum volume of the CD holder?

5-2 Practice
Form K

Polynomials, Linear Factors, and Zeros

Write each polynomial in factored form. Check by multiplication.

1. $x^3 + 11x^2 + 30x$

To start, factor out the GCF, x. $x(x^2 + 11x + 30)$

2. $x^3 - 3x^2 - x + 3$ **3.** $x^2 - 4x - 12$

4. $x^3 - 81x$ **5.** $x^3 + 9x^2 + 18x$

Find the zeros of each function. Then graph the function.

6. $y = (x + 2)(x + 3)$ **7.** $y = x(x - 1)(x + 3)$

8. $y = (x - 4)(x - 1)$ **9.** $y = x(x - 5)(x + 2)$

Write a polynomial function in standard form with the given zeros.

10. $x = -2, 1, 4$

To start, write a linear factor for each zero. $(x - (-2))(x - 1)(x - 4)$

Simplify $(x + 2)(x - 1)(x - 4)$

11. $x = 3, 0$ **12.** $3, -8, 0$

13. $x = 3, -2, 1$ **14.** $x = -4, 1$

Lesson 5-2

5-2 Practice (continued) Form K

Polynomials, Linear Factors, and Zeros

Find the zeros of each function. State the multiplicity of multiple zeros.

15. $y = (x - 3)^2(x + 1)$

To start, identify the zeros.   The zeros are 3 and -1.

16. $y = x^2 + 3x + 2$ **17.** $y = (x + 5)^2$

18. $y = (x - 9)^2$ **19.** $y = 2x^2 - 2x$

Find the relative maximum and relative minimum of the graph of each function.

20. $f(x) = -3x^3 + 10x^2 + 6x - 3$

To start, use a graphing calculator.

(An approximate viewing window is

$-5 \leq x \leq 5$ and $-10 \leq y \leq 30$.)

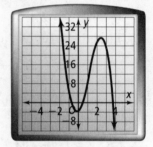

21. $f(x) = x^3 + 4x^2 - x + 1$ **22.** $f(x) = x^3 - 6x + 9$

23. Reasoning A polynomial function has a zero at $x = b$. Find one of its factors.

24. The side of a cube measures $2x + 1$ units long. Express the volume of the cube as a polynomial.

25. The length of a box is 2 times the height. The sum of the length, width, and height of the box is 10 centimeters.
   a. Write an expression for the dimensions of the box.
   b. Write a polynomial function for the volume of the box. (To start, write the function in factored form).
   c. Find the maximum volume of the box and the dimensions of the box that generates this volume.

5-2 Standardized Test Prep

Polynomials, Linear Factors, and Zeros

Multiple Choice

For Exercises 1–6, choose the correct letter.

1. What are the zeros of the polynomial function $y = (x - 3)(2x + 1)(x - 1)$?

(A) $\frac{1}{2}, 1, 3$ (B) $-1, 1, 3$ (C) $-\frac{1}{2}, 1, 3$ (D) $-3, \frac{1}{2}, -1$

2. What is the factored form of $2x^3 + 5x^2 - 12x$?

(F) $(x + 4)(2x - 3)$ (H) $x(x + 4)(2x - 3)$

(G) $(x - 4)(2x + 3)$ (I) $x(x - 4)(2x + 3)$

3. Which is the cubic polynomial in standard form with roots 3, −6, and 0?

(A) $x^2 - 3x - 18$ (C) $x^3 - 3x^2 - 18x$

(B) $x^2 + 3x - 18$ (D) $x^3 + 3x^2 - 18x$

4. What is the relative minimum and relative maximum of $f(x) = 6x^3 - 5x + 12$?

(F) min = 0, max = 0   (H) min = −1.5, max = 12

(G) min = −5, max = 6   (I) min = 10.2, max = 13.8

5. What is the multiplicity of the zero of the polynomial function $f(x) = (x + 5)^4$?

(A) 4   (B) 5   (C) 20   (D) 625

6. For the polynomial function $y = (x - 2)^3$, which behavior will the graph exhibit at the x-intercept?

(F) linear   (G) quadratic   (H) cubic   (I) quartic

Short Response

7. A rectangular box is 24 in. long, 12 in. wide, and 18 in. high. If each dimension is increased by x in., what is the polynomial function in standard form that models the volume V of the box? Show your work.

5-3 Think About a Plan

Solving Polynomial Equations

Geometry The width of a box is 2 m less than the length. The height is 1 m less than the length. The volume is 60 m^3. What is the length of the box?

Know

1. The volume of the box is [   ].

2. The formula for the volume of a rectangular prism is [   ].

3. The width of the box is equal to [   ] − 2 m.

4. The height of the box is equal to [   ] − 1 m.

Need

5. To solve the problem I need to:

   _____

   _____.

Plan

6. Define a variable. Let $x =$ [   ].

7. What variable expressions represent the width and height of the box?

   [   ] and [   ]

8. What equation expresses the volume of the box in two ways?

9. How can you use a graphing calculator to help you solve the equation?

   _____

   _____.

10. What are the solutions of the equation?

11. Are the solutions reasonable?

   _____

   _____.

5-3 Practice

Form K

Solving Polynomial Equations

Find the real or imaginary solutions of each equation by factoring.

1. $x^3 + 512 = 0$

To start, write $x^3 + 512$ as a sum
of cubes and factor.

$x^3 + 8^3 = 0$
$(x + 8)(x^2 - 8x + 64) = 0$

2. $x^4 - 3x^2 = -2x^2$

3. $x^4 + 5x^2 = 6$

4. $x^4 + 2x^3 = 10x^2$

5. $27x^3 - 1 = 0$

6. $x^2 + 4 = -4x$

7. $x^3 + 10x^2 + 24x = 0$

Solve each equation.

8. $x^3 + 4x^2 - 2x - 8 = 0$

9. $x^5 - 6x^3 + 5x = 0$

10. $x^3 = 9x$

11. $2x^3 + 8x^2 + 4x = -16$

12. $x^4 - 25 = 0$

13. $27x^3 - 216 = 0$

14. Writing Show how you can rewrite $\frac{x^6}{y^9} - \frac{1}{27}$ as a difference of two cubes.

Lesson 5-3

5-3   **Practice** (continued)   *Form K*

Solving Polynomial Equations

Find the real solutions of each equation by graphing.

15. $x^3 - 3x^2 - 9x = -15$

To start, rewrite the equation with $x^3 - 3x^2 - 9x + 15 = 0$
one side equal to zero.

16. $3x^2 = 22x$ **17.** $2x^4 - 2x^3 + 4x^2 = 3$

18. $-x^3 + 1 = 2x^2$ **19.** $x^4 - 2x^3 - 5x^2 + 1 = 0$

20. $2x^2 = -6x$ **21.** $x^3 + 5x^2 = 9x$

For Exercises 22–25, write an equation to model each situation. Then solve each equation by graphing.

22. The volume V of a container is 61 in.^{3}. The width, the length, and the height are x, $x - 2$, and $x + 3$ respectively. What are the container's dimensions?

To start, write the equation of $x(x - 2)(x + 3) = 61$
the volume of the container. $x^3 + x^2 - 6x = 61$

23. The product of three consecutive integers is 720. What are the numbers?

24. The height of a box is 3 cm less than the width. The length is 2 cm less than the width. The volume is 50 cm^3. What is the width of the box?

25. Your sister is 8 years older than you. Your mother is 25 years older than your sister. The product of all three ages is 18,816. How old is your mother?

5-3 Standardized Test Prep

Solving Polynomial Equations

Multiple Choice

For Exercises 1–6, choose the correct letter.

1. If you factor $x^3 - 8$ in the form $(x - a)(x^2 + bx + c)$, what is the value of a?

   Ⓐ 2   Ⓑ −2   Ⓒ 4   Ⓓ −4

2. The product of three integers x, $x + 2$, and $x - 5$ is 240. What are the integers?

   Ⓕ 5.9, 7.9, 0.9   Ⓖ 7.5, 9.5, 2.5   Ⓗ 5, 6, 8   Ⓘ 8, 10, 3

3. Over 3 years, you save \$550, \$600, and \$650 from babysitting jobs. The polynomial $550x^3 + 600x^2 + 650x$ represents your total bank account balance after 3 years. The annual interest rate is $x - 1$. What is the interest rate needed so that you will have \$2000 after 3 years?

   Ⓐ 0.06%   Ⓑ 1.06%   Ⓒ 5.52%   Ⓓ 24%

4. Which polynomial equation has the zeros 5, −3, and $\frac{1}{2}$?

   Ⓕ $x^3 + 4x^2 + 4x - 45$ Ⓗ $2x^3 - 5x^2 - 28x + 15$

   Ⓖ $x^3 - 4x^2 + 4x + 15$ Ⓘ $2x^3 + 5x^2 - 28x - 45$

5. Your brother is 3 years older than you. Your sister is 4 years younger than you. The product of your ages is 1872. How old is your sister?

   Ⓐ 9 years   Ⓑ 13 years   Ⓒ 16 years   Ⓓ 17 years

6. What are the real roots of $x^3 + 8 = 0$?

   Ⓕ 2   Ⓖ −2   Ⓗ $-2 \pm \sqrt{3}$ Ⓘ $-2 \pm \sqrt{5}$

Short Response

7. You have a block of wood with a depth of x units, a length of $5x$ units, and a height of $2x$ units. You need to cut a slice off the top of the block to decrease the height by 2 units. The new block will have a volume of 480 cubic units.

   a. What are the dimensions of the new block?

   b. What is the volume of the slice?

5-4   Think About a Plan

Dividing Polynomials

Geometry The expression $\frac{1}{3}(x^3 + 5x^2 + 8x + 4)$ represents the volume of a square pyramid. The expression $x + 1$ represents the height of the pyramid. What expression represents the side length of the base? (*Hint:* The formula for the volume of a pyramid is $V = \frac{1}{3}Bh$.)

Understanding the Problem

1. What expression represents the height of the pyramid?

2. What does B represent in the formula for the volume of a pyramid?

   _____

3. What is the problem asking you to determine?

   _____

Planning the Solution

4. How can you find an expression that represents B?

   _____

   _____.

5. How can polynomial division help you solve this problem?

   _____

   _____.

6. How can you find the side length of the base once you find an expression for B?

   _____

   _____.

Getting an Answer

7. What expression represents B, the area of the base?

8. What expression represents the side length of the base?

5-4 Practice
Dividing Polynomials

Divide using long division. Check your answers.

1. $(2x^2 + 7x - 5) \div (x + 1)$

To start, divide $\frac{2x^2}{x} = 2x$

Then, multiply $2x(x + 1) = 2x^2 + 2x$.

$$\begin{array}{r} 2x \\ x + 1 \overline{)\,2x^2 + 7x - 5} \\ \underline{2x^2 + 2x} \end{array}$$

2. $(x^3 + x^2 - 14x - 27) \div (x + 3)$

3. $(2x^3 + 13x^2 + 16x + 5) \div (x + 5)$

4. $(x^2 + 9x + 22) \div (x + 2)$

5. $(6x^2 + 4x - 16) \div (2x - 2)$

6. $(8x^3 + 18x^2 + 7x - 3) \div (4x - 1)$

7. $(12x^2 + 18x - 17) \div (6x - 3)$

Determine whether each binomial is a factor of $x^3 - 3x^2 - 4x$.

8. $x - 4$

9. $x + 2$

10. $x - 3$

11. $x + 1$

Determine whether each binomial is a factor of $x^3 - 9x^2 + 15x + 25$.

12. $x - 2$

13. $x + 1$

14. $x - 5$

15. $x - 3$

5-4 Practice (continued) Form K

Dividing Polynomials

Divide using synthetic division.

16. $(x^3 - 7x^2 - 36) \div (x - 2)$

To start, write the coefficients of
the polynomial. Use 2 for the divisor.

$$\underline{2}|1 \quad -7 \quad 0 \quad -36$$
$$\underline{ \quad 2 \quad -10 \quad -20}$$
$$1 \quad -5 \quad -10 \quad -56$$

17. $(x^3 + x^2 - 14x - 27) \div (x + 3)$

18. $(x^3 - 6x^2 + 3x - 2) \div (x - 2)$

19. $(x^3 - 15) \div (x - 1)$

20. $(x^2 + 8) \div (x - 4)$

21. $(3x^3 - 70x + 2) \div (x - 5)$

22. $(2x^3 + x^2 - 8x + 4) \div (x + 2)$

Use synthetic division and the given factor to completely factor each polynomial function.

23. $y = 2x^3 + 9x^2 + 13x + 6; (x + 1)$

24. $y = x^3 + 4x^2 - 7x - 10; (x - 2)$

Use synthetic division and the Remainder Theorem to find $P(a)$.

25. $P(x) = 5x^3 - 12x^2 + 2x + 1, a = 3$

26. $P(x) = 2x^3 - 4x^2 + 3x - 6, a = -2$

27. $P(x) = x^3 + 6x^2 - 2, a = 3$

28. $P(x) = 7x^3 + x^2 - 2x + 10, a = 1$

29. $P(x) = x^3 - 412, a = 8$

30. $P(x) = 2x^3 + x^2 - 3x - 3, a = -3$

5-4 Standardized Test Prep

Dividing Polynomials

Gridded Response

Solve each exercise and enter your answer in the grid provided.

1. What is $P(-2)$ given that $P(x) = x^4 - 3x^2 + 5x + 10$?

2. What is the missing value in the following synthetic division?

$$
\begin{array}{r|rrrrr}
-4 & 1 & 0 & -5 & 4 & 12 \\
   &   & -4 & \blacksquare & -44 & 160 \\
\hline
   & 1 & -4 & 11 & -40 & 172 \\
\end{array}
$$

3. What is the remainder when $x^6 - 4x^4 + 4x^2 - 10$ is divided by $x + 3$?

4. How many unique factors does $x^4 + 4x^3 - 3x^2 - 14x - 8$ have, including $(x + 4)$?

5. How many terms are there in the simplified form of $\dfrac{x^4 - 2x^3 - 23x^2 - 12x + 36}{x - 6}$?

Answers

1.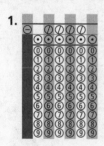
2.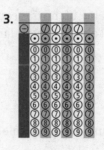
3.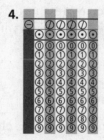
4.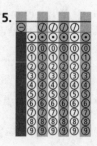
5.

5-5 Think About a Plan

Theorems About Roots of Polynomial Equations

Gardening A gardener is designing a new garden in the shape of a trapezoid. She wants the shorter base to be twice the height and the longer base to be 4 feet longer than the shorter base. If she has enough topsoil to create a 60 ft^2 garden, what dimensions should she use for the garden?

Understanding the Problem

1. What is the formula for the area of a trapezoid?

2. How can drawing a diagram help you solve the problem?

   _____
   _____.

3. What is the problem asking you to determine?

   _____

Planning the Solution

4. Define a variable. Let $x = $ ⬚ .

5. What variable expression represents the shorter base? The longer base?

   ⬚   ⬚

6. What expression represents the area of the trapezoid? What number is this equal to? Write the equation you obtain in standard form.

Getting an Answer

7. Solve your equation. Are the solutions reasonable?

   _____.

8. What are the dimensions of the garden?

   _____

5-5 **Practice** Form K

Theorems About Roots of Polynomial Equations

Use the Rational Root Theorem to list all possible rational roots for each equation. Then find any actual rational roots.

1. $x^3 - 5x^2 + 17x - 13$

To start, list the constant term's factors and the leading coefficient's factors.

constant term factors: $\pm 1, \pm 13$

leading coefficient factors: ± 1

2. $2x^3 - 5x^2 + x - 7$

3. $x^3 - 4x^2 - 15x + 18$

4. $x^3 - 8x^2 - 2$

5. $x^3 - x^2 + 6x - 6$

6. $4x^3 + 12x^2 + x + 3$

7. $x^3 - 3x^2 - 16x - 12$

8. $x^3 + 8x^2 - x - 8$

9. $x^3 - 3x^2 - 24x - 28$

Find all rational roots for $P(x) = 0$.

10. $P(x) = x^3 + 5x^2 + 2x - 8$

11. $P(x) = x^4 - 4x^3 - 13x^2 + 4x + 12$

12. $P(x) = x^3 + 14x^2 + 53x + 40$

13. $P(x) = x^3 + 3x^2 - 4x - 12$

14. $P(x) = x^3 + 5x^2 - 9x - 45$

15. $P(x) = x^3 + 9x^2 - x - 9$

16. $P(x) = x^3 - 7x^2 - x + 7$

17. $P(x) = x^3 - 7x^2 + 14x - 8$

Lesson 5-5

5-5 **Practice** (continued)   *Form K*

Theorems About Roots of Polynomial Equations

A polynomial function $P(x)$ with rational coefficients has the given roots. Find two additional roots of $P(x) = 0$.

18. $1 + 4i$ and $\sqrt{3}$

19. $3 - \sqrt{2}$ and $1 + \sqrt{3}$

20. $-8i$ and $7 - i$

21. $6 - \sqrt{7}$ and $-3 + \sqrt{10}$

22. $\sqrt{2}$ and $-\sqrt{13}$

23. $1 - \sqrt{3}$ and $1 + \sqrt{2}$

Write a polynomial function with rational coefficients so that $P(x) = 0$ has the given roots.

24. $3i$

    To start, use the Conjugate Root Theorem   Since $3i$ is a root, $-3i$
    to identify a second root.   is also a root.

25. -2 and -8

26. 4 and 1

27. $2i$ and $\sqrt{2}$

28. $3 + i$ and $1 - \sqrt{3}$

29. -4 and $5i$

30. $2i$ and i

What does Descartes' Rule of Signs say about the number of positive real roots and negative real roots for each polynomial function?

31. $P(x) = x^3 - x^2 - 8x + 12$

    To start, count and identify   There are 2 sign changes in $P(x)$.
    the number of sign changes in $P(x)$.   So there are 0 or 2 positive real roots.

32. $P(x) = 2x^3 + 2x^2 - 5x - 2$

33. $P(x) = x^4 - 3x^3 - x + 5$

5-5 Standardized Test Prep

Theorems About Roots of Polynomial Equations

Multiple Choice

For Exercises 1–5, choose the correct letter.

1. A fourth-degree polynomial with integer coefficients has roots at 1 and $3 + \sqrt{5}$. Which number *cannot* also be a root of this polynomial?

   Ⓐ -1 Ⓑ -3 Ⓒ $3 - \sqrt{5}$ Ⓓ $3 + \sqrt{2}$

2. A quartic polynomial $P(x)$ has rational coefficients. If $\sqrt{7}$ and $6 + i$ are roots of $P(x) = 0$, what is one additional root?

   Ⓕ 7 Ⓖ $-\sqrt{7}$ Ⓗ $i - 6$ Ⓘ $6i$

3. What is a quartic polynomial function with rational coefficients that has roots i and $2i$?

   Ⓐ $x^4 - 5x^2 - 4$ Ⓑ $x^4 - 5x^2 + 4$ Ⓒ $x^4 + 5x^2 + 4$ Ⓓ $x^4 + 5x^2 - 4$

4. What does Descartes' Rule of Signs tell you about the real roots of $6x^4 + 29x^3 + 40x^2 + 7x - 12$?

   Ⓕ 1 positive real root and 1 or 3 negative real roots

   Ⓖ 0 positive real roots and 1 negative real root

   Ⓗ 1 or 3 positive real roots and 1 negative real root

   Ⓘ 0 or 1 positive real roots and 3 negative real roots

5. What is a rational root of $x^3 + 3x^2 - 6x - 8 = 0$?

   Ⓐ 1   Ⓑ -1 Ⓒ 8   Ⓓ -8

Extended Response

6. A third-degree polynomial with rational coefficients has roots -4 and $-4i$. If the leading coefficient of the polynomial is $\frac{3}{2}$, what is the polynomial? Show your work.

5-6 Think About a Plan
The Fundamental Theorem of Algebra

Bridges A twist in a river can be modeled by the function $f(x) = \frac{1}{3}x^3 + \frac{1}{2}x^2 - x$, $-3 \le x \le 2$. A city wants to build a road that goes directly along the x-axis. How many bridges would it have to build?

Know

1. The function has exactly ☐ complex roots.

2. _____
   _____

3. _____
   _____

Need

4. To solve the problem I need to:
   _____
   _____ .

Plan

5. Graph the function on a graphing calculator. What viewing window should you use?
   _____

6. What does the graph tell you?
   _____ .

7. How many bridges would the city have to build? ☐
   Explain.
   _____
   _____ .

5-6 Practice

The Fundamental Theorem of Algebra

Form K

Without using a calculator, find all the roots of each equation.

1. $x^3 - 5x^2 + x - 5 = 0$

To start, identify the possible rational roots.

The possible rational roots are $\pm 1, \pm 5$

2. $x^5 + 3x^4 - 8x^3 - 24x^2 - 9x - 27 = 0$ **3.** $x^3 + 4x^2 + 9x + 36 = 0$

4. $x^3 + x^2 - 2x - 2 = 0$ **5.** $x^4 + 15x^2 - 16 = 0$

6. $x^4 - 8x^3 + 19x^2 - 32x + 60 = 0$ **7.** $x^3 + 5x^2 - 3x - 15 = 0$

Find all the zeros of each function.

8. $y = x^3 - x^2 - 3x + 3$

To start, use a graphing calculator to find the possible rational roots.

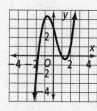

9. $y = x^4 - 4x^3 + 7x^2 - 16x + 12$ **10.** $f(x) = x^3 + x^2 + 16x + 16$

11. $g(x) = x^3 - 4x^2 + 4x - 3$ **12.** $y = x^3 + 6x^2 - 5x - 30$

13. $f(x) = x^4 - 2x^3 + 2x^2 - 2x + 1$ **14.** $y = x^4 + 2x^3 - 5x^2 - 4x + 6$

5-6 Practice (continued) Form K
The Fundamental Theorem of Algebra

For each equation, state the number of complex roots, the possible number of positive real roots, and the possible rational roots.

15. $x^2 + 8x - 5 = 0$

16. $2x^3 - 18x + 4 = 0$

17. $x^4 + 8x^2 + 2 = 0$

18. $x^6 - 8x^4 + 2x^2 - 10 = 0$

19. $x^3 - 2x + 6 = 0$

20. $8x + x^2 - 12 = 0$

Find the number of complex roots for each equation.

21. $5x^6 + 3x^4 + x - 10 = 0$

22. $-4x^3 + 2x^2 - x + 5 = 0$

23. $2x^5 + 2x^3 - x^2 + 12x - 8 = 0$

24. $-x^3 + 7x^2 - 12x + 9 = 0$

25. $3x^8 + 4x^6 + 5x^2 - x + 15 = 0$

26. $12x^5 + 3x^4 + 2x^2 - 12 = 0$

27. $-5x^3 + 2x^3 + 2x - 32 = 0$

28. $x^{10} - 25 = 0$

29. Error Analysis Your friend says that the function $3x^4 - 2x^3 - x + 12 = 0$ has 3 complex roots. You say that the function has 4 complex roots. Who is correct? What mistake was made?

30. A section of a bridge can be modeled by the function $f(x) = x^4 - 5x^3 - 10x^2 + 20x + 24$. Support beams for this bridge will be placed at one of the zeros. What are the possible locations for the support beams?

31. How many complex roots does the equation $x^4 = 81$ have? What are they?

5-6 Standardized Test Prep

The Fundamental Theorem of Algebra

Multiple Choice

For Exercises 1–6, choose the correct letter.

1. Which number is a zero of $f(x) = x^3 + 6x^2 + 9x$ with multiplicity 1?

   Ⓐ -3 Ⓑ 0 Ⓒ 1 Ⓓ 3

2. One root of the equation $x^3 + x^2 - 2 = 0$ is 1. What are the other two roots?

   Ⓕ $-1 \pm i$ Ⓖ $1 \pm 2i$ Ⓗ $\pm 1 + 2i$ Ⓘ $\pm 1 - i$

3. A polynomial with real coefficients has 3, $2i$, and $-i$ as three of its zeros. What is the least possible degree of the polynomial?

   Ⓐ 3   Ⓑ 4   Ⓒ 5   Ⓓ 6

4. How many times does the graph of $x^3 + 27$ cross the x-axis?

   Ⓕ 0   Ⓖ 1   Ⓗ 2   Ⓘ 4

5. Which of the following is the polynomial with zeros at 1, $-\frac{3}{2}$, $2i$, and $-2i$?

   Ⓐ $2x^4 + x^3 + 5x^2 + 4x - 12$ Ⓒ $2x^4 + x^3 - 11x^2 - 4x + 12$

   Ⓑ $2x^4 - x^3 + 5x^2 - 4x - 12$ Ⓓ $2x^4 - x^3 - 11x^2 + 4x + 12$

6. A polynomial with real coefficients has roots of 6, -2, $-4i$, and $\sqrt{5}$. Which of the following *must* be another root of this polynomial?

   Ⓕ -6 Ⓖ $-\sqrt{5}$ Ⓗ 2   Ⓘ $4i$

Short Response

7. One root of the equation $x^4 - 4x^3 - 6x^2 + 4x + 5 = 0$ is -1. How many complex roots does this equation have? What are all the roots? Show your work.

Lesson 5-6

5-7   Think About a Plan

The Binomial Theorem

Geometry The side length of a cube is given by the expression $(2x + 8)$. Write a binomial expression for the area of a face of the cube and the volume of the cube. Then use the Binomial Theorem to expand and rewrite the expressions in standard form.

Understanding the Problem

1. What is the formula for the area of a face of a cube?

2. What is the formula for the volume of a cube?

3. What is the problem asking you to determine?

   _____

   _____

Planning the Solution

4. What is a binomial expression for the area of a face of this cube?

5. What is a binomial expression for the volume of this cube?

6. How can you use the Binomial Theorem to expand these expressions?

   _____

   _____

   _____.

Getting an Answer

7. What is an expression for the area of a face of the cube written in standard form?

8. What is an expression for the volume of the cube written in standard form?

5-7   **Practice**   *Form K*

The Binomial Theorem

Expand each binomial.

1. $(x + 4)^3$

   To start, identify the third row of

   Pascal's Triangle.   1   3   3   1

2. $(5 + a)^6$ 3. $(y + 1)^4$

4. $(3a + 2)^4$ 5. $(x - 3)^5$

6. $(b + 1)^8$ 7. $(x + 2)^3$

Find the specified term of each binomial expansion.

8. second term of $(x - 4)^8$ 9. third term of $(x + 3)^{12}$

10. fourth term of $(x - 2)^7$ 11. third term of $(x^2 - 2y)^6$

12. fifth term of $(3x - 1)^5$ 13. seventh term of $(x - 4y)^6$

14. third term of $(x^2 + y^2)^8$ 15. second term of $(2 + x)^4$

16. The term $56a^5b^3$ appears in the expansion of $(a + b)^n$. What is n?

17. The coefficient of the second term in the expansion of $(c + d)^n$ is 6. Find the value of n, and write the complete term.

State the number of terms in each expansion and give the first two terms.

18. $(2a + b)^7$ 19. $(c - d)^8$

20. $(x + y)^3$ 21. $(3x - y)^5$

22. $(x + y^2)^5$ 23. $(4 - 2x)^7$

5-7

Practice (continued)
The Binomial Theorem

24. The side of a dice is $x + 6$ units long. Write a binomial for the volume of the dice. Use the Binomial Theorem to expand and rewrite the expression in standard form.

Expand each binomial.

25. $(m + 1)^4$

26. $(2y + 8)^3$

27. $(2x + 2)^3$

28. $(x - 1)^8$

29. $(x + 4)^5$

30. $(3b + 1)^6$

31. **Open-Ended** Write a binomial in the form of $(a + b)^n$ that will have a first term coefficient equal to 7.

32. Use Pascal's Triangle to determine the binomial of the expanded expression $x^8 + 8x^7 + 28x^6 + 56x^5 + 70x^4 + 56x^3 + 28x^2 + 8x + 1$.

33. **Error Analysis** Your friend expands the binomial $(x - 4)^5$ as $x^5 + 20x^4 + 160x^3 + 640x^2 + 1280x + 1024$. What mistake did your friend make? What is the correct expansion?

34. **Reasoning** Without writing any of the previous terms, how do you know that 64 is the seventh term of the expansion of the binomial $(x + 2)^6$.

35. In the expansion of $2(m - n)^7$, one of the terms contains n^2.
    a. What is the exponent of $2m$ in this term?
    b. What is the coefficient of this term?

5-7 Standardized Test Prep

The Binomial Theorem

Multiple Choice

For Exercises 1–7, choose the correct letter.

1. What is the expanded form of $(a - b)^3$?

   A. $a^3 + a^2b + ab^2 + b^3$

   B. $a^3 - a^2b + ab^2 - b^3$

   C. $a^3 + 3a^2b + 3ab^2 + b^3$

   D. $a^3 - 3a^2b + 3ab^2 - b^3$

2. What is the third term in the expansion of $(x - y)^7$?

   F. $21x^5y^2$ G. $-7x^6y$ H. $7x^6y$ I. $-21x^5y^2$

3. What is the coefficient of the third term in the expansion of $(2x - y)^5$?

   A. -80 B. 32 C. 40 D. 80

4. Which term in the expansion of $(2a - 3b)^6$ has coefficient 2160?

   F. second term   G. third term   H. fourth term   I. fifth term

5. What is n if $-448x^5y^3$ appears in the expansion of $(x - 2y)^n$?

   A. 6 B. 7 C. 8 D. 9

6. What is the 6th term in the 12th line of Pascal's Triangle?

   F. 252 G. 462 H. 792 I. 1287

7. What is the expanded form of $(2x - y)^5$?

   A. $32x^5 + 80x^4y + 80x^3y^2 + 40x^2y^3 + 10xy^4 + y^5$

   B. $32x^5 - 80x^4y + 80x^3y^2 - 40x^2y^3 + 10xy^4 - y^5$

   C. $2x^5 + 5x^4y + 20x^3y^2 + 20x^2y^3 + 10xy^4 + y^5$

   D. $2x^5 - 5x^4y + 20x^3y^2 - 20x^2y^3 + 10xy^4 - y^5$

Short Response

8. The coefficient of the fourth term in the expansion of $(x + y)^n$ is 84.

   a. What is the value of n?

   b. What is the complete term?

5-8 Think About a Plan

Polynomial Models in the Real World

Air Travel The table shows the percent of on-time flights for selected years. Find a polynomial function to model the data.

Year	1998	2000	2002	2004	2006
On-time Flights (%)	76.04	73.1	81.07	77.6	76.19

1. How can you plot the data? (*Hint*: Let *x* equal the number of years after 1990.)

   _____

2. What types of models can you find for the data? _____

3. Which model will fit the data points exactly? _____

4. Find r^2 or R^2 for the models you listed in exercise 2.

   _____

5. What does the value of r^2 or R^2 tell you about each model?

   _____

   _____ .

6. Graph each model on your graphing calculator. Sketch and label each model.

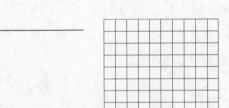
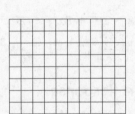

7. Which model seems more likely to represent the percent of on-time flights over time?

   _____

   _____

   _____ .

5-8 Practice   Form K

Polynomial Models in the Real World

Find a polynomial function whose graph passes through each set of points.

1. $(-4, 31)$, $(2, 25)$, and $(0, 3)$

To start, substitute the x- and y-values of
the points into the quadratic polynomial
$y = ax^2 + bx + c$ to get three linear equations
in three unknowns.

$31 = a(-4)^2 + b(-4) + c$
$25 = a(2)^2 + b(2) + c$
$3 = a(0)^2 + b(0) + c$

2. $(1, 3)$ and $(4, -6)$

3. $(-2, -19)$, $(0, 5)$, $(1, 8)$ and $(4, 53)$

4. $(-4, -47)$, $(-1, 7)$, and $(1, 3)$

5. $(-3, 16)$, $(1, 0)$, and $(5, 16)$

6. $(-4, -3)$, $(-1, 12)$, $(0, 5)$ and $(1, 2)$

7. $(-3, 8)$, $(0, -1)$, and $(2, 13)$

Find a polynomial function that best models each set of values.

8. Let $x = 0$.

Life Expectancy

Exact Age	Male (years)
5	70.5
10	65.6
15	60.6
20	55.9

Source: 2004 U.S. Social Security

9. Let x = the number of years since 1950.

World Silver

Year	Production (metric tons)
1950	6323
1955	9967
1960	7505
1965	8007

Source: The World Almanac & Book of Facts 2002

Lesson 5-8

5-8 Practice (continued)   *Form K*

Polynomial Models in the Real World

Find a cubic and a quartic model for each set of values. Then determine which model best represents the values.

10.

x	−2	−1	0	1	2
y	−6	−2	2	7	−2

11.

x	−2	−1	0	1	2
y	5	3	−5	−8	5

12.

x	−2	−1	0	1	2
y	−10	−8	3	4	−3

13.

x	−2	−1	0	1	2
y	4	−2	−1	0	2

Use your models from Exercises 8 and 9 to make predictions.

14. Estimate the life expectancy for a 40 year-old male.

15. Estimate world silver production for 2000.

5-8 Standardized Test Prep

Polynomial Models in the Real World

Multiple Choice

For Exercises 1–4, choose the correct letter.

1. Which of the following is the polynomial function whose graph passes through $(0, 4)$, $(-2, 30)$, and $(1, 6)$?

   Ⓐ $y = -9x + 10$

   Ⓒ $y = 9x - 10$

   Ⓑ $y = 5x^2 - 3x + 4$

   Ⓓ $y = -5x^2 + 3x - 4$

2. Which model type best represents the set of values at the right?

   Ⓕ linear

   Ⓗ quadratic

   Ⓖ cubic

   Ⓘ quartic

x	−2	−1	0	1	2
y	−17	4	1	−2	−5

3. Which polynomial function best models the data set at the right?

   Ⓐ $y = 0.00006006x^4 + 0.000119x^3 - 0.025x^2 + 2.13x + 71.6$

   Ⓑ $y = 0.00002163x^4 + 0.001267x^3 - 0.155x^2 + 8.24x + 81.2$

   Ⓒ $y = 0.00000312x^4 + 0.000197x^3 - 0.219x^2 + 5.22x + 86.3$

   Ⓓ $y = 0.00000606x^4 + 0.000217x^3 - 0.079x^2 + 3.90x + 83.5$

Paying Taxes for 1 Day

Year	Time Spent (minutes)
1940	83
1950	117
1960	130
1970	141
1980	145
1990	145
2000	160

SOURCE: Tax Foundation

4. Using a cubic model for the data set at the right, what is the estimated Consumer Price Index for 1965?

   Ⓕ 102.5

   Ⓗ 116.564

   Ⓖ 130.034

   Ⓘ 147.384

Consumer Prices

Year	Index
1920	60.0
1930	50.0
1940	42.0
1950	72.1
1960	88.7
1970	116.3
1980	248.8
1990	391.4
2000	515.8

SOURCE: Bureau of Labor Statistics

Short Response

5. Find both a cubic and quartic model for the set of values at the right. Which model is a better fit? How do you know?

x	1.2	1.4	1.6	1.8	2.0	2.2
y	3.1	−4.2	4.1	7.5	−8.9	10

Lesson 5-8

5-9 | Think About a Plan

Transforming Polynomial Functions

Physics The formula $K = \frac{1}{2}mv^2$ represents the kinetic energy of an object. If the kinetic energy of a ball is 10 lb–ft^2/s^2 when it is thrown with a velocity of 4 ft/s, how much kinetic energy is generated if the ball is thrown with a velocity of 8 ft/s?

Know

1. The kinetic energy of a ball is [_____] when the velocity of the ball is [_____].

2. _____

   _____

Need

3. To solve the problem I need to:

   _____ .

Plan

4. What equation can you use to find the value of m for the ball?

5. Solve the equation.

6. What equation can you use to find the kinetic energy generated if the ball is thrown with a velocity of 8 ft/sec?

7. Simplify.

8. Is the solution reasonable? Explain.

   _____

   _____

   _____ .

5-9 Practice

Form K

Transforming Polynomial Functions

Determine the cubic function that is obtained from the parent function $y = x^3$ after each sequence of transformations.

1. a vertical stretch by a factor of 2
a vertical translation 5 units down;
and a horizontal translation 3 units left
To start, multiply by 2 to stretch. $y = 2x^3$

2. a reflection across the x-axis;
a vertical translation 6 units up;
and a horizontal translation 4 units right

3. a vertical stretch by a factor of 3;
a reflection across the x-axis;
and a horizontal translation 6 units left

4. a vertical stretch by a factor of $\frac{1}{2}$;
a reflection across the x-axis;
and a vertical translation 5 units down
and a horizontal translation 2 units left

5. a vertical stretch by a factor of 2;
a reflection across the y-axis;
a vertical translation 2 units down

Find all the real zeros of each function.

6. $y = 3(x - 1)^3 + 2$

7. $y = -5(x - 2)^3 + 20$

8. $y = (x + 4)^3 - 1$

9. $y = 5(-x + 1)^3 + 10$

10. $y = 2(x - 5)^3 - 6$

11. $y = -(x - 6)^3 + 1$

Lesson 5-9

5-9 **Practice** (continued)   *Form K*

Transforming Polynomial Functions

Find a quartic function with the given x-values as its only real zeros.

12. $x = 1$ and $x = 4$

To start, use the Factor Theorem to write the
equation of a quartic with real roots at 1 and $y = (x - 1)(x - 4) \cdot Q(x)$
4 and complex zeros where $Q(x)$ has zeros.

13. $x = -2$ and $x = -5$ **14.** $x = -3$ and $x = 2$

15. $x = 7$ and $x = 2$ **16.** $x = -3$ and $x = -4$

17. $x = -3$ and $x = -5$ **18.** $x = -5$ and $x = 5$

19. You are swinging a bucket in a circle at a velocity of 8.2 ft/sec. The radius of the circle you
are making is 1.5 ft. The acceleration is equal to one over the radius times the velocity
squared.
   a. What is the acceleration of the bucket?
   b. What is the velocity if the acceleration is 28 ft/sec^2?

5-9 Standardized Test Prep

Transforming Polynomial Functions

Multiple Choice

For Exercises 1–5, choose the correct letter.

1. Which of the following describes the transformation of the parent function $y = x^3$ shown in the graph at the right?

   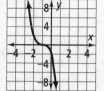

   (A) reflection across x-axis, vertical stretch by a factor of 2, and horizontal translation 1 unit left
   (B) reflection across y-axis, vertical translation 1 unit up
   (C) horizontal translation 2 units left, vertical translation 1 unit down
   (D) vertical stretch by a factor of $\frac{1}{2}$, horizontal translation 1 unit right, and vertical translation 2 units down

2. What are all the real zeros for $y = 5(x - 4)^3 + 6$?

   (F) $\sqrt[3]{\frac{-6}{5}} - 4$ (G) $\sqrt[3]{\frac{6}{5}} - 4$ (H) $\sqrt[3]{\frac{-6}{5}} + 4$ (I) $\sqrt[3]{\frac{6}{5}} + 4$

3. Which of the following polynomial functions *cannot* be obtained from the parent function $y = x^n$ using basic transformations?

   (A) $y = 6(x + 2)^3 - 3$ (B) $y = (-x - 1)^4$ (C) $y = \frac{x^2}{5}$ (D) $y = x^2 + x$

4. Which quartic function has $x = 3$ and $x = 9$ as its only real zeros?

   (F) $y = (x + 6)^4 - 81$ (H) $y = (x + 3)^4 - 81$

   (G) $y = (x - 6)^4 - 81$ (I) $y = (x - 3)^4 - 81$

5. Which graph represents the polynomial $y = 2(-x + 6)^3 - 1$?

   (A) 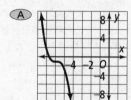   (B) 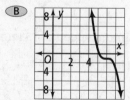   (C) 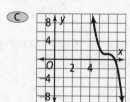   (D)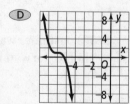

Short Response

6. The formula $s = \frac{1}{2}at^2$ represents the distance an object will travel in a specific amount of time if it travels at a constant acceleration. You roll a ball 20 ft in 6 s. How long will it take to roll the ball 45 ft? Show your work.

149

Lesson 5-9

6-1 Think About a Plan

Roots and Radical Expressions

Boat Building Boat builders share an old rule of thumb for sailboats. The maximum speed K in knots is 1.35 times the square root of the length L in feet of the boat's waterline.

    a. A customer is planning to order a sailboat with a maximum speed of 12 knots. How long should the waterline be?

    b. How much longer would the waterline have to be to achieve a maximum speed of 15 knots?

1. Write an equation to relate the maximum speed K in knots to the length L in feet of a boat's waterline.

2. How can you find the length of a sailboat's waterline if you know its maximum speed?

    _____ .

3. A customer is planning to order a sailboat with a maximum speed of 12 knots. How long should the waterline be?

4. How can you find how much longer the waterline would have to be to achieve a maximum speed of 15 knots, compared to a maximum speed of 12 knots?

    _____

    _____ .

5. If a customer wants a sailboat with a maximum speed of 15 knots, how long should the waterline be?

6. How much longer would the waterline have to be to achieve a maximum speed of 15 knots?

6-1

Practice   *Form K*

Roots and Radical Expressions

Find all the real square roots of each number.

1. 625

2. -1.44

3. $\frac{16}{81}$

Find all the real cube roots of each number.

4. -216

5. $\frac{1}{64}$

6. 0.027

Find all the real fourth roots of each number.

7. 0.2401

8. 1

9. -1296

Find each real root. To start, find a number whose square is equal to the radicand.

10. $\sqrt{400}$
$= \sqrt{(20)^2}$

11. $-\sqrt[4]{256}$

12. $\sqrt[3]{-729}$

Simplify each radical expression. Use absolute value symbols when needed. To start, write the factors of the radicand as perfect squares, cubes, or fourths.

13. $\sqrt{25x^6}$
$= \sqrt{(5)^2(x^3)^2}$

14. $\sqrt[3]{343x^9y^{12}}$

15. $\sqrt[4]{16x^{16}y^{20}}$

6-1 Practice (continued) Form K
Roots and Radical Expressions

16. The formula for the volume of a sphere is $V = \frac{4}{3}\pi r^3$. Solving for r, the radius of a sphere is $r = \sqrt[3]{\frac{3V}{4\pi}}$. If the volume of a sphere is 20 ft^3, what is the radius of the sphere to the nearest hundredth?

Find the two real solutions of each equation.

17. $x^4 = 81$

18. $x^2 = 144$

19. $x^4 = \frac{2401}{625}$

20. **Writing** Explain how you know whether or not to include the absolute value symbol on your root.

21. Arrange the numbers $\sqrt[3]{-64}$, $-\sqrt[3]{-64}$, $\sqrt{64}$, and $\sqrt[6]{64}$, in order from least to greatest.

22. **Open-Ended** Write a radical that has no real values.

23. **Reasoning** There are no real nth roots of a number b. What can you conclude about the index n and the number b?

6-1 Standardized Test Prep

Roots and Radical Expressions

Multiple Choice

For Exercises 1–6, choose the correct letter.

1. What is the real square root of 0.0064?

   Ⓐ 0.4   Ⓒ 0.04

   Ⓑ 0.08   Ⓓ no real square root

2. What is the real cube root of -64?

   Ⓕ 4   Ⓗ -8

   Ⓖ -4 Ⓘ no real cube root

3. What is the real fourth root of $-\frac{16}{81}$?

   Ⓐ $\frac{2}{3}$ Ⓒ $-\frac{4}{9}$

   Ⓑ $-\frac{2}{3}$ Ⓓ no real fourth root

4. What is the value of $\sqrt[3]{-0.027}$?

   Ⓕ -0.3 Ⓖ 0.3   Ⓗ -0.03 Ⓘ 0.03

5. What is the simplified form of the expression $\sqrt{4x^2y^4}$?

   Ⓐ $2xy^2$ Ⓑ $2|x|y^2$ Ⓒ $4xy^2$ Ⓓ $2|xy|$

6. What are the real solutions of the equation $x^4 = 81$?

   Ⓕ $-9, 9$ Ⓖ 3   Ⓗ $-3, 3$ Ⓘ -3

Short Response

7. The volume V of a cube with side length s is $V = s^3$. A cubical storage bin has volume 5832 cubic inches. What is the length of the side of the cube? Show your work.

6-2 Think About a Plan

Multiplying and Dividing Radical Expressions

Satellites The circular velocity v, in miles per hour of a satellite orbiting Earth is given by the formula $v = \sqrt{\dfrac{1.24 \times 10^{12}}{r}}$, where r is the distance in miles from the satellite to the center of the Earth. How much greater is the velocity of a satellite orbiting at an altitude of 100 mi than the velocity of a satellite orbiting at an altitude of 200 mi? (The radius of the Earth is 3950 mi.)

Know

1. The first satellite orbits at an altitude of [ ].

2. The second satellite orbits at an altitude of [ ].

3. The distance from the surface of the Earth to its center is [ ].

Need

4. To solve the problem I need to find:

   _____

   _____ .

Plan

5. Rewrite the formula for the circular velocity of a satellite using a for the altitude of the satellite.

6. Use your formula to find the velocity of a satellite orbiting at an altitude of 100 mi.

7. Use your formula to find the velocity of a satellite orbiting at an altitude of 200 mi.

8. How much greater is the velocity of a satellite orbiting at an altitude of 100 mi than one orbiting at an altitude of 200 mi?

6-2 Practice

Form K

Multiplying and Dividing Radical Expressions

Multiply, if possible. Then simplify. To start, identify the index of each radical.

1. $\sqrt[3]{4} \cdot \sqrt[3]{6}$

   index of both radicals is 3

   $\sqrt[3]{4 \cdot 6}$

2. $\sqrt{5} \cdot \sqrt{8}$

3. $\sqrt[3]{6} \cdot \sqrt[4]{9}$

Simplify. Assume all variables are positive. To start, find all perfect square factors.

4. $\sqrt[3]{27x^6}$

   $= \sqrt[3]{3^3 \cdot (x^2)^3}$

5. $\sqrt{48x^3y^4}$

6. $\sqrt[5]{128x^2y^{25}}$

Multiply and simplify. Assume all variables are positive.

7. $\sqrt{12} \cdot \sqrt{3}$

8. $\sqrt[4]{7x^6} \cdot \sqrt[4]{32x^2}$

9. $2\sqrt[3]{6x^4y} \cdot 3\sqrt[3]{9x^5y^2}$

Simplify each expression. Assume all variables are positive.

10. $\sqrt[3]{4} \cdot \sqrt[3]{80}$

11. $5\sqrt{2xy^6} \cdot 2\sqrt{2x^3y}$

12. $\sqrt{5}(\sqrt{5} + \sqrt{15})$

13. **Error Analysis** Your classmate simplified $\sqrt{5x^3} \cdot \sqrt[3]{5xy^2}$ to $5x^2y$. What mistake did she make? What is the correct answer?

14. A square rug has sides measuring $\sqrt[3]{16}$ ft by $\sqrt[3]{16}$ ft. What is the area of the rug?

Lesson 6-2

6-2 **Practice** (continued)   *Form K*

Multiplying and Dividing Radical Expressions

Divide and simplify. Assume all variables are positive. To start, write the quotient of roots as a root of a quotient.

15. $\dfrac{\sqrt{36x^6}}{\sqrt{9x^4}}$

$= \sqrt{\dfrac{36x^6}{9x^4}}$

16. $\dfrac{\sqrt[4]{405x^8y^2}}{\sqrt[4]{5x^3y^2}}$

17. $\dfrac{\sqrt[3]{75x^7y^2}}{\sqrt[3]{25x^4}}$

Rationalize the denominator of each quotient. Assume all variables are positive. To start, multiply the numerator and denominator by the denominator so that the denominator becomes a whole number.

18. $\dfrac{\sqrt{26}}{\sqrt{3}}$

$= \dfrac{\sqrt{26}}{\sqrt{3}} \cdot \dfrac{\sqrt{3}}{\sqrt{3}}$

19. $\dfrac{\sqrt[3]{x}}{\sqrt[3]{2}}$

20. $\dfrac{\sqrt{7x^4y}}{\sqrt{5xy}}$

21. Einstein's famous formula $E = mc^2$ relates energy E, mass m, and the speed of light c. Solve the formula for c. Rationalize the denominator.

22. The formula $h = 16t^2$ is used to measure the time t it takes for an object to free fall from height h. If an object falls from a height of $h = 18a^5$ ft, how long did it take for the object to fall in terms of a?

6-2

Standardized Test Prep

Multiplying and Dividing Radical Expressions

Multiple Choice

For Exercises 1–5, choose the correct letter. Assume that all variables are positive.

1. What is the simplest form of $\sqrt[3]{-49x} \cdot \sqrt[3]{7x^2}$?

   Ⓐ $7x\sqrt{7x}$ Ⓑ $-7x$ Ⓒ $7x$ Ⓓ $-7\sqrt[3]{x^2}$

2. What is the simplest form of $\sqrt{80x^7y^6}$?

   Ⓕ $2x^3y^3\sqrt{20x}$ Ⓖ $4x^6y^6\sqrt{5x^3}$ Ⓗ $4\sqrt{5x^7y^6}$ Ⓘ $4x^3y^3\sqrt{5x}$

3. What is the simplest form of $\sqrt[3]{25xy^2} \cdot \sqrt[3]{15x^2}$?

   Ⓐ $5x\sqrt[3]{3y^2}$ Ⓑ $5x\sqrt[3]{3y}$ Ⓒ $15xy\sqrt[3]{y}$ Ⓓ $5xy\sqrt{15x}$

4. What is the simplest form of $\dfrac{\sqrt{75x^5}}{\sqrt{12xy^2}}$?

   Ⓕ $\dfrac{5\sqrt{3x^4}}{2\sqrt{3y^2}}$ Ⓖ $\dfrac{5x^2}{2y}$ Ⓗ $\dfrac{5x\sqrt{x}}{2y}$ Ⓘ $\dfrac{5x^2y}{2}$

5. What is the simplest form of $\dfrac{2\sqrt[3]{x^2y}}{\sqrt[3]{4xy^2}}$?

   Ⓐ $\dfrac{\sqrt[3]{x^2y}}{2y}$ Ⓑ $\dfrac{x\sqrt[3]{2y}}{y}$ Ⓒ $\dfrac{\sqrt[3]{2xy^2}}{y}$ Ⓓ $\dfrac{\sqrt[3]{2y}}{xy}$

Short Response

6. The volume V of a wooden beam is $V = ls^2$, where l is the length of the beam and s is the length of one side of its square cross section. If the volume of the beam is 1200 in.^{3} and its length is 96 in., what is the side length? Show your work.

6-3 Think About a Plan

Binomial Radical Expressions

Geometry Show that the right triangle with legs of length $\sqrt{2} - 1$ and $\sqrt{2} + 1$ is similar to the right triangle with legs of length $6 - \sqrt{32}$ and 2.

Understanding the Problem

1. What is the length of the shortest leg of the first triangle? Explain.

   _____

2. What is the length of the shortest leg of the second triangle? Explain.

   _____

   _____

3. Which legs in the two triangles are corresponding legs?

   _____

   _____

   _____

Planning the Solution

4. Write a proportion that can be used to show that the two triangles are similar.

Getting an Answer

5. Simplify your proportion to show that the two triangles are similar.

Name _____ Class _____ Date _____

6-3 Practice

Binomial Radical Expressions

Form K

Simplify if possible. To start, determine if the expressions contain like radicals.

1. $3\sqrt{5} + 4\sqrt{5}$

both radicals

2. $8\sqrt[3]{4} - 6\sqrt[3]{4}$

3. $2\sqrt{xy} + 2\sqrt{y}$

4. A floor tile is made up of smaller squares. Each square measures 3 in. on each side. Find the perimeter of the floor tile.

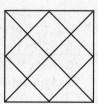

Simplify. To start, factor each radicand.

5. $\sqrt{18} + \sqrt{32}$
$= \sqrt{9 \cdot 2} + \sqrt{16 \cdot 2}$

6. $\sqrt[4]{324} - \sqrt[4]{2500}$

7. $\sqrt[3]{192} + \sqrt[3]{24}$

Multiply.

8. $(3 - \sqrt{6})(2 - \sqrt{6})$

9. $(5 + \sqrt{5})(1 - \sqrt{5})$

10. $(4 + \sqrt{7})^2$

Multiply each pair of conjugates.

11. $(7 - \sqrt{2})(7 + \sqrt{2})$

12. $(1 + 3\sqrt{3})(1 - 3\sqrt{3})$

13. $(6 + 4\sqrt{7})(6 - 4\sqrt{7})$

Lesson 6-3

6-3 Practice (continued) Form K

Binomial Radical Expressions

Rationalize each denominator. Simplify the answer.

14. $\dfrac{3}{2 + \sqrt{6}}$

$= \dfrac{3}{2 + \sqrt{6}} \cdot \dfrac{2 - \sqrt{6}}{2 - \sqrt{6}}$

15. $\dfrac{7 + \sqrt{5}}{6 - \sqrt{5}}$

16. $\dfrac{1 - 2\sqrt{10}}{4 + \sqrt{10}}$

17. A section of mosaic tile wall has the design shown at the right. The design is made up of equilateral triangles. Each side of the large triangle is 4 in. and each side of a small triangle is 2 in. Find the total area of the design to the nearest tenth of an inch.

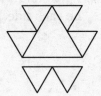

Simplify. Assume that all variables are positive.

18. $\sqrt{45} - \sqrt{80} + \sqrt{245}$

19. $\left(2 - \sqrt{98}\right)\left(3 + \sqrt{18}\right)$

20. $6\sqrt{192xy^2} + 4\sqrt{3xy^2}$

21. Error Analysis A classmate simplified the expression $\dfrac{1}{1 - \sqrt{2}}$ using the steps shown. What mistake did your classmate make? What is the correct answer?

$\dfrac{1}{1 - \sqrt{2}} \cdot \dfrac{1 - \sqrt{2}}{1 - \sqrt{2}}$

$= \dfrac{1 - \sqrt{2}}{1 - 2} = \dfrac{1 - \sqrt{2}}{-1} = -1 + \sqrt{2}$

22. Writing Explain the first step in simplifying $\sqrt{405} + \sqrt{80} - \sqrt{5}$.

6-3 Standardized Test Prep

Binomial Radical Expressions

Multiple Choice

For Exercises 1–5, choose the correct letter.

1. What is the simplest form of $2\sqrt{72} - 3\sqrt{32}$?

   (A) $2\sqrt{72} - 3\sqrt{32}$ (B) $24\sqrt{2}$ (C) $-2\sqrt{2}$ (D) 0

2. What is the simplest form of $(2 - \sqrt{7})(1 + 2\sqrt{7})$?

   (F) $-12 + 3\sqrt{7}$ (H) $16 + 5\sqrt{7}$

   (G) $-12 - 3\sqrt{7}$ (I) $3 + \sqrt{7}$

3. What is the simplest form of $(\sqrt{2} + \sqrt{7})(\sqrt{2} - \sqrt{7})$?

   (A) $9 + 2\sqrt{14}$ (B) $9 - 2\sqrt{14}$ (C) -5 (D) 9

4. What is the simplest form of $\dfrac{7}{2 + \sqrt{5}}$?

   (F) $-14 + 7\sqrt{5}$ (H) $-14 - 7\sqrt{5}$

   (G) $14 + 7\sqrt{5}$ (I) $14 - 7\sqrt{5}$

5. What is the simplest form of $8\sqrt[3]{5} - \sqrt[3]{40} - 2\sqrt[3]{135}$?

   (A) $16\sqrt[3]{5}$ (B) $12\sqrt[3]{5}$ (C) $4\sqrt[3]{5}$ (D) 0

Short Response

6. A hiker drops a rock from the rim of the Grand Canyon. The distance it falls d in feet after t seconds is given by the function $d = 16t^2$. How far has the rock fallen after $(3 + \sqrt{2})$ seconds? Show your work.

6-4 Think About a Plan

Rational Exponents

Science A desktop world globe has a volume of about 1386 cubic inches. The radius of the Earth is approximately equal to the radius of the globe raised to the 10th power. Find the radius of the Earth. (*Hint:* Use the formula $V = \frac{4}{3}\pi r^3$ for the volume of a sphere.)

Know

1. The volume of the globe is $\boxed{}$.

2. The radius of the Earth is equal to _____.

Need

3. To solve the problem I need to find _____.

Plan

4. Write an equation relating the radius of the globe r_G to the radius of the Earth r_E.

5. How can you represent the radius of the globe in terms of the radius of the Earth?

6. Write an equation to represent the volume of the globe.

7. Use your previous equation and your equation from Exercise 5 to write an equation to find the radius of the Earth.

8. Solve your equation to find the radius of the Earth.

6-4

Practice

Rational Exponents

Form K

Simplify each expression.

1. $16^{\frac{1}{4}}$

$\sqrt[4]{16}$

2. $(-3)^{\frac{1}{3}} \cdot (-3)^{\frac{1}{3}} \cdot (-3)^{\frac{1}{3}}$

3. $5^{\frac{1}{2}} \cdot 45^{\frac{1}{2}}$

Write each expression in radical form.

4. $x^{\frac{1}{4}}$

5. $x^{\frac{4}{5}}$

6. $x^{\frac{2}{9}}$

Write each expression in exponential form.

7. $\sqrt[3]{2}$

8. $\sqrt[3]{2x^2}$

9. $\sqrt[3]{(2x)^2}$

10. Bone loss for astronauts may be prevented with an apparatus that rotates to simulate gravity. In the formula $N = \dfrac{a^{0.5}}{2\pi r^{0.5}}$, N is the rate of rotation in revolutions per second, a is the simulated acceleration in m/s^2, and r is the radius of the apparatus in meters. How fast would an apparatus with the following radii have to rotate to simulate the acceleration of 9.8 m/s^2 that is due to Earth's gravity?

a. $r = 1.7$ m

b. $r = 3.6$ m

c. $r = 5.2$ m

d. Reasoning Would an apparatus with radius 0.8 m need to spin faster or slower than the one in part (a)?

Lesson 6-4

6-4

Practice (continued)

Rational Exponents

Simplify each number.

11. $(-216)^{\frac{1}{3}}$

$\sqrt[3]{-216}$

12. $243^{1.2}$

13. $32^{-0.4}$

Find each product or quotient. To start, rewrite the expression using exponents.

14. $\left(\sqrt[4]{6}\right)\left(\sqrt[3]{6}\right)$

$= \left(6^{\frac{1}{4}}\right)\left(6^{\frac{1}{3}}\right)$

15. $\dfrac{\sqrt[5]{x^2}}{\sqrt[10]{x^2}}$

16. $\sqrt{20} \cdot \sqrt[3]{135}$

Simplify each number.

17. $(125)^{\frac{2}{3}}$

18. $(216)^{\frac{2}{3}}(216)^{\frac{2}{3}}$

19. $(-243)^{\frac{2}{5}}$

Write each expression in simplest form. Assume that all variables are positive.

20. $\left(16x^{-8}\right)^{-\frac{3}{4}}$

21. $\left(8x^{15}\right)^{-\frac{1}{3}}$

22. $\left(\dfrac{x^2}{x^{-10}}\right)^{\frac{1}{3}}$

23. Error Analysis Explain why the following simplification is incorrect. What is the correct simplification?

$$5\left(4 - 5^{\frac{1}{2}}\right)$$
$$= 5(4) - 5\left(5^{\frac{1}{2}}\right) = 20 - 25^{\frac{1}{2}} = 15$$

6-4 Standardized Test Prep

Rational Exponents

Multiple Choice

For Exercises 1–5, choose the correct letter.

1. What is $12^{\frac{1}{3}} \cdot 45^{\frac{1}{3}} \cdot 50^{\frac{1}{3}}$ in simplest form?

   Ⓐ $\sqrt{27,000}$ Ⓑ 30   Ⓒ $107^{\frac{1}{3}}$ Ⓓ 27,000

2. What is $x^{\frac{1}{3}} \cdot y^{\frac{2}{3}}$ in simplest form?

   Ⓕ $x^3\sqrt{y^3}$ Ⓖ $\sqrt{xy^3}$ Ⓗ $\sqrt[3]{(xy)^2}$ Ⓘ $\sqrt[3]{xy^2}$

3. What is $x^{\frac{1}{3}} \cdot x^{\frac{1}{2}} \cdot x^{\frac{1}{4}}$ in simplest form?

   Ⓐ $x^{\frac{13}{12}}$ Ⓑ $x^{\frac{1}{24}}$ Ⓒ $x^{\frac{1}{9}}$ Ⓓ $x^{\frac{5}{24}}$

4. What is $\left(\dfrac{x^{\frac{2}{3}}y^{\frac{1}{3}}}{x^{\frac{1}{2}}y^{\frac{3}{4}}}\right)^6$ in simplest form?

   Ⓕ $xy^{\frac{5}{2}}$ Ⓖ $x^7y^{\frac{5}{2}}$ Ⓗ $\dfrac{1}{xy^{\frac{5}{2}}}$ Ⓘ $\dfrac{x}{y^{\frac{5}{2}}}$

5. What is $(-32x^{10}y^{35})^{-\frac{1}{5}}$ in simplest form?

   Ⓐ $2x^2y^7$ Ⓑ $-\dfrac{2}{x^2y^7}$ Ⓒ $-\dfrac{1}{2x^2y^7}$ Ⓓ $\dfrac{2}{x^2y^7}$

Short Response

6. The surface area S, in square units, of a sphere with volume V, in cubic units, is given by the formula $S = \pi^{\frac{1}{3}}(6V)^{\frac{2}{3}}$. What is the surface area of a sphere with volume $\frac{4}{3}$ mi^3? Write your answer in terms of $\pi^{\frac{1}{3}}$. Show your work.

6-5 Think About a Plan

Solving Square Root and Other Radical Equations

Traffic Signs A stop sign is a regular octagon, formed by cutting triangles off the corners of a square. If a stop sign measures 36 in. from top to bottom, what is the length of each side?

Understanding the Problem

1. How can you use the diagram at the right to find a relationship between *s* and *x*?

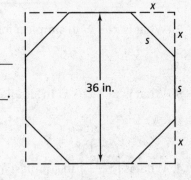

   _____

   _____ .

2. How can you use the diagram at the right to find another relationship between *s* and *x*?

   _____

   _____ .

3. What is the problem asking you to determine?

   _____

Planning the Solution

4. What are two equations that relate *s* and *x*?

5. How can you use your equations to find *s*?

   _____ .

Getting an Answer

6. Solve your equations for *s*.

7. Is your answer reasonable? Explain.

   _____

   _____ .

6-5 Practice

Solving Square Root and Other Radical Equations

Solve. To start, rewrite the equation to isolate the radical.

1. $\sqrt{x + 2} - 2 = 0$

$\sqrt{x + 2} = 2$

2. $\sqrt{2x + 3} - 7 = 0$

3. $2 + \sqrt{3x - 2} = 6$

Solve.

4. $2(x - 2)^{\frac{2}{3}} = 50$

5. $2(x + 3)^{\frac{3}{2}} = 54$

6. $(6x - 5)^{\frac{1}{3}} + 3 = -2$

7. A cylindrical can holds 28 in.^{3} of soup. If the can is 4 in. tall, what is the radius of the can to the nearest tenth of an inch? (*Hint:* $V = \pi r^2 h$)

8. Writing Explain the difference between a radical equation and a polynomial equation.

9. Reasoning If you are solving $4(x + 3)^{\frac{3}{4}} = 7$, do you need to use the absolute value to solve for x? Why or why not?

6-5 **Practice** (continued) Form K

Solving Square Root and Other Radical Equations

Solve. Check for extraneous solutions. To start, square each side of the equation.

10. $\sqrt{4x + 5} = x + 2$

$(\sqrt{4x + 5})^2 = (x + 2)^2$

11. $\sqrt{-3x - 5} - 3 = x$

12. $\sqrt{x + 7} + 5 = x$

13. $\sqrt{2x - 7} = \sqrt{x + 2}$

$(\sqrt{2x - 7})^2 = (\sqrt{x + 2})^2$

14. $\sqrt{3x + 2} - \sqrt{2x + 7} = 0$ **15.** $\sqrt{2x + 4} - 2 = \sqrt{x}$

16. Find the solutions of $\sqrt{x + 2} = x$.

  a. Are there any extraneous solutions?

  b. **Reasoning** How do you know the answer to part (a)?

17. A floor is made up of hexagon-shaped tiles. Each hexagon tile has an area of 1497 cm². What is the length of each side of the hexagon? (*Hint:* Six equilateral triangles make one hexagon.)

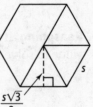

6-5 Standardized Test Prep

Solving Square Root and Other Radical Equations

Gridded Response

Solve each exercise and enter your answer in the grid provided.

1. What is the solution? $\sqrt{2x - 4} - 3 = 1$

2. What is the solution? $5x^{\frac{1}{2}} - 8 = 7$

3. What is the solution? $\sqrt{2x - 6} = 3 - x$

4. What is the solution? $\sqrt{5x - 3} = \sqrt{2x + 3}$

5. Kepler's Third Law of Orbital Motion states that the period P (in Earth years) it takes a planet to complete one orbit of the sun is a function of the distance d (in astronomical units, AU) from the planet to the sun. This relationship is $P = d^{\frac{3}{2}}$. If it takes Neptune 165 years to orbit the sun, what is the distance (in AU) of Neptune from the sun? Round your answer to two decimal places.

Answers

1. 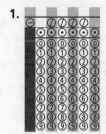 2. 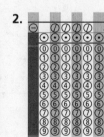 3. 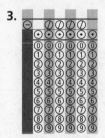 4. 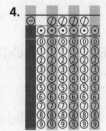 5.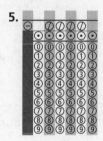

6-6 Think About a Plan

Function Operations

Sales A salesperson earns a 3% bonus on weekly sales over $5000. Consider the following functions.

$$g(x) = 0.03x \qquad h(x) = x - 5000$$

a. Explain what each function above represents.

b. Which composition, $(h \circ g)(x)$ or $(g \circ h)(x)$, represents the weekly bonus? Explain.

1. What does x represent in the function $g(x)$?

_____

2. What does the function $g(x)$ represent?

_____

3. What does x represent in the function $h(x)$?

_____

4. What does the function $h(x)$ represent?

_____

5. What is the meaning of $(h \circ g)(x)$?

_____.

6. Assume that x is $7000. What is $(h \circ g)(x)$?

7. What is the meaning of $(g \circ h)(x)$?

_____.

8. Assume that x is $7000. What is $(g \circ h)(x)$?

9. Which composition represents the weekly bonus? Explain

_____

_____

_____.

6-6

Practice   Form K

Function Operations

Let $f(x) = 4x + 8$ and $g(x) = 2x - 12$. Perform each function operation and then find the domain of the result.

1. $(f + g)(x)$ **2.** $(f - g)(x)$ **3.** $(f \cdot g)(x)$ **4.** $\left(\dfrac{f}{g}\right)(x)$

$f(x) + g(x)$

Let $f(x) = x + 2$ and $g(x) = \sqrt{x} - 1$. Perform each function operation and then find the domain of the result.

5. $(f + g)(x)$ **6.** $(f \cdot g)(x)$ **7.** $\left(\dfrac{f}{g}\right)(x)$ **8.** $\left(\dfrac{g}{f}\right)(x)$

Let $f(x) = x - 2$ and $g(x) = x^2$. Find each value. To start, use the definition of composing functions to find a function rule.

9. $(g \circ f)(4)$ **10.** $(f \circ g)(-1)$ **11.** $(g \circ f)(-3)$

$f(4) = 4 - 2 = 2$

Let $f(x) = \sqrt{x}$ and $g(x) = (x + 2)^2$. Find each value.

12. $(f \circ g)(-5)$ **13.** $(f \circ g)(0)$ **14.** $(g \circ f)(4)$

Lesson 6-6

6-6 Practice (continued) Form K

Function Operations

15. A car dealer offers a 15% discount off the list price x of any car on the lot. At the same time, the manufacturer offers a $1000 rebate for each purchase of a car.

  a. Write a function $f(x)$ to represent the price after discount.

  b. Write a function $g(x)$ to represent the price after the $1000 rebate.

  c. Suppose the list price of a car is $18,000. Use a composite function to find the price of the car if the discount is applied before the rebate.

  d. Suppose the list price of a car is $18,000. Use a composite function to find the price of the car if the discount is applied after the rebate.

  e. Reasoning Between parts (c) and (d), will the dealer want to apply the discount before or after the rebate? Why?

16. Error Analysis $f(x) = 2\sqrt{x}$ and $g(x) = 3x - 6$. Your friend gives a domain for $\left(\dfrac{f}{g}\right)(x)$ as $x \geq 0$. Is this correct? If not, what is the correct domain?

Let $f(x) = 2x^2 - 3$ and $g(x) = \dfrac{x+1}{2}$. Find each value.

17. $f(g(2))$ **18.** $g(f(-3))$ **19.** $(f \circ f)(-1)$

20. Reasoning A local bookstore has a sale on all their paperbacks giving a 10% discount. You also received a coupon in the mail for $4 off your purchase. If you buy 2 paperbacks at $8 each, is it less expensive for you to apply the discount before the coupon or after the coupon? How much will you save?

6-6

Standardized Test Prep

Function Operations

Multiple Choice

For Exercises 1–5, choose the correct letter.

1. Let $f(x) = -2x + 5$ and $g(x) = x^3$. What is $(g - f)(x)$?

   (A) $x^3 - 2x + 5$

   (B) $x^3 + 2x - 5$

   (C) $-x^3 - 2x + 5$

   (D) $-x^3 + 2x - 5$

2. Let $f(x) = 3x$ and $g(x) = x^2 + 1$. What is $(f \cdot g)(x)$?

   (F) $9x^2 + 3x$

   (G) $9x^2 + 1$

   (H) $3x^3 + 3x$

   (I) $3x^3 + 1$

3. Let $f(x) = x^2 - 2x - 15$ and $g(x) = x + 3$. What is the domain of $\frac{f}{g}(x)$?

   (A) all real numbers

   (B) $x \neq 5, -3$

   (C) $x \neq -3$

   (D) $x > 0$

4. Let $f(x) = \sqrt{x} + 1$ and $g(x) = 2x + 1$. What is $(g \circ f)(x)$?

   (F) $2\sqrt{x} + 3$

   (G) $2x\sqrt{x} + 2x + \sqrt{x} + 1$

   (H) $\sqrt{2x + 1} + 1$

   (I) $2x + \sqrt{x} + 2$

5. Let $f(x) = \frac{1}{x}$ and $g(x) = x^2 - 2$. What is $(f \circ g)(-3)$?

   (A) $\frac{17}{9}$

   (B) $\frac{1}{7}$

   (C) $-\frac{17}{9}$

   (D) $-\frac{7}{3}$

Short Response

6. Suppose the function $f(x) = 0.035x$ represents the number of U.S. dollars equivalent to x Russian rubles and the function $g(x) = 90x$ represents the number of Japanese yen equivalent to x U.S. dollars. Write a composite function that represents the number of Japanese yen equivalent to x Russian rubles. Show your work.

Lesson 6-6

6-7 Think About a Plan

Inverse Relations and Functions

Geometry Write a function that gives the length of the hypotenuse of an isosceles right triangle with side length *s*. Evaluate the inverse of the function to find the side length of an isosceles right triangle with a hypotenuse of 6 in.

Know

1. An equation that relates the length of each side *s* and the length of the hypotenuse *h* of an isosceles right triangle is

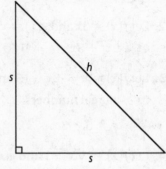

Need

2. To solve the problem I need to:

_____

_____.

Plan

3. A function that gives the length of the hypotenuse *h* in terms of the side length

   s is [   ].

4. An inverse function that gives the side length *s* in terms of the length of the

   hypotenuse *h* is [   ].

5. What is the inverse function evaluated for *h* = 6 in.?

6. Is the side length reasonable? Explain.

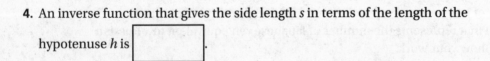

6-7 Practice

Form K

Inverse Relations and Functions

Find the inverse of each relation. Graph the given relation and its inverse.

1.

x	y
0	−1
1	1
2	3
3	5

2.

x	y
−2	7
0	3
2	7
4	19

3.

x	y
−3	2
−2	2
−1	2
0	2

Find the inverse of each function. Is the inverse a function? To start, switch x and y.

4. $y = \frac{x}{2}$

$x = \frac{y}{2}$

5. $y = x^2 + 4$

6. $y = (3x - 4)^2$

Graph each relation and its inverse.

7. $y = 3x - 4$

8. $y = -x^2$

9. $y = (3 - 2x)^2$

Lesson 6-7

6-7 Practice (continued) Form K

Inverse Relations and Functions

Find the inverse of each function. Is the inverse a function?

10. $f(x) = (x + 1)^2$ **11.** $f(x) = \frac{2x^3}{5}$ **12.** $f(x) = \sqrt{3x} + 4$

13. Multiple Choice What is the inverse of $y = 5x - 1$?

$\circledA$ $f^{-1}(x) = 5x + 1$ $\circledB$ $f^{-1}(x) = \frac{x + 1}{5}$ $\circledC$ $f^{-1}(x) = \frac{x}{5} + 1$ $\circledD$ $f^{-1}(x) = \frac{x}{5} - 1$

For each function, find its inverse and the domain and range of the function and its inverse. Determine whether the inverse is a function.

14. $f(x) = \sqrt{x + 1}$ **15.** $f(x) = 10 - 3x$ **16.** $f(x) = 4x^2 + 25$

17. The formula for the area of a circle is $A = \pi r^2$.

    a. Find the inverse of the formula. Is the inverse a function?

    b. Use the inverse to find the radius of a circle that has an area of 82 in.^{2}.

For Exercises 18–20, $f(x) = 5x + 11$. Find each value. To start, rewrite $f(x)$ as y and switch x and y.

18. $(f \circ f^{-1})(5)$ **19.** $(f^{-1} \circ f)(-3)$ **20.** $(f^{-1} \circ f)(0)$

    $y = 5x + 11$

6-7 Standardized Test Prep

Inverse Relations and Functions

Multiple Choice

For Exercises 1–4, choose the correct letter.

1. What is the inverse of the relation?

x	−2	−1	0	2
y	3	1	−1	−2

A)

x	−2	−1	1	3
y	2	0	−1	−2

C)

x	−2	−1	0	2
y	−2	−1	1	3

B)

x	−2	−1	0	2
y	−3	−1	1	2

D)

x	−2	−1	1	3
y	2	1	−1	−2

2. What is the inverse of the function? $y = 5(x - 3)$

F) $y = \frac{x + 3}{5}$ G) $y = \frac{1}{5}x + 3$ H) $y = 5(x + 3)$ I) $y = \frac{1}{5}x - 3$

3. What function with domain $x \geq 5$ is the inverse of $y = \sqrt{x} + 5$?

A) $y = x^2 + 5$ B) $y = x^2 - 5$ C) $y = (x - 5)^2$ D) $y = (x + 5)^2$

4. What is the domain and range of the inverse of the function? $y = \sqrt{x - 5}$

F) domain is the set of all real numbers ≥ 0; range is the set of all real numbers ≥ 5

G) domain is the set of all real numbers ≥ 5; range is the set of all real numbers ≥ 0

H) domain and range is the set of all real numbers ≥ 5

I) domain and range is the set of all real numbers

Extended Response

5. A high school principal uses the formula $y = 150x + 180$ to predict a student's score on a state achievement test using the student's 11th-grade GPA number x.
   a. What is the inverse of the formula?
   b. Is the inverse a function?
   c. Using the inverse, what GPA does a student need to get a passing score of 510 on the state exam?

Lesson 6-7

6-8

Think About a Plan

Graphing Radical Functions

Electronics The size of a computer monitor is given as the length of the screen's diagonal d in inches. The equation $d = \frac{5}{6}\sqrt{3A}$ models the length of a diagonal of a monitor screen with area A in square inches.

a. Graph the equation on your calculator.

b. Suppose you want to buy a new monitor that has twice the area of your old monitor. Your old monitor has a diagonal of 15 inches. What will be the diagonal of your new monitor?

1. How can you use a graph to approximate the area of the old monitor?

_____

_____ .

2. Graph the equation on your calculator. Make a sketch of the graph.

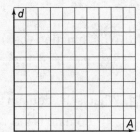

3. What is the area of the old monitor?

4. How can you check your answer algebraically?

_____ .

5. Show that your answer checks.

6. How can you find the diagonal of a new monitor with twice the area of the old monitor?

_____ .

7. Use your method to find the diagonal of your new monitor.

8. What will be the diagonal of your new monitor?

6-8 Practice

Form K

Graphing Radical Functions

Graph each function.

1. $y = \sqrt{x} + 3$

2. $y = \sqrt{x - 4}$

3. $y = \sqrt{x} - 7$

Graph each function.

4. $y = 4\sqrt{x}$

5. $y = -2\sqrt{x + 1}$

6. $y = 5\sqrt{x} - 4$

Solve each square root equation by graphing. Round the answer to the nearest hundredth, if necessary. If there is no solution, explain why.

7. $\sqrt{x + 2} = 7$

8. $\sqrt{4x + 1} = 5$

9. $3\sqrt{3 - x} = 10$

10. A periscope on a submarine is at a height h, in feet, above the surface of the water. The greatest distance d, in miles, that can be seen from the periscope on a clear day is given by $d = \sqrt{\dfrac{3h}{2}}$.

   a. If a ship is 3 miles from the submarine, at what height above the water would the submarine have to raise its periscope in order to see the ship?

   b. If a ship is 1.5 miles from the submarine, to what height would it have to be raised?

Lesson 6-8

6-8

Practice (continued)

Form K

Graphing Radical Functions

Graph each function. To start, graph the parent function, $y = \sqrt[3]{x}$.

11. $y = \sqrt[3]{x} - 4$ **12.** $y = 3 - \sqrt[3]{x + 1}$ **13.** $y = \frac{1}{2}\sqrt[3]{x - 1} + 3$

14. A center-pivot irrigation system can water from 1 to 130 acres of crop land. The length l in feet of rotating pipe needed to irrigate A acres is given by the function $l = 117.75\sqrt{A}$.

   a. Graph the equation on your calculator. Make a sketch of the graph.

   b. What length of pipe is needed to irrigate 40, 80, and 130 acres?

Graph each function. Find the domain and range.

15. $y = 2\sqrt[3]{x} - 4$ **16.** $y = -\sqrt[3]{8x} + 5$ **17.** $y = -3\sqrt{x - 4} - 3$

18. Open Ended Write a cube root function in which the vertical translation of $y = \sqrt[3]{x}$ is twice the horizontal translation.

6-8

Standardized Test Prep

Graphing Radical Functions

Multiple Choice

For Exercises 1–4, choose the correct letter.

1. What is the graph of $y = \sqrt{x} + 4$?

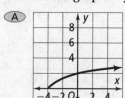 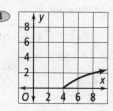 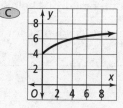 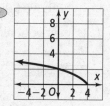

2. What is the graph of $y = \sqrt{x - 3} - 2$?

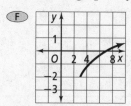 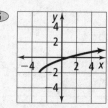 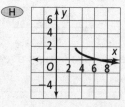 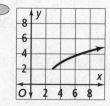

3. What is the graph of $y = 1 - \sqrt[3]{x + 3}$?

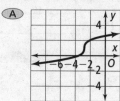 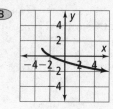 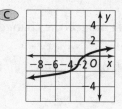 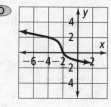

4. What is the description of $y = \sqrt{9x - 3}$ to make it easy to graph using transformations of its parent function?

F the graph of $y = 3\sqrt{x}$, shifted right 3 units

G the graph of $y = 3\sqrt{x}$, shifted right $\frac{1}{3}$ unit

H the graph of $y = \sqrt{x}$, shifted right 3 units and up 9 units

I the graph of $y = \sqrt{x}$, shifted right $\frac{1}{3}$ unit and up 9 units

Short Response

5. What is the graph of $y = 2\sqrt{x - 1} + 3$?

7-1 Think About a Plan

Exploring Exponential Models

Population The population of a certain animal species decreases at a rate of 3.5% per year. You have counted 80 of the animals in the habitat you are studying.

    a. Write a function that models the change in the animal population.

    b. Graphing Calculator Graph the function. Estimate the number of years until the population first drops below 15 animals.

1. Is an exponential model reasonable for this situation? Explain.

_____

_____ .

2. Write the function that models exponential growth or decay. $A(t) =$ ☐

3. The initial population is ☐ .

4. Is the rate of change positive or negative? Explain.

_____ .

5. The rate of change is ☐ .

6. Write a function that models the change in the animal population. $P(t) =$ ☐

7. Graph your function on a graphing calculator. Sketch your graph.

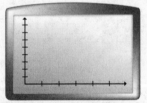

8. How can you find the x-value that produces a given y-value?

_____ .

9. Use your graph to estimate the number of years until the population first drops below 15 animals.

7-1 | **Practice** | *Form K*
Exploring Exponential Models

Complete the table of values for each function. Then graph the function.

1. $y = 3^x$

x	3^x	y
−2	3^{-2}	0.11
−1	3^{-1}	
0		
1		
2		

2. $y = 0.5(2)^x$

x	$0.5(2)^x$	y
−1	$0.5(2)^{-1}$	
0		
1		
2		
3		
4		

3. $y = 3(2)^x$

x	$3(2)^x$	y
−2		
−1		
0		
1		
2		

4. $y = 2(0.5)^x$

x	$2(0.5)^x$	y
−2		
−1		
0		
1		
2		

Without graphing, determine whether the function represents exponential growth or exponential decay.

5. $y = 3(7)^x$

6. $y = 4(2.5)^x$

7. $y = 5(0.75)^x$

8. $y = 0.5(0.2)^x$

9. $y = 10(6)^x$

10. $y = 0.6^x$

Find the *y*-intercept of each function.

11. $y = 2(0.75)^x$

12. $y = 0.75(3)^x$

13. $y = 3^x$

7-1 **Practice** (continued) — Form K

Exploring Exponential Models

For each annual rate of change, find the corresponding growth or decay factor.

14. 35%   **15.** −20%   **16.** 62%

17. Identify the meaning of the variables in the exponential growth or decay function.

$$A(t) = a(1 + r)^t$$

  a. $a =$ _____

  b. $r =$ _____

  c. $t =$ _____

18. The population of Bainsville is 2000. The population is supposed to grow by 10% each year for the next 5 years. How many people will live in Bainsville in 5 years?

19. Writing Describe a situation that could be modeled by the function $A(t) = 200(1.05)^x$.

20. A music store sold 200 guitars in 2007. The store sold 180 guitars in 2008. The number of guitars that the store sells is decreasing exponentially. If this trend continues, how many guitars will the store sell in 2012?

$r = \dfrac{y_2 - y_1}{y_1}$ $A(t) = a(1 + r)^t$

$r = \dfrac{180 - 200}{200}$ $A(5) =$

$r =$

7-1 Standardized Test Prep

Exploring Exponential Models

Multiple Choice

For Exercises 1 and 2, choose the correct letter.

1. Which of the following functions represents exponential decay and has a y-intercept of 2?

   Ⓐ $y = 2\left(\frac{4}{3}\right)^x$

   Ⓑ $y = \frac{1}{2}(0.95)^x$

   Ⓒ $y = \frac{1}{4}(2)^x$

   Ⓓ $y = 2\left(\frac{2}{5}\right)^x$

2. Suppose you deposit $3000 in a savings account that pays interest at an annual rate of 4%. If no other money is added or withdrawn from the account, how much will be in the account after 10 years?

   Ⓕ $3122.18

   Ⓖ $4994.50

   Ⓗ $4440.73

   Ⓘ $86,776.40

Extended Response

3. In 2009 there was an endangered population of 270 cranes in a western state. Due to wildlife efforts, the population is increasing at a rate of 5% per year.

   a. What exponential function would be a good model for this population of cranes? Explain in words or show work for how you determined the exponential function.

   b. If this trend continues, how many cranes will there be in this population in 2020? Show your work.

7-2   Think About a Plan

Properties of Exponential Functions

Investment How long would it take to double your principal in an account that pays 6.5% annual interest compounded continuously?

Know

1. The equation for continuously compounded interest is $\boxed{}$.

2. The principal is $\boxed{}$.

3. The interest rate is $\boxed{}$.

Need

4. To solve the problem I need to:

_____ .

Plan

5. If the principal is P, then twice the principal is $\boxed{}$.

6. What equation can you use to find the time it takes to double your principal?

7. Solve your equation for t.

8. Is your solution reasonable? Explain.

_____

_____ .

Name _____ Class _____ Date _____

7-2 | **Practice** | Form K

Properties of Exponential Functions

Write the parent function of each function.

1. $y = 5 \cdot 3^x$

2. $y = 7^{(x-3)}$

3. $y = 6^{(x-2)} + 9$

Graph each of the following functions.

4. $y = 4^x$

5. $y = 0.5 \cdot 2^x$

Identify each function as a compression, a reflection, or a translation of the parent function.

6.
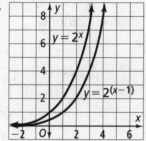

7.
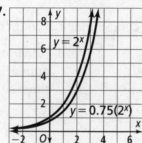

8.
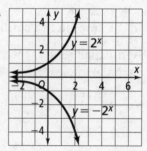

Write a function for the indicated transformation.

9. the function $y = 5^{(x-2)}$ vertically stretched by the factor 3

10. the function $y = 7 \cdot 2^x$ translated up 8 units

Lesson 7-2

7-2 Practice (continued)   Form K

Properties of Exponential Functions

Use the graph of $y = e^x$ to evaluate each expression to four decimal places.

11. e^3 **12.** $e^{0.5}$ **13.** e^{-4}

Identify the meaning of the following variables in the formula for continuously compounded interest.

$$A(t) = P \cdot e^{rt}$$

14. P **15.** r **16.** t

Find the amount in a continuously compounded account for the given conditions.

17. principal: $300
annual interest rate: 5%
time: 4 yr

$A(t) = P \cdot e^{rt}$
$A(4) = \$300 \cdot e^{(0.05)(4)}$
$A(4) =$

18. principal: $650
annual interest rate: 6.5%
time: 20 yr

$A(t) = P \cdot e^{rt}$
$A(t) =$

19. Sarah received a paycheck for $1200. She deposited $\frac{1}{4}$ of the money into a bank account. The account has an interest rate of 6% compounded continuously. This is the first and last deposit that Sarah makes into this account. How much money will be in the account in 15 years?

7-2 Standardized Test Prep

Properties of Exponential Functions

Gridded Response

Solve each exercise and enter your answer in the grid provided.

1. Suppose you deposit $6000 in a savings account that pays interest at an annual rate of 4% compounded continuously. How many years will it take for the balance in your savings account to reach $8000? Round your answer up to the nearest number of years.

2. Suppose you make $1500 at your summer job and you decide to invest this money in a savings account that pays interest at an annual rate of 5.5% compounded continuously. How many dollars will be in the account after 5 years? Express the answer to the nearest whole dollar.

3. The half-life of a radioactive substance is the time it takes for half of the material to decay. Phosphorus-32 is used to study a plant's use of fertilizer. It has a half-life of 14.3 days. How many milligrams of phosphorus-32 remain after 92 days from a 100-mg sample? Express the answer to the nearest whole milligram.

4. A scientist notes the bacteria count in a petrie dish is 40. Three hours later, she notes the count has increased to 75. Using an exponential model, how many hours will it take for the bacteria count to grow from 75 to 120? Express the answer to the nearest tenth of an hour.

Answers

1.
2.
3.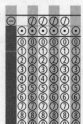
4.

7-3 Think About a Plan

Logarithmic Functions as Inverses

Chemistry Find the concentration of hydrogen ions in seawater, if the pH level of seawater is 8.5.

Understanding the Problem

1. What is the pH of seawater?

2. How do you represent the concentration of hydrogen ions?

3. What is the problem asking you to determine?

Planning the Solution

4. Write the formula for the pH of a substance.

5. Write an equation relating the pH of seawater to the concentration of hydrogen ions in seawater.

Getting an Answer

6. Solve your equation to find the concentration of hydrogen ions in seawater.

7-3 Practice
Logarithmic Functions as Inverses

Form K

Write each equation in logarithmic form.

1. $32 = 2^5$

2. $243 = 3^5$

3. $625 = 5^4$

Write each equation in exponential form.

4. $\log_3 9 = 2$

5. $\log_5 125 = 3$

6. $\log_8 512 = 3$

Evaluate each logarithm.

7. $\log_9 27$

$\log_9 27 = x$

$27 = 9^x$

$3^3 = \left(3^2\right)^x$

$3^3 = 3^{2x}$

$3 = 2x$

$x =$

8. $\log_8 256$

$\log_8 256 = x$

$256 = 8^x$

9. $\log_{125} \frac{1}{25}$

The formula $\log \dfrac{I_1}{I_2} = M_1 - M_2$ is used to compare the intensity levels of earthquakes. The variable I is the intensity measured by a seismograph. The variable M is the measurement on the Richter scale. Use the formula to answer the following problem.

10. In 1906, an earthquake of magnitude 8.25 hit San Francisco, California. Indonesia was hit by an earthquake of magnitude 8.5 in 1938. Compare the intensity of the two earthquakes.

Lesson 7-3

7-3 **Practice** (continued)   *Form K*

Logarithmic Functions as Inverses

11. Error Analysis A student drew the graph below to represent the function $y = \log_4 x$. What mistake did the student make when she drew her graph?

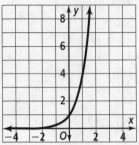

Graph each logarithmic function.

12. $y = \log_2 x$

13. $y = \log_{\frac{1}{3}} x$

Identify each function as a compression, a stretch, or a translation of the parent function.

14. $y = 4 \log_3 x$ **15.** $y = \log_2 x + 10$ **16.** $y = 0.25 \log_4 x$

Transform the function $y = \log_5 x$ as indicated below.

17. stretch by a factor of 3 and translate 6 units up

18. compress by a factor of 0.4 and reflect in the x-axis

7-3 Standardized Test Prep

Logarithmic Functions as Inverses

Multiple Choice

For Exercises 1–4, choose the correct letter.

1. Which of the following is the logarithmic form of the equation $4^{-3} = \frac{1}{64}$?

   Ⓐ $\log_{-3}\left(\frac{1}{64}\right) = 4$

   Ⓒ $\log_4\left(\frac{1}{64}\right) = -3$

   Ⓑ $\log_{-3} 4 = \frac{1}{64}$

   Ⓓ $\log_{\frac{1}{64}} 4 = -3$

2. What is the value of $\log_2 8$?

   Ⓕ 64

   Ⓗ 16

   Ⓖ 8

   Ⓘ 3

3. How does the graph of $y = \log_5(x - 3)$ compare with the graph of the parent function, $y = \log_5 x$?

   Ⓐ translated 3 units to the left

   Ⓒ translated 3 units to the right

   Ⓑ translated 3 units down

   Ⓓ translated 3 units up

4. In 2009, an earthquake of magnitude 6.7 shook the Kermadec Islands off the coast of New Zealand. Also in 2009, an earthquake of magnitude 5.1 occurred in the Alaska Peninsula. How many times stronger was the Kermadec earthquake than the Alaska earthquake?

   Ⓕ 39.811

   Ⓗ 5.77

   Ⓖ 20.593

   Ⓘ 0.025

Short Response

5. A single-celled bacterium divides every hour. The number N of bacteria after t hours is given by the formula $\log_2 N = t$.
   a. After how many hours will there be 64 bacteria?
   b. Explain in words or show work for how you determined the number of hours.

7-4

Think About a Plan

Properties of Logarithms

Construction The foreman of a construction team puts up a sound barrier that reduces the intensity of the noise by 50%. By how many decibels is the noise reduced? Use the formula $L = 10 \log \frac{I}{I_0}$ to measure loudness. (*Hint*: Find the difference between the expression for loudness for intensity I and the expression for loudness for intensity $0.5I$.)

Know

1. You can represent the intensity of the original noise by [   ].

2. You can represent the intensity of the reduced noise by [   ].

3. The formula for loudness is [   ].

Need

4. To solve the problem I need to find:

_____

_____.

Plan

5. What is an expression for the loudness of the original construction noise?

6. What is an expression for the loudness of the reduced construction noise?

7. Use your expressions to find the difference between the loudness of the original construction noise and the loudness of the reduced construction noise.

8. The sound barrier reduced the loudness by [   ].

7-4 Practice

Properties of Logarithms

Form K

Properties of Logarithms		
Product Property	**Quotient Property**	**Power Property**
$\log_b mn = \log_b m + \log_b n$	$\log_b \frac{m}{n} = \log_b m - \log_b n$	$\log_b m^n = n \log_b m$

Write each expression as a single logarithm.

1. $\log_3 9 + \log_3 24$

2. $\log_4 16^3$

3. $\log_2 7 - \log_2 9$

4. $\log_3 8^5$

5. $\log_4 x - \log_4 y$

6. $\log 5 + \log 7$

Expand each logarithm. Simplify if possible.

7. $\log_3 27x$

8. $\log \frac{3}{7}$

9. $\log_4 y^2 z^3$

10. $\log_5 \frac{3^2}{x}$

11. $\log_3 15xy$

12. $\log 8xz^4$

13. Open-Ended Write three different logarithms. You should be able to expand each logarithm by one of the properties of logarithms.

Lesson 7-4

7-4

Practice (continued)   *Form K*

Properties of Logarithms

Change of Base Formula

For any positive numbers m, b, and c, with $b \neq 1$ and $c \neq 1$,

$$\log_b m = \frac{\log_c m}{\log_c b}$$

Use the Change of Base Formula to evaluate each expression.

14. $\log_{32} 4$ **15.** $\log_9 27$ **16.** $\log_4 12$

$\dfrac{\log_2 4}{\log_2 32} =$

17. Error Analysis Your friend used the Change of Base Formula to evaluate the expression $\log_4 8$. Her answer was $\frac{2}{3}$. What error did your friend make? What is the correct answer?

Use the following formula to solve Exercise 18.

Formula for Loudness of a Sound (decibels)

$$L = 10 \log \frac{I}{I_0}$$

- I is the intensity of a sound in watts per square meter (W/m²).
- I_0 is the intensity of a sound that can barely be heard.
- $I_0 = 10^{-12}$ W/m²

---

18. Your classmate went to a rock concert. At the loudest point during the concert, the sound had an intensity of 2.35×10^{-3} W/m². What was the loudness of this sound in decibels?

7-4 Standardized Test Prep

Properties of Logarithms

Multiple Choice

For Exercises 1–4, choose the correct letter.

1. Which statement correctly demonstrates the Power Property of Logarithms?

   Ⓐ $\frac{1}{2} \log_5 9 = \log_5 81$ 　　　　Ⓒ $\frac{1}{2} \log_5 9 = \log_5 18$

   Ⓑ $\frac{1}{2} \log_5 9 = \log_5 \frac{9}{2}$ 　　　　Ⓓ $\frac{1}{2} \log_5 9 = \log_5 3$

2. Which expression is the correct expansion of $\log_4 (3x)^2$?

   Ⓕ $\frac{1}{2} (\log_4 3 - \log_4 x)$ 　　　　Ⓗ $2 (\log_4 3 - \log_4 x)$

   Ⓖ $2 (\log_4 3 + \log_4 x)$ 　　　　Ⓘ $2 \log_4 3 + \log_4 x$

3. Which expression is equivalent to $\log_7 16$?

   Ⓐ $\dfrac{\log_7 16}{\log 10}$ 　　　　Ⓒ $\dfrac{\log 16}{\log 7}$

   Ⓑ $\dfrac{\log_{16} 10}{\log_7 10}$ 　　　　Ⓓ $\dfrac{\log 7}{\log 16}$

4. Which statement correctly expresses $4 \log_3 x + 7 \log_3 y$ as a single logarithm?

   Ⓕ $\log_3 x^4 y^7$ 　　　　Ⓗ $\log_3 (x^4 + y^7)$

   Ⓖ $\log_3 (4x + 7y)$ 　　　　Ⓘ $\log_3 (4x - 7y)$

Short Response

5. The pH of a substance equals $-\log[H^+]$, where $[H^+]$ is the concentration of hydrogen ions. The concentration of hydrogen ions in pure water is 10^{-7} and the concentration of hydrogen ions in a sodium hydroxide solution is 10^{-14}.
   a. Without using a calculator, what is the difference of the pH levels of pure water and the sodium hydroxide solution?
   b. Explain in words or show work for how you determined the difference of the pH levels.

7-5

Think About a Plan

Exponential and Logarithmic Equations

Seismology An earthquake of magnitude 7.6 occurred in 2001 in Gujarat, India. It was 251 times as strong as the greatest earthquake ever to hit Pennsylvania. What is the magnitude of the Pennsylvania earthquake? (*Hint*: Refer to the Richter scale on page 453.)

Know

1. The magnitude of the Gujarat earthquake is [   ].

2. The ratio of the intensity of the Gujarat earthquake to the intensity

   of Pennsylvania's greatest earthquake is [   ].

Need

3. To solve the problem I need to find:

   _____ .

Plan

4. Let I_1 and M_1 be the intensity and magnitude of the Gujarat earthquake. Let I_2 and M_2 be the intensity and magnitude of Pennsylvania's greatest earthquake. What equation should you use to model this situation?

5. What does $\dfrac{I_1}{I_2}$ represent? _____

   _____

6. What can you substitute for $\dfrac{I_1}{I_2}$ in your equation?

7. Solve your equation for the magnitude of Pennsylvania's greatest earthquake.

8. The magnitude of Pennsylvania's greatest earthquake is [   ].

7-5 Practice   Form K

Exponential and Logarithmic Equations

Solve each equation. To start, rewrite each side with a common base.

1. $125^{2x} = 25$

$(5^3)^{2x} = 5^2$

$5^{6x} = 5^2$

$6x = 2$

$x =$

2. $2^{3x-3} = 64$

$2^{3x-3} = 2^6$

3. $81^{3x} = 27$

Solve each equation. Round to the nearest ten-thousandth. Check your answers. To start, take the logarithm of each side.

4. $6^{4x} = 234$

$\log 6^{4x} = \log 234$

$4x \log 6 = \log 234$

$x = \dfrac{\log 234}{4 \log 6}$

$x \approx$

5. $3^{5x} = 375$

$\log 3^{5x} = \log 375$

6. $7^{3x} - 24 = 184$

Graphing Calculator Solve by graphing. Round to the nearest ten-thousandth.

7. $3^{6x} = 2000$

Let $Y_1 = 3^{6x}$ and $Y_2 = 2000$.

$x \approx$

8. $8^{3x} = 154$

9. $12^{4x} = 4600$

Use the following formula for Exercise 10.

$$T(m) = a(1 + r)^m$$

- m = the number of minutes it takes for $\frac{3}{4}$ of the crowd to leave the stadium
- $T(m)$ = the number of people in the stadium after m minutes
- a = the number of people currently in the stadium
- r = the percent change in the number of people in the stadium

10. There are currently 100,000 people in a stadium watching a soccer game. When the game ends, about 3% of the crowd will leave the stadium each minute. At this rate, how many minutes will it take for $\frac{3}{4}$ of the crowd to leave the stadium?

Lesson 7-5

7-5 Practice (continued)   Form K

Exponential and Logarithmic Equations

Convert from Logarithmic Form to Exponential Form to solve each equation.

Exponential and Logarithmic Form	
Logarithmic Form $\log_b x = y$	Exponential Form $b^y = x$

11. $\log(2x + 4) = 3$

$2x + 4 = 10^3$
$2x = 996$
$x =$

12. $\log 4z - 3 = 2$

$\log 4z = 5$

13. $\log(2x - 8) = 2$

Use the properties of logarithms to solve each equation.

Product Property	Quotient Property	Power Property
$\log_b mn = \log_b m + \log_b n$	$\log_b \frac{m}{n} = \log_b m - \log_b n$	$\log_b m^n = n \log_b m$

14. $2 \log x + \log 4 = 3$

$\log x^2 + \log 4 = 3$
$\log 4x^2 = 3$
$4x^2 = 10^3$
$x^2 = 250$
$x \approx$

15. $\log y - \log 4 = 2$

$\log \frac{y}{4} = 2$

16. $\log 10 + \log 2x = 3$

17. Error Analysis Your friend used the following steps to solve the equation
$\log x + \log 6 = 4$. What error did he make? What is the correct answer?

$\log x + \log 6 = 4$
$\log \frac{x}{6} = 4$
$\frac{x}{6} = 10^4$
$x = 6000$

7-5 Standardized Test Prep

Exponential and Logarithmic Equations

Multiple Choice

For Exercises 1–5, choose the correct letter.

1. If $9^x = 243$, what is the value of x?

   (A) 2   (B) 5   (C) 2.5   (D) 10

2. If $2^{3x+2} = 64$, what is the value of x?

   (F) $\frac{8}{3}$ (G) $\frac{4}{3}$ (H) 2   (I) $\frac{3}{4}$

3. If $\log(3x + 25) = 2$, what is the value of x?

   (A) 25   (B) 75   (C) $41\frac{2}{3}$ (D) 100

4. Which best approximates the solution of $16^{2x} = 124$?

   (F) 0.869   (G) 1.150   (H) 1.739   (I) 3.477

5. Which equation represents the solution of $2^{3x+1} = 7$?

   (A) $x = 3\left(\dfrac{\log 7}{\log 2} - 1\right)$ (C) $x = \dfrac{1}{3}\left(\dfrac{\log 2}{\log 7} - 1\right)$

   (B) $x = \dfrac{\log 7}{3\log 2} - 1$ (D) $x = \dfrac{1}{3}\left(\dfrac{\log 7}{\log 2} - 1\right)$

Short Response

6. In 2007, the population of Tallahassee, Florida was 168,979. Some researchers believe that the population of Tallahassee will increase at a rate of 1% each year for the 10 years following this.

   a. If the researchers are correct, how many years will it take for the population of Tallahassee to reach 180,000?

   b. Explain in words or show your work for how you determined the number of years found in part (a).

8-1

Think About a Plan

Inverse Variation

The spreadsheet shows data that could be modeled by an equation of the form $PV = k$. Estimate P when $V = 62$.

	A	B
1	P	V
2	140.00	100
3	147.30	95
4	155.60	90
5	164.70	85
6	175.00	80
7	186.70	75

Understanding the Problem

1. The data can be modeled by [ ].

2. What is the problem asking you to determine?

   _____

   _____

Planning the Solution

3. What does it mean that the data can be modeled by an inverse variation?

   _____.

4. How can you estimate the constant of the inverse variation?

   _____

   _____.

5. What is the constant of the inverse variation?

6. Write an equation that you can use to find P when $V = 62$.

Getting an Answer

7. Solve your equation.

8. What is an estimate for P when $V = 62$?

8-1

Practice

Inverse Variation

Form K

Is the relationship between the values in each table a *direct variation*, an *inverse variation*, or *neither*? Write an equation to model the direct and inverse variations.

1.

x	y
0.1	3
3	0.1
6	0.05
24	0.0125

2.

x	y
1	3
2	6
5	15
6	18

3.

x	y
0	1
2	5
4	7
6	8

Suppose that x and y vary inversely. Write a function that models each inverse variation. Graph the function and find y when x = 10.

4. $x = 2$ when $y = -4$ **5.** $x = -9$ when $y = -1$ **6.** $x = 1.5$ when $y = 10$

7. Suppose the table at the right shows the time t it takes to drive home when you travel at various average speeds s.

  a. Write a function that models the relationship between the speed and the time it takes to drive home.

  b. At what speed would you need to drive to get home in 50 min or $\frac{5}{6}$ h?

Time t (h)	Speed s (mi/h)
$\frac{1}{6}$	60
$\frac{1}{4}$	40
$\frac{1}{3}$	30
$\frac{3}{4}$	13.3

Lesson 8-1

8-1 Practice (continued)

Inverse Variation

Form K

Use combined variation to solve each problem.

8. The height h of a cylinder varies directly with the volume of the cylinder and inversely with the square of the cylinder's radius with the constant equal to $\frac{1}{\pi}$.
   a. Write a formula that models this combined variation.
   b. What is the height of a cylinder with radius 4 m and volume 500 m³? Use 3.14 for π and round to the nearest tenth of a meter.

9. Some students volunteered to clean up a highway near their school. The amount of time it will take varies directly with the length of the section of highway and inversely with the number of students who will help. If 25 students clean up 5 mi of highway, the project will take 2 h. How long would it take 85 students to clean up 34 mi of highway?

Write the function that models each variation. Find z when $x = 2$ and $y = 6$.

10. z varies inversely with x and directly with y. When $x = 5$ and $y = 10, z = 2$.

11. z varies directly with the square of x and inversely with y. When $x = 2$ and $y = 4, z = 3$.

Each ordered pair is from an inverse variation. Find the constant of variation.

12. $(2, 2)$ 13. $(1, 8)$ 14. $(9, 4)$

Each pair of values is from an inverse variation. Find the missing value.

15. $(9, 5), (x, 3)$ 16. $(8, 7), (5, y)$ 17. $(2, 7), (x, 1)$

8-1

Standardized Test Prep

Inverse Variation

Multiple Choice

For Exercises 1–5, choose the correct letter.

1. Which equation represents inverse variation between x and y?

   A $4y = kx$ **B** $xy = 4k$ **C** $y = 4kx$ **D** $4k = \frac{x}{y}$

2. The ordered pair (3.5, 1.2) is from an inverse variation. What is the constant of variation?

   F 2.3   **G** 2.9   **H** 4.2   **I** 4.7

3. Suppose x and y vary inversely, and $x = 4$ when $y = 9$. Which function models the inverse variation?

   A $y = \frac{36}{x}$ **B** $x = \frac{y}{36}$ **C** $y = \frac{x}{36}$ **D** $\frac{x}{y} = 36$

4. Suppose x and y vary inversely, and $x = -3$ when $y = \frac{1}{3}$. What is the value of y when $x = 9$?

   F -9 **G** -1 **H** $-\frac{1}{9}$ **I** $\frac{1}{9}$

5. In which function does t vary jointly with q and r and inversely with s?

   A $t = \frac{kq}{rs}$ **B** $t = \frac{ks}{qr}$ **C** $t = \frac{s}{kqr}$ **D** $t = \frac{kqr}{s}$

Short Response

6. A student suggests that the graph at the right represents the inverse variation $y = \frac{3}{x}$. Is the student correct? Explain.

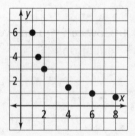

8-2 Think About a Plan

The Reciprocal Function Family

a. **Gasoline Mileage** Suppose you drive an average of 10,000 miles each year. Your gasoline mileage (mi/gal) varies inversely with the number of gallons of gasoline you use each year. Write and graph a model for your average mileage m in terms of the gallons g of gasoline used.

b. After you begin driving on the highway more often, you use 50 gal less per year. Write and graph a new model to include this information.

c. Calculate your old and new mileage assuming that you originally used 400 gal of gasoline per year.

1. Write a formula for gasoline mileage in words.

   _____.

2. Write and graph an equation to model your average mileage m in terms of the gallons g of gasoline used.

3. Write and graph an equation to model your average mileage m in terms of the gallons g of gasoline used if you use 50 gal less per year.

4. How can you find your old and your new mileage from your equations?

   _____.

5. What is your old mileage?

6. What is your new mileage?

8-2 Practice

The Reciprocal Function Family

Graph each function. Identify the x- and y-intercepts and asymptotes of the graph. Also, state the domain and range of the function.

1. $y = -\dfrac{2}{x}$ **2.** $y = \dfrac{4}{x}$ **3.** $y = -\dfrac{5}{x}$

Graph the equations $y = \dfrac{1}{x}$ and $y = \dfrac{a}{x}$ using the given value of a. Then identify the effect of a on the graph.

  4. $a = -3$ **5.** $a = 4$ **6.** $a = -0.25$

Sketch the asymptotes and the graph of each function. Identify the domain and range.

  7. $y = \dfrac{1}{x} + 2$ **8.** $y = \dfrac{1}{x - 2} + 3$ **9.** $y = \dfrac{-10}{x + 1} - 8$

8-2 Practice (continued) Form K

The Reciprocal Function Family

Write an equation for the translation of $y = \frac{3}{x}$ that has the given asymptotes.

10. $x = 0$ and $y = 2$ **11.** $x = -2$ and $y = 4$ **12.** $x = 5$ and $y = -3$

Sketch the graph of each function.

13. $3xy = 1$ **14.** $xy - 8 = 0$ **15.** $2xy = -6$

16. Writing Explain the difference between what happens to the parent function $y = \frac{a}{x}$ when $|a| > 1$ and what happens to the parent function $y = \frac{a}{x}$ when $0 < |a| < 1$.

17. Suppose your class wants to get your teacher an end-of-year gift of a weekend package at her favorite spa. The package costs $250. Let c equal the cost each student needs to pay and s equal the number of students.

  a. If there are 22 students, how much will each student need to pay?

  b. Using the information, how many total students (including those from other classes) need to contribute to the teacher's gift, if no student wants to pay more than $7?

  c. Reasoning Did you need to round your answer up or down? Explain.

Name _____ Class _____ Date _____

8-2 Standardized Test Prep

The Reciprocal Function Family

Multiple Choice

For Exercises 1–3, choose the correct letter.

1. What is an equation for the translation of $y = -\dfrac{4.5}{x}$ that has asymptotes at $x = 3$ and $y = -5$?

   Ⓐ $y = -\dfrac{4.5}{x - 3} - 5$ Ⓒ $y = -\dfrac{4.5}{x - 5} + 3$

   Ⓑ $y = -\dfrac{4.5}{x + 3} - 5$ Ⓓ $y = -\dfrac{4.5}{x + 5} + 3$

2. What is the equation of the vertical asymptote of $y = \dfrac{2}{x - 5}$?

   Ⓕ $x = -5$ Ⓖ $x = 0$ Ⓗ $x = 2$ Ⓘ $x = 5$

3. Which is the graph of $y = \dfrac{1}{x + 1} - 2$?

   Ⓐ 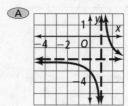   Ⓑ 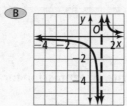   Ⓒ 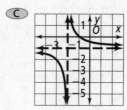   Ⓓ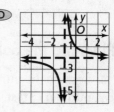

Extended Response

4. A race pilot's average rate of speed over a 720-mi course is inversely proportional to the time in minutes t the pilot takes to fly a complete race course. The pilot's final score s is the average speed minus any penalty points p earned.

   a. Write a function to model the pilot's score for a given t and p. (*Hint: d = rt*)

   b. Graph the function for a pilot who has 2 penalty points.

   c. What is the maximum time a pilot with 2 penalty points can take to finish the course and still earn a score of at least 3?

Lesson 8-2

8-3 Think About a Plan

Rational Functions and Their Graphs

Grades A student earns an 82% on her first test. How many consecutive 100% test scores does she need to bring her average up to 95%? Assume that each test has equal impact on the average grade.

Understanding the Problem

1. One test score is [   ] .

2. The average of all the test scores is [   ] .

3. What is the problem asking you to determine?

_____

_____

Planning the Solution

4. Let x be the number of 100% test scores. Write an expression for the total number of test scores.

5. Write an expression for the sum of the test scores.

6. How can you model the student's average as a rational function?

Getting an Answer

7. How can a graph help you answer this question?

_____

_____ .

8. What does a fractional answer tell you? Explain.

_____

_____ .

9. How many consecutive 100% test scores does the student need to bring her average up to 95%?

8-3

Practice

Form K

Rational Functions and Their Graphs

Find the domain, points of discontinuity, and *x*- and *y*-intercepts of each rational function. Determine whether the discontinuities are removable or non-removable.

To start, factor the numerator and denominator, if possible.

1. $y = \frac{x+5}{x-2}$

2. $y = \frac{1}{x^2+2x+1}$

3. $y = \frac{x+4}{x^2+2x-8}$

Find the vertical asymptotes and holes for the graph of each rational function.

4. $y = \frac{x+6}{x+4}$

5. $y = \frac{(x-2)(x-1)}{x-2}$

6. $y = \frac{x+1}{(3x-2)(x-3)}$

Find the horizontal asymptote of the graph of each rational function.

To start, identify the degree of the numerator and denominator.

7. $y = \frac{x+1}{x+5}$

8. $y = \frac{x+2}{2x^2-4}$

9. $y = \frac{3x^3-4}{4x+1}$

$\frac{x+1}{x+5}$ ← degree 1
← degree 1

Sketch the graph of each rational function.

10. $y = \frac{x+2}{(x+3)(x-4)}$

11. $y = \frac{x+3}{(x-1)(x-5)}$

12. $y = \frac{2x}{3x-1}$

Lesson 8-3

8-3 Practice (continued) Form K

Rational Functions and Their Graphs

13. The CD-ROMs for a computer game can be manufactured for $.25 each. The development cost is $124,000. The first 100 discs are samples and will not be sold.
    a. Write a function for the average cost of a disc that is not a sample.
    b. What is the average cost if 2000 discs are produced? If 12,800 discs are produced?
    c. **Reasoning** How could you find the number of discs that must be produced to bring the average cost under $8?
    d. How many discs must be produced to bring the average cost under $8?

14. **Error Analysis** For the rational function $y = \dfrac{x^2 - 2x - 8}{x^2 - 9}$, your friend said that the vertical asymptote is $x = 1$ and the horizontal asymptotes are $y = 3$ and $y = -3$. Without doing any calculations, you know this is incorrect. Explain how you know.

Sketch the graph of each rational function.

15. $y = \dfrac{4x^2 - 100}{2x^2 + x - 15}$

16. $y = \dfrac{2x^2}{5x + 1}$

17. $y = \dfrac{2}{x^2 - 4}$

18. **Multiple Choice** What are the points of discontinuity for the graph of
    $y = \dfrac{(2x + 3)(x - 5)}{(x + 5)(2x - 1)}$?

    Ⓐ $-5, 1$

    Ⓑ $-\frac{3}{2}, 5$

    Ⓒ $-5, \frac{1}{2}$

    Ⓓ $5, -\frac{1}{2}$

8-3

Standardized Test Prep

Rational Functions and Their Graphs

Multiple Choice

For Exercises 1–4, choose the correct letter.

1. What function has a graph with a removable discontinuity at $\left(5, \frac{1}{9}\right)$?

    Ⓐ $y = \dfrac{(x - 5)}{(x + 4)(x - 5)}$

    Ⓒ $y = \dfrac{4x - 1}{5x + 1}$

    Ⓑ $y = \dfrac{4}{x - 5}$

    Ⓓ $y = \dfrac{x + 1}{5x - 4}$

2. What is the vertical asymptote of the graph of $y = \dfrac{(x + 2)(x - 3)}{x(x - 3)}$?

    Ⓕ $x = -3$ Ⓖ $x = -2$ Ⓗ $x = 0$ Ⓘ $x = 3$

3. What best describes the horizontal asymptote(s), if any, of the graph of
    $y = \dfrac{x^2 + 2x - 8}{(x + 6)^2}$?

    Ⓐ $y = -6$

    Ⓒ $y = 1$

    Ⓑ $y = 0$

    Ⓓ The graph has no horizontal asymptote.

4. Which rational function has a graph that has vertical asymptotes at $x = a$ and $x = -a$, and a horizontal asymptote at $y = 0$?

    Ⓕ $y = \dfrac{(x - a)(x + a)}{x}$

    Ⓗ $y = \dfrac{x^2}{x^2 - a^2}$

    Ⓖ $y = \dfrac{1}{x^2 - a^2}$

    Ⓘ $y = \dfrac{x - a}{x + a}$

Short Response

5. How many milliliters of 0.30% sugar solution must you add to 75 mL of 4% sugar solution to get a 0.50% sugar solution? Show your work.

8-4

Think About a Plan

Rational Expressions

Manufacturing A toy company is considering a cube or sphere-shaped container for packaging a new product. The height of the cube would equal the diameter of the sphere. Compare the ratios of the volumes to the surface areas of the containers. Which packaging will be more efficient? For a sphere, $SA = 4\pi r^2$.

Understanding the Problem

1. Let x be the height of the cube. What are expressions for the cube's volume and surface area?

   Volume: ☐   Surface area: ☐

2. Let x be the diameter of the sphere. What are expressions for the sphere's volume and surface area?

   Volume: ☐   Surface area: ☐

3. What is the problem asking you to do?

   _____

   _____ .

Planning the Solution

4. Write an expression for the ratio of the cube's volume to its surface area. Simplify your expression.

5. Write an expression for the ratio of the sphere's volume to its surface area. Simplify your expression.

Getting an Answer

6. Compare the ratios of the volumes to the surface areas of the containers. Which packaging will be more efficient?

   _____

   _____ .

8-4 Practice

Form K

Rational Expressions

Simplify each rational expression. State any restrictions on the variables.

1. $\dfrac{-27x^3y}{9x^4y}$

2. $\dfrac{-6 + 3x}{x^2 - 6x + 8}$

3. $\dfrac{2x^2 - 3x - 2}{x^2 - 5x + 6}$

Multiply. State any restrictions on the variables.

To start, factor all polynomials.

4. $\dfrac{4x^2 - 1}{2x^2 - 5x - 3} \cdot \dfrac{x^2 - 6x + 9}{2x^2 + 5x - 3}$

$\dfrac{(2x + 1)(2x - 1)}{(2x + 1)(x - 3)} \cdot \dfrac{(x - 3)(x - 3)}{(2x - 1)(x + 3)}$

5. $\dfrac{2x^2 + 7x + 3}{x - 4} \cdot \dfrac{x^2 - 16}{x^2 + 8x + 15}$

6. $\dfrac{4x^2}{5y} \cdot \dfrac{7y}{12x^4}$

Divide. State any restrictions on the variables.

To start, rewrite the division as multiplication by the reciprocal.

7. $\dfrac{16x^5}{3y^3} \div \dfrac{8x^3}{9y^2}$

8. $\dfrac{x^2 + 2x - 15}{x^2 - 16} \div \dfrac{x + 1}{3x - 12}$

9. $\dfrac{3y - 12}{2y + 4} \div \dfrac{6y - 24}{4y + 8}$

$\dfrac{16x^5}{3y^3} \cdot \dfrac{9y^2}{8x^3}$

Lesson 8-4

8-4 **Practice** (continued) Form K

Rational Expressions

10. Your school wants to build a courtyard surrounded by a low brick wall. It wants the maximum area for a given amount of brick wall. The courtyard can be either a circle or an equilateral triangle. Which shape provides the most efficient use of brick wall: a circle or an equilateral triangle?

Simplify each rational expression. State any restrictions on the variables.

11. $\dfrac{x^2 - 2x - 8}{3x^2 + 4x - 4}$

12. $\dfrac{6x + 15}{2x^2 + 3x - 5}$

13. $\dfrac{x^2 - y^2}{6x^2 + 6xy}$

14. **Writing** How can you tell whether a rational expression is in simplest form? Include an example with your explanation.

15. The width of a rectangle is given by the expression $\dfrac{x + 10}{3x + 24}$ and the area can be represented by $\dfrac{2x + 20}{6x + 15}$. What is the length of the rectangle?

16. **Multiple Choice** Which expression can be simplified to $\dfrac{x - 1}{x - 3}$?

Ⓐ $\dfrac{x^2 - x - 6}{x^2 - x - 2}$
Ⓑ $\dfrac{x^2 - 2x + 1}{x^2 + 2x - 3}$
Ⓒ $\dfrac{x^2 - 3x - 4}{x^2 - 7x + 12}$
Ⓓ $\dfrac{x^2 - 4x + 3}{x^2 - 6x + 9}$

8-4 Standardized Test Prep

Rational Expressions

Multiple Choice

For Exercises 1–4, choose the correct letter.

1. Which expression equals $\dfrac{x^2 - 4x - 5}{x^2 + 6x + 5}$?

   Ⓐ $x + 1$ Ⓑ $-10x - 10$ Ⓒ $\dfrac{x - 5}{x + 5}$ Ⓓ $\dfrac{4x - 5}{6x + 5}$

2. Which expression equals $\dfrac{42a^2 b^4}{12a^5 b^{-2}}$?

   Ⓕ $\dfrac{7b^6}{2a^3}$ Ⓖ $\dfrac{30a^7}{b^2}$ Ⓗ $\dfrac{7ab^3}{2}$ Ⓘ $\dfrac{30b^2}{a^3}$

3. Which expression equals $\dfrac{t^2 - 1}{t - 2} \cdot \dfrac{t^2 - 3t + 2}{t^2 + 4t + 3}$?

   Ⓐ $\dfrac{t^2 - 2t + 1}{t + 3}$ Ⓑ $\dfrac{t^2 - 1}{t + 3}$ Ⓒ $\dfrac{(t + 1)^2 (t + 3)}{(t - 2)^2}$ Ⓓ $\dfrac{2t^2 - 3t + 1}{t^2 + 5t + 1}$

4. What is the area of the triangle shown at the right?

   Ⓕ $\dfrac{2x + 8}{x^2 - 6x + 9}$ Ⓗ $\dfrac{x + 4}{x^2 - 6x + 9}$

   Ⓖ $\dfrac{x^2 + 6x + 9}{x + 4}$ Ⓘ $\dfrac{2x^2 + 12x + 18}{x + 4}$

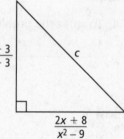

Short Response

5. What is the quotient $\dfrac{y + 2}{2y^2 - 3y - 2} \div \dfrac{y^2 - 4}{y^2 + y - 6}$ expressed in simplest form? State any restrictions on the variable. Show your work.

Lesson 8-4

8-5 | Think About a Plan

Adding and Subtracting Rational Expressions

Optics To read small font, you use the magnifying lens with the focal length 3 in. How far from the magnifying lens should you place the page if you want to hold the lens at 1 foot from your eyes? Use the thin-lens equation.

Know

1. The focal length of the magnifying lens is [   ].

2. The distance from the lens to your eyes is [   ].

3. The thin-lens equation is [   ].

Need

4. To solve the problem I need to find:

   _____.

Plan

5. What are the known variables in the thin-lens equation?

   _____

   _____

6. Solve the thin-lens equation for the unknown variable.

7. Substitute the known values into your equation and solve.

8. How far from the page should you hold the magnifying lens?

Name _____ Class _____ Date _____

8-5 Practice   *Form K*

Adding and Subtracting Rational Expressions

Find the least common multiple of each pair of polynomials.

To start, completely factor each expression.

1. $4x^2 - 36$ and $6x^2 + 36x + 54$ **2.** $(x - 2)(x + 3)$ and $10(x + 3)^2$

$(2)(2)(x - 3)(x + 3)$ and $(2)(3)(x + 3)(x + 3)$

Simplify each sum or difference. State any restrictions on the variables.

To start, factor the denominators and identify the LCD.

3. $\dfrac{6x - 1}{x^2y} + \dfrac{3y + 2}{2xy}$ **4.** $\dfrac{1}{x^2 - 4x - 12} - \dfrac{3x}{4x + 8}$ **5.** $\dfrac{2x}{x^2 + 5x + 4} + \dfrac{2x}{3x + 3}$

$\dfrac{6x - 1}{(x)(x)(y)} + \dfrac{3y + 2}{(2)(x)(y)}$

Add or subtract. Simplify where possible. State any restrictions on the variables.

6. $\dfrac{x + 2}{x - 1} + \dfrac{x - 3}{2x + 1}$ **7.** $\dfrac{x}{x^2 - x} + \dfrac{1}{x}$ **8.** $4y - \dfrac{y + 2}{y^2 + 3y}$

9. Error Analysis A classmate said that the sum of $\dfrac{4}{x^2 - 9}$ and $\dfrac{7}{x + 3}$ is $\dfrac{7x + 25}{x^2 - 9}$.
What mistake did your classmate make? What is the correct sum?

219

Lesson 8-5

8-5

Practice (continued)   Form K

Adding and Subtracting Rational Expressions

Simplify each complex fraction.

To start, multiply the numerator and the denominator by the LCD of all the rational expressions.

10. $\dfrac{\frac{1}{x} + 3}{\frac{5}{y} + 4}$

11. $\dfrac{-3}{\frac{5}{x} + y}$

12. $\dfrac{\frac{4}{x+2}}{\frac{3}{x-1}}$

$\dfrac{(\frac{1}{x} + 3)xy}{(\frac{5}{y} + 4)xy}$

13. Reasoning What real numbers are not in the domain of the function $f(x) = \dfrac{\frac{x+1}{x+2}}{\frac{x+3}{x+4}}$? Explain.

14. If you jog 12 mi at an average rate of 4 mi/h and walk the same route back at an average rate of 3 mi/h, you have traveled 24 mi in 7 h and your overall rate is $\frac{24}{7}$ mi/h. What is your overall average rate if you travel d mi at 3 mi/h and d mi at 4 mi/h?

15. Multiple Choice Simplify: $\dfrac{\frac{2}{x} - 5}{\frac{6}{x} - 3}$.

Ⓐ $\dfrac{2 - 5x}{6 - 3x}$ Ⓑ $\dfrac{2 + 5x}{6 - 3x}$ Ⓒ $\dfrac{2x - 5}{6x + 3}$ Ⓓ $\dfrac{6 + 3x}{2 - 5x}$

8-5

Standardized Test Prep

Adding and Subtracting Rational Expressions

Multiple Choice

For Exercises 1–4, choose the correct letter.

1. Which is the least common denominator of fractions that have denominators $5x + 10$ and $25x^2 - 100$?

   (A) $5(x - 2)$

   (C) $25(x^2 - 4)$

   (B) $5(x^2 - 20)$

   (D) $75(x + 2)(x^2 - 4)$

2. Which expression equals $\dfrac{\frac{2}{x} + 6}{\frac{1}{y}}$?

   (F) $\dfrac{12y}{x}$

   (G) $\dfrac{2y + 6xy}{x}$

   (H) $\dfrac{6x + 2}{xy}$

   (I) $\dfrac{x}{2y + 6xy}$

3. Which expression equals $\dfrac{4}{x^2 - 3x} + \dfrac{6}{3x - 9}$?

   (A) $\dfrac{2(x + 2)}{x(x - 3)}$

   (B) $\dfrac{10}{x^2 - 9}$

   (C) $\dfrac{4x + 18}{3x(x - 3)}$

   (D) $\dfrac{2}{x}$

4. The harmonic mean of two numbers a and b equals $\dfrac{2}{\frac{1}{a} + \frac{1}{b}}$. Which expression equals the harmonic mean of x and $x + 1$?

   (F) $\dfrac{2}{x^2 + x}$

   (G) $\dfrac{4x + 2}{x^2 + x}$

   (H) $2x + 1$

   (I) $\dfrac{2x^2 + 2x}{2x + 1}$

Short Response

5. Subtract $3 - \dfrac{1}{x^2 + 5}$. Write your answer in simplest form. State any restrictions on the variable. Show your work.

8-6 Think About a Plan

Solving Rational Equations

Storage One pump can fill a tank with oil in 4 hours. A second pump can fill the same tank in 3 hours. If both pumps are used at the same time, how long will they take to fill the tank?

Understanding the Problem

1. How long does it take the first pump to fill the tank?

2. How long does it take the second pump to fill the tank?

3. What is the problem asking you to determine?

_____

_____

Planning the Solution

4. If V is the volume of the tank, what expressions represent the portion of the tank that each pump can fill in one hour?

First pump: ☐   Second pump: ☐

5. What expression represents the part of the tank the two pumps can fill in one hour if they are used at the same time?

6. Let t be number of hours. Write an equation to find the time it takes for the two pumps to fill one tank.

Getting an Answer

7. Solve your equation to find how long the pumps will take to fill the tank if both pumps are used at the same time.

8-6 **Practice** $\qquad$ Form K

Solving Rational Equations

Solve each equation. Check each solution.

To start, multiply each side by the LCD.

1. $\frac{x}{4} - \frac{3}{x} = \frac{1}{4}$

$4x\left(\frac{x}{4} - \frac{3}{x}\right) = (4x)\left(\frac{1}{4}\right)$

2. $x + \frac{6}{x} = -5$

3. $\frac{5}{2x - 2} = \frac{15}{x^2 - 1}$

4. The aerodynamic covering on a bicycle increases a cyclist's average speed by 10 mi/h. The time for a 75-mi trip is reduced by 2 h.
   a. Using t for time, write a rational equation you can use to determine the average speed using the aerodynamic covering.
   b. What is the average speed for the trip using the aerodynamic covering?

Using a graphing calculator, solve each equation. Check each solution.

5. $\frac{4}{2x - 3} = \frac{x}{5}$

6. $x + 5 = \frac{6}{x}$

7. $\frac{2}{x + 7} = \frac{x}{x^2 - 49}$

Solve each equation for the given variable.

8. $F = \frac{mv^2}{r}$ for v

9. $\frac{c}{dt} = Qm$ for d

10. $\frac{F}{Gm_1} = \frac{m_2}{r^2}$ for r

Lesson 8-6

8-6 **Practice** (continued)   *Form K*

Solving Rational Equations

11. You can travel 40 mi on your motorbike in the same time it takes your friend to travel 15 mi on his bicycle. If your friend rides his bike 20 mi/h slower than you ride your motorbike, find the speed for each bike.

12. A passenger train travels 392 mi in the same time that it takes a freight train to travel 322 mi. If the passenger train travels 20 mi/h faster than the freight train, find the speed of each train.

13. You can paint a fence twice as fast as your sister can. Working together, the two of you can paint a fence in 6 h. How many hours would it take each of you working alone?

Solve each equation. Check each solution.

14. $\dfrac{2}{x-3} - \dfrac{4}{x+3} = \dfrac{8}{x^2-9}$

15. $\dfrac{3}{x+5} + \dfrac{2}{5-x} = \dfrac{-4}{x^2-25}$

16. $\dfrac{3}{x^2-1} + \dfrac{4x}{x+1} = \dfrac{1.5}{x-1}$

17. You are planning a school field trip to a local theater. It costs $60 to rent the bus. Each theater ticket costs $5.50.
    a. Write a function $c(x)$ to represent the cost per student if x students sign up for the trip.
    b. How many students must sign up if the cost is to be no more than $10 per student?

8-6

Standardized Test Prep

Solving Rational Equations

Gridded Response

For Exercises 1–8, what are the solutions of each rational equation? Enter your answer in the grid provided. If necessary, enter your answer as a fraction.

1. $\dfrac{3-x}{6} = \dfrac{6-x}{12}$

2. $\dfrac{2}{6x+2} = \dfrac{x}{3x^2+11}$

3. $\dfrac{3}{2x-4} = \dfrac{5}{3x+7}$

4. $\dfrac{2}{x+2} + \dfrac{5}{x-2} = \dfrac{6}{x^2-4}$

5. $\dfrac{7}{x^2-5x} + \dfrac{2}{x} = \dfrac{3}{2x-10}$

6. $\dfrac{1}{4-5x} = \dfrac{3}{x+9}$

7. $\dfrac{7}{2} = \dfrac{7x}{8} - 4$

8. $4 + \dfrac{2y}{y-5} = \dfrac{8}{y-5}$

Answers

1.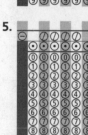

2.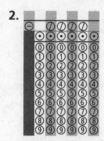

3.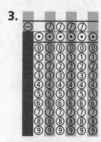

4.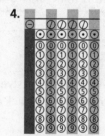

5.

6.

7.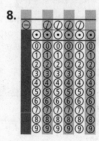

8.

9-1 Think About a Plan

Mathematical Patterns

Geometry Suppose you are stacking boxes in levels that form squares. The numbers of boxes in successive levels form a sequence. The figure at the right shows the top four levels as viewed from above.

a. How many boxes of equal size would you need for the next lower level?

b. How many boxes of equal size would you need to add three levels?

c. Suppose you are stacking a total of 285 boxes. How many levels will you have?

1. How many boxes are in each of the first four levels?

Level 1: [   ]   Level 2: [   ]   Level 3: [   ]   Level 4: [   ]

2. How many boxes of equal size would you need for the next lower level?

3. What is a recursive or explicit formula that describes the number of boxes in the nth level?

4. How many boxes would you need to add three levels?

[   ] + [   ] + [   ] = [   ]

5. What is a recursive or explicit formula that describes the total number of boxes in a stack of n levels?

6. How can you use your formula to find the number of levels you will have with a stack of 285 boxes?

_____

_____.

7. Suppose you are stacking a total of 285 boxes. Use your formula to find how many levels you will have. Show your work.

8. You need [   ] levels to make a stack of 285 boxes.

9-1 Practice

Mathematical Patterns

Form K

Find the first five terms of each sequence.

1. $a_n = 4n - 1$

Substitute 1 for n and simplify.

$a_1 = 4(1) - 1 = 3$

Substitute 2 for n and simplify.

$a_2 = 4(2) - 1 = 7$

Continue for the numbers 3, 4, and 5.

The first five terms are 3, 7, ☐, ☐, and ☐.

2. $a_n = n^2 + 4$

3. $a = \frac{1}{2}n + 2$

4. $a_n = 3^n$

5. $a_n = -6n^2$

6. Write an explicit formula for a sequence with 3, 5, 7, 9, and 11 as its first five terms.

Write a recursive definition for each sequence.

7. 2, 6, 12, 20, . . .

Identify the initial condition.

$a_1 = 2$

Use n to express the relationship between successive terms.

8. 120, 60, 30, 15, . . .

9. 3, 8, 13, 18, . . .

10. 1, 3, 9, 27, . . .

11. 2, 3, 8, 63, . . .

12. Writing Explain the difference between a recursive definition and an explicit formula.

Lesson 9-1

9-1 **Practice** (continued)   *Form K*

Mathematical Patterns

Write an explicit formula for each sequence. Then find the tenth term.

13. 7, 10, 13, 16, . . .   **14.** 8, 9, 10, 11, 12, . . .   **15.** $-\frac{1}{2}, 0, \frac{1}{2}, 1, 1\frac{1}{2}, \ldots$

$a_n = 3n + 4$

$a_{10} = 3(10) + 4 = \boxed{}$

16. 1, 4, 9, 16, . . .   **17.** 3, 1, −1, −3, −5, . . .   **18.** 1, 7, 25, 79, 241

19. Reasoning You and your friend are trying to find the 80th term in the sequence 8, 14, 20, 26, 32, ... You use a recursive definition and your friend uses an explicit formula. Who will find the 80th term first? Why?

20. Your neighbor recently began learning to play the guitar. On the first day, she practiced for 0.4 h. On the second day, she practiced for 0.5 h. She practiced for 0.65 h on the third day, and 0.85 h on the fourth day. If this pattern continues, how long will she practice on the seventh day?

21. Charles lost two rented movies, so he owes the rental store a fee of $40. At the end of each month, the amount that Charles owes will increase by 5%, plus a $2 billing fee. How much money will Charles owe the rental store after 8 months?

9-1 Standardized Test Prep

Mathematical Patterns

Multiple Choice

For Exercises 1–6, choose the correct letter.

1. What are the first five terms of the sequence?

   $$a_n = 3^n - 1$$

   (A) 2, 5, 8, 11, 14

   (B) 3, 9, 27, 81, 243

   (C) 2, 8, 26, 80, 242

   (D) 2, 4, 8, 16, 32

2. The formula $a_n = 3n + 2$ best represents which sequence?

   (F) 3, 6, 9, 12, 15

   (G) 5, 8, 11, 14, 17

   (H) 4, 7, 10, 13, 16

   (I) 5, 9, 29, 83, 245

3. Which pattern can be represented by $a_n = n^2 - 3$?

   (A) −1, 0, 5, 12, 21   (B) 4, 7, 12, 19, 28   (C) 1, 4, 9, 16, 25   (D) −2, 1, 6, 13, 22

4. The sequence 4, 16, 36, 64, 100, . . . can best be represented by which formula?

   (F) $a_n = 4n$ (G) $a_n = 4n^2$ (H) $a_n = 4n^3$ (I) $a_n = 2n^4$

5. For the sequence 0, 6, 16, 30, 48, . . . , what is the 40th term?

   (A) 3198   (B) 3200   (C) 4000   (D) 16,000

6. A student sets up a savings plan to transfer money from his checking account
   to his savings account. The first week $10 is transferred, the second week $12
   is transferred, the third week $16 is transferred, and the fourth week $24 is
   transferred. If this pattern continues and he starts with $100 in his checking
   account, how many weeks will pass before his balance is zero?

   (F) 4   (G) 5   (H) 6   (I) 7

Short Response

7. After training for and running a marathon, an athlete wants to reduce her daily run
   by half each day. The marathon is about 26 mi. How many days will it take after the
   marathon before she runs less than a mile a day? Show your work.

9-2 Think About a Plan

Arithmetic Sequences

Transportation Suppose a trolley stops at a certain intersection every 14 min. The first trolley of the day gets to the stop at 6:43 A.M. How long do you have to wait for a trolley if you get to the stop at 8:15 A.M.? At 3:20 P.M.?

Know

1. If you define 12:00 A.M. as minute 0, then 6:43 A.M. is [   ] from 0.

2. 8:15 A.M. is [   ] from 0 and 3:20 P.M. is [   ] from 0.

3. The trolley stops every [   ].

Need

4. To solve the problem I need to find:

   _____

   _____.

Plan

5. What is an explicit formula for the number of minutes after 12:00 A.M. that the trolley gets to the stop?

6. Use your formula to find the smallest n that gives the minutes just after 8:15 A.M. that the trolley arrives at the stop.

7. Using this n in your formula, when does the trolley stop? How long do you have to wait for this trolley?

8. Use your formula to find the smallest n that gives the minutes just after 3:20 P.M. that the trolley arrives at the stop.

9. Using this n in your formula, when does the trolley stop? How long do you have to wait for this trolley?

9-2 Practice

Form K

Arithmetic Sequences

Determine whether each sequence is arithmetic. If so, identify the common difference.

1. $1, 4, 7, 10, \ldots$

$4 - 1 = 3$

$7 - 4 = 3$

$10 - 7 = 3$

This sequence is arithmetic.

The common difference is $\boxed{}$.

2. $6, 10, 14, 18, 22, \ldots$

3. $1, 3, 6, 10, 15, \ldots$

4. $-16, -13, -9, -4, 2, \ldots$

5. $2, 9, 16, 23, 30, \ldots$

6. $43, 56, 69, 82, \ldots$

7. Reasoning Is the sequence represented by the formula $a_n = 4n + 8$ arithmetic? Explain.

Find the 24th term of each arithmetic sequence.

8. $4, 6, 8, 10, 12, \ldots$

$a_n = a_1 + (n - 1)d$

$a_{24} = 4 + (24 - 1)2$

$a_{24} = 4 + 46$

$a_{24} = \boxed{}$

9. $2, 5, 8, 11, 14, \ldots$

$a_n = a_1 + (n - 1)d$

10. $9, 5, 1, -3, -7, \ldots$

Find the missing terms in the following arithmetic sequences.

11. $2, \underline{}, \underline{}, 14, \ldots$

$14 = 2 + 3d$

$12 = 3d$

$d = 4$

$2 + 4 = \boxed{}$

$6 + 4 = \boxed{}$

12. $3, \boxed{}, \boxed{}, 21, \ldots$

13. $65, \boxed{}, \boxed{}, 32, \ldots$

14. Error Analysis Noah used the formula $a_n = a + (n - 1)d$ to find the 12th term in the sequence $2, 4, 7, 11, 16, \ldots$. Did Noah find the correct term? How do you know?

Lesson 9-2

9-2 **Practice** (continued)   *Form K*

Arithmetic Sequences

Find the missing term of each arithmetic sequence.

15. . . . 4, ___, 18, . . .   **16.** . . . 9, ☐ , 37, . . .

Find the arithmetic mean of the given terms.

$4 + 18 = 22$

$22 \div 2 = 11$

The missing term is ☐ .

17. 46, ☐ , 28, . . .   **18.** −12, ☐ , −4, . . .   **19.** . . . 4, ☐ , −44, . . .

20. Error Analysis Your friend used the arithmetic mean to find the missing term in the following sequence: 3, ___, 29, 42, ... His answer was 13. What error did your friend make? What is the correct answer?

21. An architect is designing a building with sides in the shape of a trapezoid. The number of windows on each floor forms an arithmetic sequence. There are 124 windows on the first floor and 116 windows on the second floor.
   a. Write an explicit formula to represent the sequence.
   b. How many windows are on the tenth floor?

22. Your cousin opened a bank account with a deposit of $256 dollars. After one week, she had $280 in her account. After two weeks, she had $304, and after three weeks she had $328. If this pattern continues, how much money will your cousin have in her account after 18 weeks?

23. There is a puddle 1.4 cm deep in your backyard. After one minute of rain, the puddle was 1.45 cm deep. The puddle was 1.5 cm deep after it rained for two minutes. If the pattern continues, how deep will the puddle be after it rains for 45 min?

9-2   Standardized Test Prep

Arithmetic Sequences

Multiple Choice

For Exercises 1–6, choose the correct letter.

1. Which sequence is an arithmetic sequence?

   A 7, 10, 13, 16, 19, . . .   **C** 7, 14, 28, 56, 112, . . .

   B 7, 8, 10, 13, 17, . . .   **D** 1, 7, 14, 22, 31, 41, . . .

2. An arithmetic sequence begins 4, 9, ... What is the 20th term?

   F 76   **G** 80   **H** 84   **I** 99

3. What are the missing terms of the arithmetic sequence 5, __, __, 62, . . . ?

   A 19, 24   **B** 19, 34   **C** 24, 43   **D** 43, 62

4. What is the missing term of the arithmetic sequence 25, __, 45, . . . ?

   F 30   **G** 35   **H** 37   **I** 40

5. The seventh and ninth terms of an arithmetic sequence are 197 and 173. What is the eighth term?

   A 161   **B** 180   **C** 185   **D** 221

6. An artist is creating a tile mosaic. She uses 4 green tiles in the first row, 11 green tiles in the second row, 18 green tiles in the third row, and 25 green tiles in the fourth row. If she continues the pattern, how many green tiles will she use in the 20th row?

   F 32   **G** 58   **H** 134   **I** 137

Extended Response

7. What is the 100th term in the arithmetic sequence beginning with 3, 19, . . . ? Show your work.

9-3 Think About a Plan

Geometric Sequences

Athletics During your first week of training for a marathon, you run a total of 10 miles. You increase the distance you run each week by twenty percent. How many miles do you run during your twelfth week of training?

Understanding the Problem

1. How can you write a sequence of numbers to represent this situation?

   _____

   _____ .

2. Is the sequence arithmetic, geometric, or neither? _____

3. What is the first term of the sequence?

4. What is the common ratio of the sequence?

5. What is the problem asking you to determine?

   _____

   _____

Planning the Solution

6. Write a formula for the sequence.

Getting an Answer

7. Evaluate your formula to find the number of miles you run during your twelfth week of training.

9-3 Practice

Form K

Geometric Sequences

Determine whether each sequence is geometric. If so, find the common ratio.

1. 1, 3, 9, 27, . . .

Find the ratios between consecutive terms.

$\frac{3}{1} = \frac{9}{3} = \frac{27}{9}$

The sequence is geometric.

The common ratio is ⬜.

2. 2, 5, 8, 11, 14, . . .

3. −2, −4, −8, −16, . . .

4. 500, 50, 5, 0.5, . . .

5. 0, 25, 50, 75, 100, . . .

6. Open-Ended Write a geometric sequence with a common ratio of $\frac{1}{4}$. Explain how you developed the sequence.

Find the ninth term of each geometric sequence.

7. 3, 12, 48, 192, . . .

Use the explicit formula.

$a_n = a_1 \cdot r^{n-1}$

$a_9 = 3(4^8)$

$a_9 = 3(65,536)$

$a_9 = $ ⬜

8. 2, 6, 18, 54, . . .

9. 1875, 375, 75, 15, . . .

Find the missing terms of each geometric sequence.

10. 2, ___, ___, 128, . . .

Identify the common ratio.

$a_n = a_1 \cdot r^{n-1}$

$a_4 = 2r^{4-1}$

$128 = 2r^3$

$64 = r^3$

$4 = r$

The second term is ⬜.

The third term is ⬜.

11. 1, ⬜, ⬜, 8, . . .

12. 108, ⬜, ⬜, 4, . . .

9-3 Practice (continued)   Form K
Geometric Sequences

Find the missing term of each geometric sequence. It could be the geometric mean or its opposite.

13. 5, ___, 45, . . .

Find the geometric mean of 5 and 45.

$\sqrt{xy}$

$\sqrt{45 \cdot 5}$

$\sqrt{225}$

14. 2, ⬚, 72, . . .

15. $\frac{1}{4}$, ⬚, $2\frac{1}{4}$, . . .   **16.** 175, ⬚, 7, . . .   **17.** 1.2, ⬚, 43.2, . . .

18. Error Analysis On a recent math test, your classmate was asked to find the missing term in the geometric sequence 4, ___, 256. Her answer was 130. What error did your classmate make? What is the correct answer?

19. The bacteria population in a petri dish was 14 at the beginning of an experiment. After 30 min, the population was 28, and after an hour the population was 56.
   a. Write an explicit definition to represent this sequence.
   b. If this pattern continues, what will be the bacteria population after 4 h?

20. A corporation earned a profit of $420,000 in its first year of operation. Over the next 10 years, the company's CEO hopes to increase the profit by 8% each year. If the CEO reaches her goal, what will be the company's profit in its seventh year, to the nearest dollar?

Name _____ Class _____ Date _____

9-3 Standardized Test Prep
Geometric Sequences

Multiple Choice

For Exercises 1–6, choose the correct letter.

1. What is the 10th term of the geometric sequence 1, 4, 16, . . .?

   A 40   B 180,224   C 262,144   D 2,883,584

2. Which sequence is a geometric sequence?

   F 1, 3, 5, 7, 9, . . .   H 2, 4, 8, 16, 32, . . .

   G 12, 9, 6, 3, 0, . . .   I −2, −6, −10, −14, −18, . . .

3. Which could be the missing term of the geometric sequence 5, __, 125, . . .?

   A 25   B 50   C 75   D 100

4. What could be the missing term of the geometric sequence -12, __, $-\frac{3}{4}$, . . .?

   F −4   G −6.375   H 3   I 4

5. In the explicit formula for the 9th term of the geometric sequence 1, 6, 36, . . . what number is a?

   A 1   B 6   C 36   D 1,679,616

6. In each successive round of a backgammon tournament, the number of players decreases by half. If the tournament starts with 32 players, which rule could predict the number of players in the nth round?

   F $32 = (0.5)^n$ G $32 = 0.5r^{n-1}$ H $a_n = 15^{n-1}$ I $a_n = (32)(0.5)^{n-1}$

Short Response

7. What is the 6th term of the geometric sequence 100, 50, . . .? Show your work using the explicit formula.

Lesson 9-3

9-4 Think About a Plan

Arithmetic Series

Architecture In a 20-row theater, the number of seats in a row increases by three with each successive row. The first row has 18 seats.

   a. Write an arithmetic series to represent the number of seats in the theater.

   b. Find the total seating capacity of the theater.

   c. Front-row tickets for a concert cost $60. After every 5 rows, the ticket price goes down by $5. What is the total amount of money generated by a full house?

1. Write the explicit formula for an arithmetic sequence.

2. What are a_1 and d for the sequence that represents the number of seats in each row?

   $a_1 =$ ☐ $d =$ ☐

3. Write an explicit formula for the arithmetic sequence that represents the number of seats in each row.

4. Write an arithmetic series to represent the number of seats in the theater.

5. How can you use a graphing calculator to evaluate the series?

   _____

   _____ .

6. Find the total seating capacity of the theater.

7. Write a series for the number of seats in each set of 5 rows.

8. Use your graphing calculator to evaluate each series. _____

9. What are the ticket prices for each set of 5 rows? _____

10. What is the total amount of money generated by a full house?

9-4

Practice

Form K

Arithmetic Series

Identify each list as a *series* or a *sequence* and *finite* or *infinite*.

1. $2, 6, 10, 14, \ldots$ **2.** $1 + 4 + 7 + 10 + 13$ **3.** $4, 10, 16, 22, 28$

4. $5 + 12 + 19 + 26 + 33$ **5.** $1.4 + 1.1 + 0.8 + 0.5 + \cdots$ **6.** $-2 - 11 - 20 - 29 - \cdots$

Find the sum of each finite arithmetic series.

7. $1 + 3 + 5 + \cdots + 99$

Find the number of terms. Find the sum.

$a_n = a_1 + (n - 1)d$ $S_n = \frac{n}{2}(a_1 + a_n)$

$99 = 1 + (n - 1)2$ $S_{50} = \frac{50}{2}(1 + 99)$

$99 = 1 + 2n - 2$ $= 25(100)$

$100 = 2n$ $= \boxed{}$

$50 = n$

8. $3 + 7 + 11 + 15 + \cdots + 55$

Find the number of terms.   Find the sum.

$a_n = a_1 + (n - 1)d$ $S_n = \frac{n}{2}(a_1 + a_n)$

9. $106 + 101 + 96 + \cdots + 1$ **10.** $2 + 10 + 18 + \cdots + 378$

11. $(-4) + (-9) + (-14) + \cdots + (299)$

12. Reasoning Is it possible to find the sum of an infinite arithmetic series? Explain.

Lesson 9-4

9-4

Practice (continued)

Arithmetic Series

Write each arithmetic series in summation notation.

13. $3 + 8 + 13 + \cdots + 268$

Find an explicit formula
for the nth term.

$a_n = a_1 + (n - 1)d$

$a_n = 3 + (n - 1)5$

$a_n = 5n - 2$

Find the value of n for 268.

$268 = 5n - 2$

$270 = 5n$

$54 = n$

Write the summation notation.

$$\sum_{n=1}^{\square} \left(\boxed{} \right)$$

14. $1 + 7 + 13 + \cdots + 343$

15. $5 + 7 + 9 + \cdots + 131$

16. Tabitha used tiles to make the design shown at the right. The first
column has 2 tiles, the second column has 4 tiles, and the pattern
continues.

   a. Write an explicit formula for the sequence.

   b. Write the summation notation for a related series with 24 tiles
in the 12th column.

   c. How many tiles are in the design if there are a total of 12 columns?

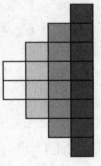

17. Your brother is preparing for basketball season. He shot 26 baskets on the first
day that he practiced. He shot 32 baskets on the second day and 38 baskets the
day after that.

   a. If this pattern continues, how many baskets will he shoot on the 30th day?

   b. How many baskets will he have shot during those 30 days?

9-4 Standardized Test Prep

Arithmetic Series

Multiple Choice

For Exercises 1–6, choose the correct letter.

1. What is the sum of the odd integers 1 to 99?
   - Ⓐ 2450
   - Ⓑ 2500
   - Ⓒ 2550
   - Ⓓ 4950

2. Which of the following is an infinite series?
   - Ⓕ 3, 8, 13, 18, 23
   - Ⓗ $3 + 8 + 13 + 18 + 23 + \cdots$
   - Ⓖ $3 + 8 + 13 + 18 + 23$
   - Ⓘ 3, 8, 13, 18, 23, . . .

3. The high school choir is participating in a fundraising sales contest. The choir will receive a bonus if they make 20 sales in their first week and improve their sales by 3 in every subsequent week. What is the minimum number of sales the choir could make in the first 12 weeks to qualify for the bonus?
   - Ⓐ 13
   - Ⓑ 53
   - Ⓒ 438
   - Ⓓ 5015

4. What is summation notation for the series $5 + 7 + 9 + \cdots + 105$?
   - Ⓕ $\displaystyle\sum_{n=1}^{51} (2n + 3)$
   - Ⓖ $\displaystyle\sum_{n=1}^{51} (n + 3)$
   - Ⓗ $\displaystyle\sum_{n=1}^{50} (2n + 3)$
   - Ⓘ $\displaystyle\sum_{n=7}^{51} (n + 3)$

5. What is the upper limit of the summation $\displaystyle\sum_{n=1}^{100} (n - 2)$?
   - Ⓐ 1
   - Ⓑ 2
   - Ⓒ 98
   - Ⓓ 100

6. What is the sum of the series $\displaystyle\sum_{n=1}^{30} (2n + 2)$?
   - Ⓕ 62
   - Ⓖ 66
   - Ⓗ 990
   - Ⓘ 1980

Short Response

7. What is the sum of the finite arithmetic series $2 + 4 + 6 + \cdots + 50$?
   Show your work.

Lesson 9-4

9-5 Think About a Plan

Geometric Series

Communications Many companies use a telephone chain to notify employees of a closing due to bad weather. Suppose a company's CEO calls three people. Then each of these people calls three others, and so on.

  a. Make a diagram to show the first three stages in the telephone chain. How many calls are made at each stage?

  b. Write the series that represents the total number of calls made through the first six stages.

  c. How many employees have been notified after stage six?

1. What type of diagram can you make to represent the telephone chain? _____

2. Make a diagram to show the first three stages in the telephone chain.

3. What expression represents the number of calls made at stage n?

4. Write the series that represents the total number of calls made through the first six stages. _____

5. What is the sum of this series?

6. Write the sum formula.

7. Use the sum formula to find how many employees have been notified after stage six.

8. Does your answer agree with your sum from exercise 5?

Name _____ Class _____ Date _____

9-5 Practice

Form K

Geometric Series

Find the sum of each finite geometric series.

1. $2 + 6 + 18 + \cdots + 4374$

Find the number of terms.   Use the sum formula.

$$a_n = a_1 r^{n-1} \qquad S_n = \frac{a_1(1 - r^n)}{1 - r}$$

$$4374 = 2 \cdot 3^{n-1} \qquad S_8 = \frac{2(1 - 3^8)}{1 - 3}$$

$$2187 = 3^{n-1} \qquad\qquad = \boxed{}$$

$$3^7 = 2187$$

$$n = 8$$

2. $1 + 2 + 4 + \cdots + 2048$

3. $8 + 4 + 2 + \cdots + \frac{1}{256}$

4. $3 + 9 + 27 + \cdots + 6561$

5. $-4 - 8 - 16 - \cdots - 2048$

6. Find the sum of the geometric series $2 - 4 + 8 - 16 + \cdots + 8192$. Explain how you found the sum.

7. A family farm produced 2400 ears of corn in its first year. For each of the next 9 yr, the farm increased its yearly corn production by 15%. How many ears of corn did the farm produce during this 10-yr period?

243

9-5 Practice (continued)
Geometric Series

Form K

Determine whether each infinite geometric series *diverges* or *converges*. Find the sum if the series converges.

8. $1 + \frac{1}{4} + \frac{1}{16} + \cdots$

9. $2 + 8 + 32 + \cdots$

Because $|r| = \left|\frac{1}{4}\right| < 1$, the series converges.

$S = \dfrac{a_1}{1-r} = \dfrac{1}{1 - \frac{1}{4}} = \dfrac{1}{\frac{3}{4}} = \boxed{}$

10. $\frac{1}{2} + \frac{1}{16} + \frac{1}{128} + \cdots$

11. $\frac{1}{4} + \frac{3}{8} + \frac{9}{16} + \cdots$

12. $2 - \frac{2}{5} + \frac{2}{25} - \cdots$

13. Your classmate is trying to cut down on the amount of time he spends watching television. In January, he spent a total of 3600 min watching television. He watched television for 3240 min in February and 2916 min in March. If this pattern continues, how many minutes of television will he watch this year?

14. Your math teacher asks you to choose between two offers. The first offer is to receive one penny on the first day, 3 pennies on the second day, 9 pennies on the third day, and so on, for 14 days. The second offer is to receive 4 pennies on the first day, 8 pennies on the second day, 16 pennies on the third day, and so on, for 14 days. Which offer is better? What is the difference between the total amounts received?

Name _____ Class _____ Date _____

9-5 Standardized Test Prep
Geometric Series

Gridded Response

Solve each exercise and enter your answer in the grid provided.

1. What is the value of a_1 in the series $\sum_{n=0}^{20} 3\left(\frac{1}{2}\right)^n$?

2. What is the sum of the geometric series $2 + 6 + 18 + \cdots + 486$?

3. A community organizes a phone tree in order to alert each family of emergencies. In the first stage, one person calls five families. In the second stage, each of the five families calls another five families, and so on. How many stages need to be reached before 600 families or more are called?

4. What is the approximate whole number sum for the finite geometric series $\sum_{n=0}^{5} 8\left(\frac{1}{4}\right)^n$?

5. What is the sum of the geometric series $1 + \frac{1}{3} + \frac{1}{9} + \ldots$? Enter your answer as a fraction.

Answers

1. 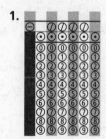 2. 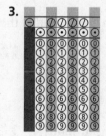 3. 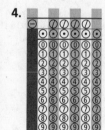 4. 5.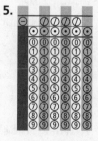

Lesson 9-5

10-1 Think About a Plan

Exploring Conic Sections

Sound An airplane flying faster than the speed of sound creates a cone-shaped pressure disturbance in the air. This is heard by people on the ground as a sonic boom. What is the shape of the path on the ground?

Know

1. The pressure disturbance is shaped like a ☐ .

2. The ground near the airplane is shaped like a ☐ .

Need

3. To solve the problem I need to find:

   _____

   _____ .

Plan

4. How can a drawing or model help you solve this problem?

   _____

   _____ .

5. Is there only one possible path on the ground? Explain.

   _____

   _____ .

6. Sketch the possible orientations to the ground of the airplane and its pressure cone.

7. What is the shape of the path on the ground?

   _____

   _____ .

10-1 Practice

Form K

Exploring Conic Sections

Graph each equation. Identify the conic section and describe the graph and its lines of symmetry. Then find the domain and range.

1. $9x^2 + y^2 = 9$

Make a table of values.   If $y = 0$, then $x = 1$ or $x = -1$.
If $y = 3$, then $x = 0$.
If $y = -3$, then $x = 0$.

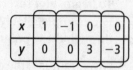

x	1	−1	0	0
y	0	0	3	−3

Plot the points in the table. Connect the points with a smooth curve. The conic section is a(n) [   ].

The conic section has two lines of symmetry: [   ] and [   ].

The smallest x-value is -1. The largest x-value is 1.

The domain is the set of all real numbers with [   ] $\leq x \leq$ [   ].

The smallest y-value is -3. The largest y-value is 3.

The range is the set of all real numbers with [   ] $\leq y \leq$ [   ].

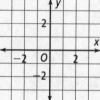

2. $x^2 - y^2 = 16$

3. $x^2 + 4y^2 = 25$

4. $x^2 + y^2 - 9 = 0$

5. $4x^2 + 9y^2 - 36 = 0$

6. $-25x^2 + 4y^2 - 100 = 0$

7. $12x^2 + 12y^2 = 192$

8. Open-Ended Describe the figures you can see that can be formed by the intersection of a plane and a rectangular prism.

10-1 Practice (continued)   Form K
Exploring Conic Sections

Graph each circle with the given radius or diameter so that the center is at the origin. Then write the equation for each graph.

9. radius 7

To begin, plot several points that are 7 units away from the origin. For example, plot $(7, 0)$, $(-7, 0)$, $(0, 7)$, and $(0, -7)$. Draw a circle through these points.

Given radius r, the equation of a circle is $x^2 + y^2 = r^2$. The equation for this circle is [   ].

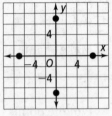

10. radius 8

11. radius $\frac{1}{3}$

12. diameter 10

13. diameter 2.2

Mental Math Each given point is on the graph of the given equation. Use symmetry to find at least one more point on the graph.

14. $(-3, 3)$, $x^2 + y^2 = 18$

15. $(4, 4\sqrt{3})$, $4x^2 - y^2 = 16$

16. $(-2, 0)$, $x^2 - 4y^2 - 4 = 0$

17. $(2\sqrt{5}, 5)$, $x^2 + y^2 - 45 = 0$

18. Error Analysis A student says that the equation $y = x + 1$ represents a line of symmetry for the circle with equation $x^2 + y^2 = 1$. What is the student's error? Identify a correct line of symmetry.

10-1 Standardized Test Prep

Exploring Conic Sections

Multiple Choice

For Exercises 1–6, choose the correct letter.

1. What shape is the conic section $x^2 + y^2 = 16$?

   Ⓐ circle   Ⓑ ellipse   Ⓒ parabola   Ⓓ hyperbola

2. Which line is not a line of symmetry for $x^2 + y^2 = 25$?

   Ⓕ $y = x$ Ⓗ $y = x + 2$

   Ⓖ $2y = 3x$ Ⓘ $3y = 3x$

3. Which equation represents the graph at the right?

   Ⓐ $4y^2 + 4x^2 = 4$ Ⓒ $x^2 + 4y^2 = 16$

   Ⓑ $4x^2 + y^2 = 16$ Ⓓ $y^2 + x^2 = 16$

   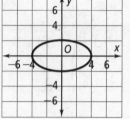

4. What are the lines of symmetry of a circle with the center at the origin?

   Ⓕ the x-axis   Ⓗ the y-axis

   Ⓖ the x- and y-axis   Ⓘ all lines that pass through the center

5. What is the range of $16x^2 + 9y^2 = 144$?

   Ⓐ $-3 \le y \le 3$ Ⓑ $-4 \le y \le 4$ Ⓒ $-16 \le y \le 16$ Ⓓ $-144 \le y \le 144$

6. What is the domain of $x^2 + y^2 = 64$?

   Ⓕ $-8 \le x \le 8$ Ⓖ $0 \le x \le 8$ Ⓗ $-8 \le y \le 8$ Ⓘ $-64 \le x \le 64$

Short Response

7. Describe the graph of $x^2 - y^2 = 16$. What is the center? What are the lines of symmetry? What are the domain and range?

10-2

Think About a Plan

Parabolas

Sound Broadcasters use a parabolic microphone on football sidelines to pick up field audio for broadcasting purposes. A certain parabolic microphone has a reflector dish with a diameter of 28 inches and a depth of 14 inches. If the receiver of the microphone is located at the focus of the reflector dish, how far from the vertex should the receiver be positioned?

Understanding the Problem

1. What is the diameter of the reflector dish?

2. What is the depth of the reflector dish?

3. What is the problem asking you to determine?

_____

Planning the Solution

4. Sketch a graph of a vertical parabola to represent the reflector dish. Place the vertex at the origin.

5. You know the coordinates of two other points on the parabola. Plot and label them on your graph.

6. What is the equation for a vertical parabola with vertex at the origin?

7. How can you find the location of the focus from the equation for the parabola?

_____

_____ .

Getting an Answer

8. What is the location of the focus?

9. If the receiver of the microphone is located at the focus of the reflector dish, how far from the vertex should the receiver be positioned?

10-2 Practice

Parabolas

Write an equation of a parabola with vertex at the origin and the given focus.

1. focus at $(0, 2)$

2. focus at $(-5, 0)$

3. focus at $(0, -1)$

4. focus at $(3, 0)$

Identify the vertex, the focus, and the directrix of the parabola with the given equation. Then sketch the graph of the parabola.

5. $y = \frac{1}{6}x^2$ This is a vertical parabola with vertex at $(0, 0)$.

The focus is at $(0, 1.5)$.

The directrix is ⬚ .

6. $x = -2y^2$

7. $y = \frac{3}{2}x^2$

Write an equation of a parabola with vertex at the origin and the given directrix.

8. directrix $x = -4$

9. directrix $y = 10$

10. directrix $y = -3$

11. directrix $x = 1$

12. A cross section of a satellite dish is a parabola. The receiver is located at the focus. Suppose the receiver is located 7 cm from the vertex of the dish. Model a cross section of the satellite dish by writing an equation of a parabola that opens to the right and has its vertex at the origin.

7 cm

10-2 Practice (continued) Form K
Parabolas

Identify the vertex, the focus, and the directrix of the parabola with the given equation. Then sketch the graph of the parabola.

13. $y = x^2 - 6x + 3$

Start by writing the equation in vertex form by completing the square.

14. $x = y^2 - 2y - 1$ **15.** $y = \frac{1}{2}x^2 + 2x - 3$

Write an equation of a parabola with the given vertex and focus.

16. vertex $(0, 4)$; focus $(0, 0)$ **17.** vertex $(3, 6)$; focus $(6, 6)$

Write an equation of a parabola with vertex at $(2, 3)$ and the given information.

18. focus $(2, 3.5)$ **19.** directrix $x = 0$

20. Writing Explain how to find the vertex of the parabola $x = y^2 + 4y - 9$.

10-2 Standardized Test Prep
Parabolas

Multiple Choice

For Exercises 1–5, choose the correct letter.

1. Which is an equation of the parabola with the vertex at the origin and focus (0, 3)?

   Ⓐ $y = \frac{1}{4}x^2$ Ⓑ $y = \frac{1}{12}x^2$ Ⓒ $x = \frac{1}{12}y^2$ Ⓓ $x = \frac{1}{3}y^2$

2. What is the focus of the parabola with the equation $y = -\frac{1}{16}x^2$?

   Ⓕ $(0, -4)$ Ⓖ $(-4, 0)$ Ⓗ $\left(0, -\frac{1}{16}\right)$ Ⓘ $\left(-\frac{1}{4}, 0\right)$

3. Which is the equation of a parabola with vertex at the origin and directrix $x = 2.5$?

   Ⓐ $x = -\frac{1}{10}y^2$ Ⓑ $x = \frac{1}{10}y^2$ Ⓒ $x = \frac{1}{2.5}y^2$ Ⓓ $x = -\frac{5}{2}y^2$

4. What is the directrix of $x = 2.25y^2$?

   Ⓕ $x = \frac{1}{4}$ Ⓖ $x = -\frac{1}{4}$ Ⓗ $x = \frac{1}{9}$ Ⓘ $x = -\frac{1}{9}$

5. What is the vertex of $y = x^2 - 8x + 10$?

   Ⓐ $(-4, 8)$ Ⓑ $(8, 10)$ Ⓒ $(10, 16)$ Ⓓ $(4, -6)$

Short Response

6. What are the vertex, focus, and directrix of the parabola with equation $y = x^2 - 14x + 5$? Show your work.

10-3

Think About a Plan

Circles

Machinery Three gears, *A*, *B*, and *C*, mesh with each other in a motor assembly. Gear *A* has a radius of 4 in., *B* has a radius of 3 in., and *C* has a radius of 1 in. If the largest gear is centered at $(-4, 0)$, the smallest gear is centered at $(4, 0)$, and Gear *B* is centered at the origin, what is the equation of each circle in standard form?

Understanding the Problem

1. The radius of gear *A* = ☐ in.

2. The radius of gear *B* = ☐ in.

3. The radius of gear *C* = ☐ in.

4. The centers of the gears are at what points?

5. What is the problem asking you to determine?

_____

Planning the Solution

6. What do you need to find an equation for each gear?

_____

Getting an Answer

7. Fill in the table to the right to find the equation of the circle that represents each gear.

Gear	(h, k)	r	Equation
A			
B			
C			

10-3 **Practice**

Circles

Form K

Write an equation of a circle with the given center and radius. Check your answers.

1. center $(1, 1)$, radius 4

2. center $(-2, 0)$, radius 6

3. center $(5, -3)$, radius 1

4. center $(-1, -5)$, radius 5

Write an equation for each translation.

5. $x^2 + y^2 = 16$; left 2 units and down 1 unit

Translate left 2 units:

$(x - (-2))^2 + y^2 = 16$

$(x + 2)^2 + y^2 = 16$

Translate down 1 unit:

$(x + 2)^2 + \left(y - \left(\boxed{}\right)\right)^2 = 16$

$(x + 2)^2 + \left(y\,\boxed{}\,\right)^2 = 16$

6. $x^2 + y^2 = 81$; right 4 units

7. $x^2 + y^2 = 1$; left 1 unit and up 1 unit

8. $x^2 + y^2 = 4$; up 7 units

9. $x^2 + y^2 = 36$; right 5 units and down 2 units

Write an equation for each circle. Each interval represents one unit.

10.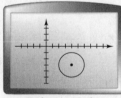

x Scale: 1   y Scale: 1

First, identify the center. $(4, -3)$

Then find the radius.   The circle is 4 units wide, so the radius is 2.

Use the standard form $(x - h)^2 + (y - k)^2 = r^2$.

11.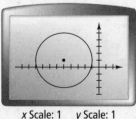

x Scale: 1   y Scale: 1

12.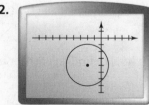

x Scale: 1   y Scale: 1

Lesson 10-3

10-3 Practice (continued)   Form K
Circles

For each equation, find the center and radius of the circle.

13. $(x + 2)^2 + (y + 2)^2 = 64$ **14.** $x^2 + (y - 5)^2 = 16$

15. $(x + 6)^2 + y^2 = 9$ **16.** $(x - 7)^2 + (y + 1)^2 = 81$

Use the center and the radius to graph each circle.

17. $(x + 3)^2 + (y - 3)^2 = 16$

     Rewrite the equation in standard form. $(x - (-3))^2 + (y - 3)^2 = 4^2$
     Find the center and radius from the equation.   center $(-3, 3)$, radius 4
     Plot the center and draw a circle with the given radius.

18. $(x - 2)^2 + (y - 1)^2 = 49$ **19.** $(x + 4)^2 + (y + 2)^2 = 25$

Write the equation of the circle that passes through the given point and has a center at the origin. (*Hint*: You can use the distance formula to find the radius.)

20. $(-2, 0)$ **21.** $(3, 4)$

Use the given information to write an equation of the circle.

22. center $(-3, 1)$, through $(-3, -1)$ **23.** radius 6, center $(4, -5)$

24. Writing Explain how to find the center and radius of the circle $x^2 + y^2 - 6y - 16 = 0$.

10-3 Standardized Test Prep
Circles

Multiple Choice

For Exercises 1–5, choose the correct letter.

1. Which is an equation of the circle with center at the origin and radius 3?

   A. $x^2 + y^2 = 3$ C. $x^2 + y^2 = 9$

   B. $x^2 + y^2 = 81$ D. $(x - 3)^2 + (y - 3)^2 = 9$

2. What is the equation for the translation of $x^2 + y^2 = 16$ two units left and one unit down?

   F. $x^2 + y^2 = 16$ H. $2x^2 + y^2 = 16$

   G. $(x - 2)^2 + (y - 1)^2 = 16$ I. $(x + 2)^2 + (y + 1)^2 = 16$

3. Which equation represents a circle with a center at $(7, -9)$ and a diameter of 8?

   A. $(x - 7)^2 + (y - 9)^2 = 64$ C. $(x - 7)^2 + (y + 9)^2 = 16$

   B. $(x - 7)^2 + (y + 9)^2 = 64$ D. $(x + 7)^2 + (y - 9)^2 = 16$

4. What is the center of the circle $(x - 3)^2 + (y + 2)^2 = 81$?

   F. $(-3, 2)$ G. $(3, -2)$ H. $(3, 2)$ I. $(9, 9)$

5. What is the radius of the circle $(x + 8)^2 + (y - 3)^2 = 100$?

   A. 10   B. 20   C. 50   D. 100

Short Response

6. What are the radius and center of a circle with the equation
   $(x + 7)^2 + (y - 8)^2 = 144$?

Lesson 10-3

10-4 Think About a Plan

Ellipses

Aerodynamics Scientists used the Transonic Tunnel at NASA Langley Research Center, Virginia, to study the dynamics of air flow. The elliptical opening of the Transonic Tunnel is 82 ft wide and 58 ft high. What is an equation of the ellipse?

Know

1. The width of the tunnel opening is [   ].

2. The height of the tunnel opening is [   ].

Need

3. To solve the problem I need to find:

   _____ .

Plan

4. How can a drawing help you solve this problem?

   _____

   _____ .

5. Make a sketch of an ellipse that represents the tunnel opening.
   Where should you put the origin? _____

6. How do the width and height of the tunnel opening relate to the
   equation of the ellipse?

   _____

   _____ .

7. How can you write the equation of the ellipse in standard form?

   _____

   _____ .

8. Write the equation of the ellipse in standard form.

10-4 Practice

Ellipses

Write an equation of an ellipse in standard form with center at the origin with the given vertex and co-vertex listed. (Note that the vertex is listed first and the co-vertex is listed second.)

1. $(3, 0), (0, 1)$

Because one vertex is at $(3, 0)$, the other vertex is at $(-3, 0)$.

The major axis is horizontal.

Because one co-vertex is at $(0, 1)$, the other co-vertex is at $(0, -1)$.

The minor axis is vertical.

$a = \boxed{}$, $b = \boxed{}$, $a^2 = \boxed{}$, and $b^2 = \boxed{}$

Write the standard form of a horizontal ellipse. $\dfrac{x^2}{a^2} + \dfrac{y^2}{b^2} = 1$

Substitute for a^2 and b^2.

2. $(0, -7), (2, 0)$

3. $(-5, 0), (0, -4)$

Find the foci for each equation of an ellipse. Then graph the ellipse.

4. $16x^2 + 25y^2 = 400$

Write the equation in standard form. $\qquad \dfrac{x^2}{25} + \dfrac{y^2}{16} = 1$

Find the vertices, co-vertices, and foci $\qquad$ vertices: $(-5, 0)$ and $(5, 0)$

from the equation. $\qquad$ co-vertices: $(0, -4)$ and $(0, 4)$

$\qquad$ foci: $(-3, 0)$ and $(3, 0)$

Plot the points to graph the ellipse.

5. $\dfrac{x^2}{4} + \dfrac{y^2}{16} = 1$

6. $4x^2 + 16y^2 = 16$

Find the distance between the foci of an ellipse. The lengths of the major and minor axes are listed respectively.

7. 26, 24

8. 30, 18

9. 18, 12

10-4 Practice (continued) Form K

Ellipses

Write an equation of an ellipse for the given foci and co-vertices.

10. foci $(0, \pm 3)$, co-vertices $(\pm 1, 0)$

The foci are on the y-axis, so the major axis is vertical.

Because $c = 3$ and $b = 1$, $c^2 = 9$ and $b^2 = 1$.

$$c^2 = a^2 - b^2$$

Find a^2: $9 = a^2 - 1$ Write the equation: $\dfrac{x^2}{b^2} + \dfrac{y^2}{a^2} = 1$

$a^2 = \boxed{}$

11. foci $(\pm 1, 0)$, co-vertices $(0, \pm 5)$ **12.** foci $(0, \pm 4)$, co-vertices $(\pm 4, 0)$

13. The decorative arch of a bridge is shaped like an ellipse. The arch is 120 ft wide and the foci are 48 ft from the center of the arch. What is the height of the arch?

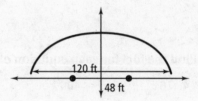

Find the foci for each equation of an ellipse.

14. $9x^2 + 18y^2 = 162$ **15.** $25x^2 + 16y^2 = 1600$

Write an equation for each ellipse.

16. 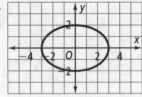   **17.**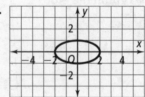

18. Reasoning How are the major and minor axes of an ellipse similar? How are they different?

10-4 Standardized Test Prep
Ellipses

Gridded Response

Solve each exercise and enter your answer on the grid provided.

1. In the equation for a horizontal ellipse $\frac{x^2}{16} + \frac{y^2}{9} = 1$, what is the positive value of the x-coordinates of the vertices?

2. What is the positive y-coordinate of the foci of the ellipse with the equation $25x^2 + 16y^2 = 400$?

3. In the equation for a vertical ellipse $\frac{x^2}{49} + \frac{y^2}{100} = 1$, what is the positive value of the y-coordinates of the vertices?

4. An ellipse has foci at $(\pm 7, 0)$ and vertices at $(\pm 16, 0)$. What is the value of c?

5. Suppose you are planning a party at an elliptical park with one game at each foci. The major axis of the ellipse is 80 yd and the minor axis is 28 yd. How many yards will the games be from one another? Round to the nearest whole number.

Answers

1. 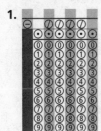 2. 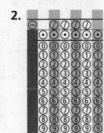 3. 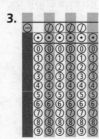 4. 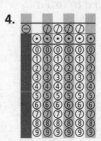 5.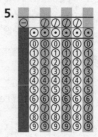

10-5 Think About a Plan

Hyperbolas

Comets The path of a comet around the sun followed one branch of a hyperbola. Find an equation that models its path around the sun, given that $a = 40$ million miles and $c = 250$ million miles. Use the horizontal model.

Know

1. a is equal to [   ].

2. c is equal to [   ].

Need

3. To solve the problem I need to find:

_____

_____ .

Plan

4. What is the equation for a horizontal hyperbola?

5. What do you need in order to write an equation for the hyperbola that models the comet?

_____

6. What is the relationship between a, b, and c in a hyperbola?

7. How can you use the relationship between a, b, and c to find an equation for the hyperbola?

_____ .

8. Write an equation for a horizontal hyperbola that models the path of the comet.

10-5 Practice

Hyperbolas

Form K

Find the equation of a hyperbola with the given values, foci, or vertices. Assume that the transverse axis is horizontal.

1. $b = 3, c = 4$

Use the equation $c^2 = a^2 + b^2$ to find a^2. $4^2 = a^2 + 3^2$

$$a^2 = \boxed{}$$

Substitute values for a^2 and b^2.

2. $b = 9, c = 12$

3. foci $(\pm 8, 0)$, vertices $(\pm 2, 0)$

Find the vertices, foci, and asymptotes of each hyperbola. Then sketch the graph.

4. $\dfrac{x^2}{25} - \dfrac{y^2}{11} = 1$

Compare to $\dfrac{x^2}{a^2} - \dfrac{y^2}{b^2} = 1: a^2 = 25, b^2 = 11.$ $a = \pm 5, b = \pm\sqrt{11}$

The vertices are given by $(\pm a, 0)$. $(-5, 0)$ and $(5, 0)$

Use the formula $c^2 = a^2 + b^2$ to find c. $c = \pm 6$

The foci are given by $(\pm c, 0)$. $\boxed{}$

Asymptotes $\left(y = \pm\dfrac{b}{a}x\right)$: $\boxed{}$

5. $\dfrac{x^2}{4} - \dfrac{y^2}{4} = 1$

6. $4y^2 - 36x^2 = 144$

10-5

Practice (continued)

Hyperbolas

7. The diagram at the right models a satellite dish and the small reflector inside it. Suppose F_1 and F_2 are 10 ft apart, and F_1 is 2 ft from the vertex of the small reflector. What equation best models the small reflector?

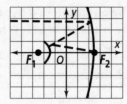

Write the equation of a hyperbola with the given foci and vertices.

8. foci $(0, \pm 10)$, vertices $(0, \pm 8)$

9. foci $(\pm 3, 0)$, vertices $(\pm 2, 0)$

Write an equation of a hyperbola with the given information. Assume the center of each hyperbola is $(0, 0)$.

10. The transverse axis is horizontal and is 8 units; the central rectangle is 8 units by 2 units.

11. The perimeter of central rectangle is 44 units; the vertices are at $(6, 0)$ and $(-6, 0)$.

Graphing Calculator Solve each equation for y. Graph each relation on your graphing calculator. Use the TRACE feature to locate the vertices.

12. $4y^2 - x^2 = 12$

13. $2y^2 - 5x^2 = 4$

Graph each equation.

14. $4x^2 - y^2 = 4$

15. $32y^2 - 18x^2 = 288$

10-5 Standardized Test Prep

Hyperbolas

Multiple Choice

For Exercises 1–4, choose the correct letter.

1. A hyperbola has vertices $(\pm 5, 0)$ and one focus at $(6, 0)$. What is the equation of the hyperbola in standard form?

   A $\dfrac{x^2}{25} + \dfrac{y^2}{11} = 1$

   B $\dfrac{x^2}{5} - \dfrac{y^2}{11} = 1$

   C $\dfrac{x^2}{11} - \dfrac{y^2}{25} = 1$

   D $\dfrac{x^2}{25} - \dfrac{y^2}{11} = 1$

2. A hyperbola with a horizontal transverse axis has asymptotes $y = \pm\dfrac{3}{4}x$. Which of the following could be the equation of the hyperbola in standard form?

   F $\dfrac{x^2}{3} + \dfrac{y^2}{4} = 1$

   G $\dfrac{x^2}{16} - \dfrac{y^2}{9} = 1$

   H $\dfrac{x^2}{4} - \dfrac{y^2}{3} = 1$

   I $\dfrac{x^2}{25} - \dfrac{y^2}{16} = 1$

3. What are the vertices of the hyperbola with the equation $8x^2 - 9y^2 = 72$?

   A $(\pm 3, 0)$ B $(\pm 2\sqrt{2}, 0)$ C $(\pm 8, 0)$ D $(\pm 9, 0)$

4. What are the foci of the hyperbola with the equation $\dfrac{y^2}{12} - \dfrac{x^2}{5} = 1$?

   F $(0, \pm 5)$ G $(0, \pm 12)$ H $(0, \pm\sqrt{13})$ I $(0, \pm\sqrt{17})$

Short Response

5. What are the vertices, foci, and asymptotes of the hyperbola with the equation $4y^2 - 16x^2 = 64$?

11-1 Think About a Plan

Permutations and Combinations

Consumer Issues A consumer magazine rates televisions by identifying two levels of price, five levels of repair frequency, three levels of features, and two levels of picture quality. How many different ratings are possible?

Understanding the Problem

1. How many levels of price are possible?

2. How many levels of repair frequency are possible?

3. How many levels of features are possible?

4. How many levels of picture quality are possible?

5. What is the problem asking you to determine?

_____

_____ .

Planning the Solution

6. What is the Fundamental Counting Principle?

_____

_____ .

7. How can the Fundamental Counting Principle help you solve the problem?

_____

_____

_____ .

Getting an Answer

8. Write an expression for the number of different ratings that are possible. [   ]

9. How many different ratings are possible?

Name _____ Class _____ Date _____

11-1 Practice   *Form K*

Permutations and Combinations

Use the Fundamental Counting Principle to solve the following problems.

1. You must make a password for your email account. The password must consist of two letters followed by four digits. How many different passwords are possible?

2. Your father is buying a sport coat, a pair of pants, and a tie. Sport coats come in 6 different colors. Pants come in 4 different colors. There are 25 different tie styles to choose from. How many different combinations are possible?

Evaluate each expression.

3. $6!$ 4. $5!4!$ 5. $\dfrac{9!}{7!}$

Find the number of permutations in the following problems.

6. Your coach has twelve team jerseys numbered from 1 through 12. He plans to give one jersey to each of the twelve members of the basketball team. In how many ways can the jerseys be assigned?

7. The owner of a car lot is lining up 7 cars in the show-room window. In how many ways can the cars be ordered?

Evaluate each expression.

8. $_5P_3$ 9. $_8P_5$ 10. $_{11}P_5$

11. Twelve different types of pizza are being judged in a contest. In how many different ways can the pizzas be judged first, second, third, and fourth?

Lesson 11-1

11-1

Practice (continued)

Permutations and Combinations

Form K

Evaluate each expression.

12. $_7C_2$

13. $_9C_5$

14. $_{12}C_7$

15. $_8C_6$

16. $5(_6C_3)$

17. $_{10}C_7 + _5C_2$

Decide whether to use a permutation or a combination for each situation. Then solve the problem.

18. An ice cream parlor offers 14 different types of ice cream. In how many different ways can you select 5 types of ice cream to sample?

19. Eleven groups entered a science fair competition. In how many ways can the groups finish first, second, and third?

20. Your aunt is ordering appetizers for her and her family. The restaurant offers 10 different appetizers. She will select 4 appetizers. How many different combinations of appetizers can your aunt possibly select?

21. Error Analysis Your friend is shopping for blue jeans. The clothing store offers 18 different types of blue jeans, and your friend will buy 5 different types. Your friend believes that she has 1,028,160 different combinations that she could possibly select. What error did your friend make? How many different combinations could she possibly select?

11-1 Standardized Test Prep

Permutations and Combinations

Multiple Choice

For Exercises 1–5, choose the correct letter.

1. You choose 5 apples from a case of 24 apples. Which best represents the number of ways you can make your selection?

    Ⓐ $_5C_{19}$ Ⓑ $_{24}C_5$ Ⓒ $_5P_{24}$ Ⓓ $_{19}P_5$

2. Which is equivalent to $_7P_3$?

    Ⓕ 28   Ⓖ 35   Ⓗ 210   Ⓘ 840

3. A traveler can choose from three airlines, five hotels, and four rental car companies. How many arrangements of these services are possible?

    Ⓐ 12   Ⓑ 60   Ⓒ 220   Ⓓ 495

4. Which is equivalent to $a!(b!)$?

    Ⓕ $(ab)!$ Ⓖ $(ab!)!$ Ⓗ $ba!$ Ⓘ $b!(a!)$

5. Which is equivalent to $_9C_5$?

    Ⓐ 126   Ⓑ 3024   Ⓒ 15,120   Ⓓ 45,000

Short Response

6. You have a $1 bill, a $5 bill, a $10 bill, a $20 bill, a quarter, a dime, a nickel, and a penny. How many different total amounts can you make by choosing 6 bills and coins? Show your work.

11-2 Think About a Plan
Probability

Lottery A lottery has 53 numbers from which five are drawn at random. Each number can only be drawn once. What is the probability of your lottery ticket matching all five numbers in any order?

Know

1. The lottery has [   ] possible numbers that can be drawn.

2. Each number can be drawn [   ] time(s).

3. A total of [   ] numbers will be drawn.

Need

4. To solve the problem I need to find:

   _____

   _____ .

Plan

5. Because order does not matter, the size of the sample space is a [   ] .

6. What is the sample space?

   _____

7. What is the size of the sample space?

8. How many of the events in the sample space represent your ticket?

9. What is the probability of your lottery ticket matching all five numbers in any order?

11-2 Practice

Probability

Form K

Find each experimental probability.

1. A baseball player got a hit in 12 of his last 40 at bats. What is the probability that he will get a hit in his next at bat?

2. A pitcher struck out 8 of the last 32 batters that he faced. What is the probability that he will strike out the next batter that he faces?

3. A student rolled a six-sided number cube 60 times. She rolled the number 4 nine times. What is the experimental probability of rolling a 4?

4. **Reasoning** There are 50 cars in a used car lot. The experimental probability that a car in the lot has two doors is 0.12. How many cars in the lot have two doors?

Explain how you could simulate each situation. Then use your simulation to find each experimental probability.

5. A quiz consists of 12 true-or-false questions. If you guess the answers at random, what is the probability of getting at least 8 correct answers?

6. There are 15 multiple-choice questions on a test. Each question has four answer choices, and only one choice is correct. What is the probability of passing the test by guessing at least 7 of the 15 answers correctly?

7. **Writing** Explain why simulations are sometimes preferable to conducting actual trials.

Lesson 11-2

11-2 Practice (continued)
Probability

Find each of the following theoretical probabilities.

8. Your classmate rolls a fair number cube. What is the theoretical probability that she will roll a number greater than 4?

9. Shawn rolls a pair of fair number cubes. What is the theoretical probability that he will roll a sum of 3?

10. A box contains 24 green markers, 16 red markers, and 10 blue markers.
    a. P(red)
    b. P(green or blue)
    c. P(not green)

Use combinatorics to find the following theoretical probability.

11. Six of the 32 players on the football team are left-handed. There are 5 starting offensive linemen. What is the theoretical probability that 2 of the starting offensive linemen are left-handed?

Use area to find the following theoretical probabilities.

12. The floor in your friend's house covers 1400 ft². The floor in her bedroom is 14 ft by 10 ft. What is the probability that a randomly selected point on the floor of the house is in your friend's bedroom?

13. A garden is 15 ft by 12 ft. Tomatoes fill a 5 foot by 4 foot section of the garden. A squirrel leaps from a tree into the garden. What is the theoretical probability that the squirrel will land in the tomato section of the garden?

11-2 Standardized Test Prep
Probability

Gridded Response

For Exercises 1-3, find each theoretical probability based on one roll of two number cubes. Enter each answer in the grid as a whole percent.

1. $P(\text{sum } 9)$

2. $P(\text{one even, one odd})$

3. $P(\text{sum} \geq 12)$

For Exercises 4-5, find each theoretical probability based on one marble drawn at random from a bag of 14 red marbles, 10 pink marbles, 18 blue marbles, and 6 gold marbles. Enter each answer in the grid as a fraction in simplest form.

4. $P(\text{not pink})$

5. $P(\text{blue or gold})$

Answers

1.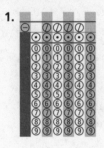

2.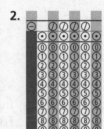

3.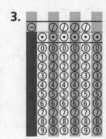

4.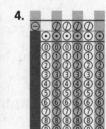

5.

Lesson 11-2

11-3 Think About a Plan

Probability of Multiple Events

Marbles A jar contains four blue marbles and two red marbles. Suppose you choose a marble at random, and do not replace it. Then you choose a second marble. Find the probability that you select a blue marble and then a red marble.

Understanding the Problem

1. How many marbles are blue?

2. How many marbles are red?

3. How many marbles are in the jar?

4. What is the problem asking you to determine?

   _____

   _____

Planning the Solution

5. What is the probability that you choose a blue marble from the jar?

6. Assuming you choose a blue marble and do not replace it, how many marbles of each color remain in the jar? What is the total number of marbles in the jar?

   _____

7. What is the probability that you now choose a red marble from the jar?

8. How can you find the probability that you select a blue marble and then a red

   marble? _____

   _____ .

Getting an Answer

9. What is the probability that you select a blue marble and then a red marble?

11-3 Practice
Probability of Multiple Events

Classify each pair of events as *dependent* or *independent*.

1. Roll a number cube. Then roll it again.

2. Pull a card from a deck of playing cards. Then pull a second card.

3. Randomly choose a student from your class. Then choose another student.

4. Flip a coin. Then spin a spinner.

Use the table shown below to answer the following questions.

Movie Collection		
	Video	**DVD**
Action	12	26
Comedy	14	8
Drama	4	16

5. You randomly pick a video and a DVD. What is the probability that you pick an action video and a comedy DVD?

6. Your friend randomly picks a video and a DVD. What is the probability that she picks a comedy video and an action DVD?

7. What is the probability of randomly picking a drama video and a comedy DVD?

8. **Writing** Explain the difference between independent events and dependent events.

11-3 Practice (continued) Form K

Probability of Multiple Events

Two fair number cubes are rolled. State whether the following events are mutually exclusive.

9. The sum is odd. The sum is less than 5. _____

10. The difference is 1. The sum is even. _____

11. The sum is a multiple of 4. The sum is odd. _____

Find the probability for the following mutually exclusive events.

12. Students can either participate in track and field or play baseball. About 13% of students participate in track and field. About 8% play baseball. What is the probability that a student chosen at random either participates in track and field or plays baseball?

13. About $\frac{1}{5}$ of a town's population has black hair. About $\frac{2}{7}$ of the population has blonde hair. What is the probability that a person chosen at random from this town will have either black hair or blonde hair?

Use the diagram at the right to answer the following questions.

14. Suppose you randomly select a shape from this circle. What is the probability that the shape is black or has five points?

15. What is the probability of randomly selecting a shape that is black or has four points?

11-3 Standardized Test Prep

Probability of Multiple Events

Multiple Choice

For Exercises 1–4, choose the correct letter.

A store display shows two red shirts, one blue shirt, and three shirts with red and white stripes. The display also shows two pairs of blue jeans, one pair of white pants, and one pair of white shorts.

1. What is the probability of randomly selecting an item with white or red on it?

(A) $\frac{1}{4}$ (B) $\frac{3}{10}$ (C) $\frac{1}{2}$ (D) $\frac{7}{10}$

2. What is the probability of randomly selecting two items and getting a pair of blue jeans, putting them back in the display, and then randomly selecting a blue shirt?

(F) $\frac{1}{50}$ (G) $\frac{1}{45}$ (H) $\frac{2}{10}$ (I) $\frac{3}{10}$

3. What is the probability of randomly selecting a complete outfit (one shirt and one pair of jeans, pants, or shorts) on two picks?

(A) $\frac{1}{24}$ (B) $\frac{1}{5}$ (C) $\frac{6}{25}$ (D) $\frac{4}{15}$

4. What is the probability of selecting an item with red or blue on it?

(F) $\frac{3}{20}$ (G) $\frac{3}{10}$ (H) $\frac{3}{5}$ (I) $\frac{4}{5}$

Short Response

5. There is a 50% chance of thunderstorms on Monday, a 50% chance on Tuesday, and a 50% chance on Wednesday. Assume these are independent events. What is the probability that there will be thunderstorms on Monday, Tuesday, and Wednesday? Show your work.

Lesson 11-3

11-4

Think About a Plan

Conditional Probability

Transportation You can take Bus 65 or Bus 79. You take the first bus that arrives. The probability that Bus 65 arrives first is 75%. There is a 40% chance that Bus 65 picks up passengers along the way. There is a 60% chance that Bus 79 picks up passengers. Your bus picked up passengers. What is the probability that it was Bus 65?

Understanding the Problem

1. What is the probability that Bus 65 arrives first?

2. What is the probability that Bus 65 picks up passengers?

3. What is the probability that Bus 79 picks up passengers?

4. What is the problem asking you to determine?

_____

Planning the Solution

5. Let B65 = Bus 65 arrived first, B79 = Bus 79 arrived first, P = passengers, NP = no passengers. What conditional probability are you looking for?

6. How can a tree diagram help you solve the problem?

_____

_____.

7. Write an equation you can use to find the probability that your bus was Bus 65.

Getting an Answer

8. Make a tree diagram for this problem.

9. Which two branches of the diagram show a bus picking up passengers?

10. What is the probability your bus was Bus 65?

11-4 Practice

Form K

Conditional Probability

Use the table to find each probability.

Guitars		
	Acoustic	**Electric**
Tan	78	42
Black	34	56
Blue	12	16

1. $P(\text{black} \mid \text{acoustic})$

$P(\text{black} \mid \text{acoustic}) = \frac{34}{124}$

$P(\text{black} \mid \text{acoustic}) = \boxed{}$

2. $P(\text{tan} \mid \text{electric})$

3. $P(\text{blue} \mid \text{electric})$

4. $P(\text{acoustic} \mid \text{tan})$

5. $P(\text{tan} \mid \text{acoustic})$

6. $P(\text{electric} \mid \text{blue})$

The following table shows national employment statistics. Use the table to find each probability.

Number of Men and Women in Different Occupations (thousands)			
	Professionals	**Sales People**	**Laborers**
Men	4190	2588	2951
Women	4747	3213	1432

Source: Equal Employment Opportunity Commission

7. $P(\text{male} \mid \text{professional})$

8. $P(\text{laborer} \mid \text{female})$

9. $P(\text{female} \mid \text{sales})$

10. $P(\text{professional} \mid \text{female})$

11. $P(\text{sales} \mid \text{male})$

12. $P(\text{male} \mid \text{laborer})$

Lesson 11-4

11-4 Practice (continued)
Conditional Probability

Form K

Use the Conditional Probability Formula and the table below to answer the following questions.

Students' Reading Preferences		
	Comic Books	Novels
Middle School	128	32
High School	86	98

13. What is the probability that a student prefers comic books, given that the student is in high school?

$$P(B \mid A) = \frac{P(A \text{ and } B)}{P(A)}$$

$P(\text{high school and comic books}) = \frac{86}{344}$ $P(\text{high school}) = \frac{184}{344}$

$P(\text{comic books} \mid \text{high school}) = \dfrac{\frac{86}{344}}{\frac{184}{344}} \approx \boxed{}$

14. What is the probability that a student prefers novels, given that the student is in middle school?

15. Writing Tony wants to know the probability that his classmate is left-handed, given that she is female. Should he use conditional probability? Explain why or why not.

Use a tree diagram to solve the following problem.

16. A car insurance company compiled the following information from a recent survey.

- 75% of drivers carefully follow the speed limit.
- Of the drivers who carefully follow the speed limit, 80% have never had an accident.
- Of the drivers who do not carefully follow the speed limit, 65% have never had an accident.

What is the probability that a driver does not carefully follow the speed limit and has never had an accident?

11-4 Standardized Test Prep

Conditional Probability

Multiple Choice

For Exercises 1–2, choose the correct letter.

A local bookstore classifies its books by type of reader, type of book, and cost. Use the table at the right for Exercises 1–2.

		< $10	$10
Child	Fiction	120	255
	Nonfiction	35	60
Adult	Fiction	200	110
	Nonfiction	75	150

1. What is the probability that a book selected at random is a child's book, given that it costs $15?

Ⓐ $\frac{315}{1005}$ Ⓑ $\frac{470}{1005}$ Ⓒ $\frac{315}{575}$ Ⓓ $\frac{470}{575}$

2. What is the probability that a book selected at random is fiction, given that it costs $6?

Ⓕ $\frac{320}{1005}$ Ⓖ $\frac{430}{1005}$ Ⓗ $\frac{120}{430}$ Ⓘ $\frac{320}{430}$

Extended Response

3. Of the photographs produced in one day at a photo shop, 25% are black-and-white, and the rest are in color. Portraits make up 65% of the black-and-white photos and 45% of the color photos. Let B, C, P, and N represent black-and-white, color, portrait, and not a portrait, respectively. Draw a tree diagram to represent this situation. What is the probability that a photo chosen at random is not a portrait? Show your work.

11-5 Think About a Plan

Analyzing Data

Meteorology On May 3, 1999, 59 tornadoes hit Oklahoma in the largest tornado outbreak ever recorded in the state. Sixteen of these were classified as strong (F2 or F3) or violent (F4 or F5).

a. Make a box-and-whisker plot of the data for length of path.
b. Identify the outliers. Remove them from the data set and make a revised box-and-whisker plot.
c. **Writing** How does the removal of the outliers affect the box-and-whisker plot? How does it affect the median of the data set?

Major Tornadoes in Oklahoma, May 3, 1999

Length of path (miles)	Intensity
6	F3
9	F3
4	F2
37	F5
7	F2
12	F3
8	F2
7	F2
15	F4
39	F4
1	F2
22	F3
15	F3
8	F2
13	F3
2	F2

1. Arrange the data in increasing order.

   _____

2. Minimum value = [   ] Q_1 = [   ]

   Maximum value = [   ] Q_2 = [   ]

                                        Q_3 = [   ]

3. Use your previous answers to make a box-and-whisker plot of the data for length of path.

4. How can you identify the outliers in the data set?

   _____

   _____.

5. What are the outliers in the data set? _____

6. Remove the outliers from the data set and make a revised box-and-whisker plot.

7. How does the removal of the outliers affect the box-and-whisker plot?

   _____

   _____.

8. How does the removal of the outliers affect the median of the data set?

   _____.

11-5 Practice
Analyzing Data

Form K

Find the mean, median, and mode of the following data set.

Points Per Game					
	Game 1	Game 2	Game 3	Game 4	Game 5
Points	24	17	15	30	24

1. mean **2.** median **3.** mode

$24 + 17 + 15 + 30 + 24 = 110$

$110 \div 5 =$ ☐

Identify the outlier in the following data set. Then find the mean, median, and mode.

Height of Students					
	Sue	Dalia	Ling	Roberto	Eleanore	Cayden
Height (in.)	58	60	74	58	62	64

4. outlier **5.** mean **6.** median **7.** mode

8. Reasoning Which measure of central tendency would be most affected by removing the outlier from the above data set? Explain your reasoning.

9. Compare the following sets of data.

Great Lakes Coastal Water Temperatures (°F)												
	Jan	Feb	Mar	Apr	May	Jun	Jul	Aug	Sep	Oct	Nov	Dec
Buffalo, NY	34	28	33	46	56	65	72	70	61	50	44	38
Oswego, NY	49	48	48	49	52	57	62	65	64	62	58	54

Lesson 11-5

11-5 Practice (continued)
Analyzing Data

Make a box-and-whisker plot for each set of values.

10. 15, 19, 24, 16, 12, 18, 20, 22, 16, 17   **11.** 26, 32, 27, 36, 28, 30, 31, 28

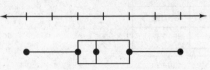

Find the following percentiles of the data set displayed below.

27, 28, 29, 29, 30, 31, 32, 33, 34, 35,

36, 36, 37, 38, 39, 40, 40, 41, 42, 43

12. 45th percentile   **13.** 70th percentile   **14.** 25th percentile

15. 95th percentile   **16.** 80th percentile   **17.** 15th percentile

18. Error Analysis Your friend calculated the tenth percentile of the data set
shown above and got 35. What error did your friend make? What is the correct
answer?

19. Open-Ended Describe a situation in which the median would be a more
useful measure of central tendency than the mean.

11-5

Standardized Test Prep
Analyzing Data

Multiple Choice

For Exercises 1–5, choose the correct letter. Use the data set below.

Day	9/1	9/2	9/3	9/4	9/5	9/6	9/7	9/8	9/9	9/10	9/11	9/12
Deliveries	14	15	19	15	15	16	19	20	21	29	16	17

1. What is the mean of the data set?

   Ⓐ 12   Ⓑ 15   Ⓒ 16.5   Ⓓ 18

2. How many modes does the data set have?

   Ⓕ 0   Ⓖ 1   Ⓗ 2   Ⓘ 3

3. What is the interquartile range of the data?

   Ⓐ 1.5   Ⓑ 3   Ⓒ 4.5   Ⓓ 15

4. What is the median value of the data set *without the outlier*?

   Ⓕ 16   Ⓖ 17   Ⓗ 19   Ⓘ 29

5. What value is at the 50th percentile?

   Ⓐ 16   Ⓑ 17   Ⓒ 19   Ⓓ 20

Short Response

6. Make a box-and-whisker plot of the data set. Label the median, minimum, maximum, first quartile, and third quartile.

11-6 Think About a Plan

Standard Deviation

Energy The data for daily energy usage of a small town during ten days in January is shown.

83.8 MWh	87.1 MWh	92.5 MWh	80.6 MWh	82.4 MWh
77.6 MWh	78.9 MWh	78.2 MWh	81.8 MWh	80.1 MWh

a. Find the mean and the standard deviation of the data.

b. How many values in the data set fall within one standard deviation of the mean? Within two standard deviations? Within three standard deviations?

Know

1. The data values are: _____

2. The mean of a set of data is [_____].

3. The standard deviation of a set of n data values is [_____].

Need

4. To solve the problem I need to find:

_____

_____ .

Plan

5. The mean of the data is [_____]. The standard deviation of the data is [_____].

6. Plot the data values on a number line. Mark off intervals of the standard deviation on either side of the mean.

7. How many values in the data set fall within one standard deviation of the mean? Within two standard deviations? Within three standard deviations?

11-6 **Practice**
Standard Deviation

Find the mean, variance, and standard deviation for each data set.

1. 6, 13, 12, 9, 10

Mean	**Variance**	**Standard Deviation**
$\bar{x} = 50 \div 5 = 10$		$\sigma = \sqrt{\sigma^2} = \sqrt{6} \approx 2.4$

x	$\bar{x}$	$x - \bar{x}$	$(x - \bar{x})^2$
6	10	−4	16
13	10	3	9
12	10	2	4
9	10	−1	1
10	10	0	0

$$\sigma^2 = \frac{\sum (x - \bar{x})^2}{n} = \frac{30}{5} = 6$$

2. 8, 16, 12, 15, 4   **3.** 25, 18, 20, 19, 22, 16   **4.** 27, 34, 45, 30, 26, 42

Use a graphing calculator to solve the following problems.

5. The most recent test scores for a math class are displayed in the table below. What are the mean and the standard deviation for this data set?

Student	1	2	3	4	5	6	7	8	9	10	11	12	13	14	15
Score	77	86	79	94	65	82	76	97	65	77	89	78	84	79	88

6. Your sister's bowling scores for the last 12 games are displayed in the table below. What are the mean and standard deviation for this data?

Game	1	2	3	4	5	6	7	8	9	10	11	12
Score	212	187	176	205	193	229	201	175	203	216	227	235

11-6 Practice (continued)
Standard Deviation

Form K

Determine the whole number of standard deviations that include all of the following data values.

7. You brother is buying his textbooks for his first semester of college. The price of each of his books is shown in the table below. The mean of the data set is $65.85, and the standard deviation is about 36. Within how many standard deviations of the mean do all of the prices fall? .

Book	1	2	3	4	5	6
Price	$25.60	$57.00	$38.25	$126.40	$84.00	$63.85

8. The table below shows the weights of the five starting players on a basketball team. Within how many standard deviations of the mean do all of the weights fall?

Player	1	2	3	4	5
Weight (lb)	146	189	246	178	203

9. **Open-Ended** Describe an example of how it can be useful to know the standard deviation of a data set.

10. **Writing** How is standard deviation similar to range and interquartile range?

11. **Error Analysis** Your classmate calculated the standard deviation of the data set shown below and got 46.53. What error did she make? What is the correct standard deviation?

Day	Mon	Tue	Wed	Thu	Fri	Sat	Sun
High Temperature (°F)	76°	82°	63°	69°	79°	84°	75°

288

11-6

Standardized Test Prep

Standard Deviation

Multiple Choice

For Exercises 1–4, choose the correct letter.

1. Of the 25 students who take a standardized test, the minimum score is 98 and the maximum score is 472. The mean score is 216, and the standard deviation is 52. What is the number of standard deviations that includes all the data values?

   (A) 3   (B) 5   (C) 8   (D) 9

2. What is the standard deviation of the data set below?
   87 21 90 43 54 23 123 110 90 44 50

   (F) 33.1   (G) 47.0   (H) 66.8   (I) 89.0

3. A data set has a mean of 255 and a standard deviation of 12. All the data values are within two standard deviations of the mean. Which could be the maximum value of the data?

   (A) 232   (B) 244   (C) 268   (D) 280

4. The scores on a math test are:
   67 69 71 75 78 78 83 85 85 85 85 86 87 89 92 95 98 98 98 100.
   Within how many standard deviations of the mean is a score of 100?

   (F) 2   (G) 3   (H) 10   (I) 15

Short Response

5. The ages of students in a club are:
   13 17 18 15 16 14 15 18 17 16 15 16 13.
   Calculate the mean and standard deviation. What is the number of standard deviations that includes all the data values? Show your work.

11-7 Think About a Plan

Samples and Surveys

Entertainment A magazine publisher mails a survey to every tenth person on a subscriber list that is alphabetized by last name. The survey asks for three favorite leisure-time activities. What sampling method is the survey using? Identify any bias in the sampling method.

Know

1. The company sending out the survey is a _____.

2. The surveys are mailed to _____
   _____.

3. The survey asks for _____.

Need

4. To solve the problem I need to find:

   _____

   _____.

Plan

5. What sampling method is the survey using? _____

6. Do the people who receive the survey represent the general population? Explain.

   _____

   _____.

7. Do the people who return the survey represent the general population? Explain.

   _____

   _____.

8. Is there any bias in the sampling method? Explain.

   _____

   _____

   _____

   _____.

11-7 Practice

Form K

Samples and Surveys

Identify the sampling methods used in each of the following situations. Then state whether the sampling method has any bias.

1. A television station invites viewers to call in and name their favorite game show.

2. A school principal gathers an alphabetical list of all the students at her school. Then she selects every 15th student to take a survey about the cafeteria's lunch menu.

3. A reporter asks people leaving a movie theater to take a survey about their television viewing habits.

4. A psychologist uses a computer program to randomly select names from a list of students at a university. The members of the sample will take a survey about student housing at the university.

5. **Writing** A group of television producers plans to survey 10-year-olds to determine their opinions about a new cartoon. Describe a sampling method that could be used to gather a biased sample in this situation. Then describe a method to gather an unbiased sample.

6. **Multiple Choice** A school psychologist sits in a school cafeteria and takes notes on students' behavior while they eat lunch. Which of the following types of studies is the researcher conducting?

   Ⓐ controlled experiment Ⓑ observational study Ⓒ survey

7. **Open-Ended** Your classmate is randomly selecting a sample of students at his high school to take a survey. You say that your classmate's sample is biased because it only contains high-school students. In what case might you be wrong?

Lesson 11-7

11-7 Practice (continued)
Samples and Surveys

Form K

Identify and describe the bias in the following survey questions.

8. Isn't summer a much more pleasant season than winter?

9. Are college students better off studying useful subjects such as math or impractical subjects such as art history?

10. Do you believe that this year's class field trip was fun and educational?

11. Do you agree that Mrs. Regis's class is more interesting than Mr. Wright's class?

Rewrite the following survey questions so that they are no longer biased.

12. Do you prefer the excitement of rock and roll or the tediousness of classical music?

13. Would you agree that dogs make better pets than cats?

14. Do you believe that Mayor Johnson is friendly and effective?

15. **Writing** A supervisor wants to determine what percent of people in his office building believe it is important to have an Internet connection at home. What sampling method can he use to gather an unbiased sample? What is an example of a survey question that is likely to yield unbiased information?

11-7 Standardized Test Prep

Samples and Surveys

Multiple Choice

For Exercises 1–4, choose the correct letter.

1. The School Dance Committee conducts a survey to find what type of music students would like to hear at the next dance. Which is an example of a random sample?

   Ⓐ Call 20% of the people in the senior class directory.

   Ⓑ Interview every 10th student as they enter the school.

   Ⓒ Ask every 5th person leaving a school orchestra concert.

   Ⓓ Set up a jazz website where students can list their 3 favorite songs.

2. Which is a characteristic of a biased survey question?

   Ⓕ It is about a controversial issue.   Ⓗ It produces inaccurate results.

   Ⓖ It is about a well-known person.   Ⓘ It is about a very unpopular person.

3. In a survey, 36% of 1600 students said they spent at least 5 h online during the past week. What is the approximate margin of error for this sample?

   Ⓐ ± 0.6%   Ⓑ ±2.5%   Ⓒ ± 6%   Ⓓ ± 25%

4. A newspaper surveys a sample of 2500 people and finds that 64% agree with a certain political position. What interval is most likely to contain the percentage of the total population who agree with the position.

   Ⓕ 62−66%   Ⓖ 62−64%   Ⓗ 63−65%   Ⓘ 64−66%

Short Response

5. A city council surveys a sample of citizens about a new law. The survey finds that 38% of citizens think the law should be repealed. The survey has a margin of error of about 8%. About how many people did the council survey? Show your work.

11-8 Think About a Plan

Binomial Distributions

Weather A scientist hopes to launch a weather balloon on one of the next three mornings. For each morning, there is a 40% chance of suitable weather. What is the probability that there will be at least one morning with suitable weather?

Understanding the Problem

1. What is the probability that a morning will have suitable weather?

2. What is the probability that a morning will have unsuitable weather?

3. How many chances does the scientist have to launch the balloon?

4. What is the problem asking you to determine?

_____

_____

Planning the Solution

5. What binomial can help you find the binomial distribution for this problem?

6. Expand your binomial.

7. What should you substitute for the variables in your binomial expansion?

_____

8. Which terms of your binomial expansion do you need to solve the problem?

Explain._____

_____

_____.

Getting an Answer

9. Use your binomial expansion to find the probability that there will be at least one morning with suitable weather.

11-8 Practice

Form K

Binomial Distributions

Find the probability of x successes in n trials for the given probability of success p on each trial.

1. $x = 5, n = 8, p = 0.6$ **2.** $x = 3, n = 9, p = 0.5$ **3.** $x = 6, n = 12, p = 0.3$

$P(x) = {}_nC_x\, p^x q^{n-x}$

$P(5) = {}_8C_5 (0.6)^5 (0.4)^3$

$P(5) = 56(0.6)^5 (0.4)^3$

$P(5) \approx \boxed{}$

4. $x = 2, n = 7, p = 0.25$ **5.** $x = 4, n = 10, p = 0.45$ **6.** $x = 5, n = 14, p = 0.2$

7. At a pet shop, 30% of the cats have short hair. The owner of the pet shop will randomly choose 6 cats to take to an animal show. What is the probability that 3 of the cats will have short hair?

8. Your brother baked a large batch of cookies. He put chocolate chips in 45% of the cookies. He randomly selects 10 cookies to give to a friend. What is the probability that 6 of the cookies contain chocolate chips?

9. Reasoning Does rolling a number cube 10 times fit all of the conditions for a binomial experiment? Explain why or why not.

10. Multiple Choice Which of the following is not one of the conditions for a binomial experiment?

    Ⓐ There is a fixed number of trials.

    Ⓑ Each trial has two possible outcomes.

    Ⓒ The trials are dependent.

    Ⓓ The probability of each outcome is constant throughout the trials.

Expand each binomial.

11. $(2x + y)^4$

     $= {}_4C_0(2x)^4 + {}_4C_1(2x)^3y + {}_4C_2(2x)^2y^2$

        $+ {}_4C_3 2xy^3 + {}_4C_4 y^4$

     $= 16x^4 + 32x^3y + 24x^2y^2 + 8xy^3 + y^4$

12. $(x + y)^3$

13. $(c + 3d)^5$

14. $(m + 2n)^4$

Find the indicated term of each binomial expansion.

15. fourth term of $(2x + 2y)^5$ **16.** second term of $(m + n)^6$ **17.** third term of $(3x + y)^5$

     $= {}_5C_3(2x)^2(2y)^3$

     $= 10(4x^2)(8y^3)$

Use the binomial expansion of $(p + q)^n$ to solve each of the following problems.

18. Your friend is shopping at a used CD store. Of all the used CDs in the store, 10% of them are badly scratched. She buys 5 used CDs.
   a. What is the probability that at least 2 of your friend's CDs are badly scratched?
   b. What is the probability that at least 4 of the CDs are badly scratched?
   c. What is the probability that none of the CDs are badly scratched?

11-8 Standardized Test Prep

Binomial Distributions

Multiple Choice

For Exercises 1–5, choose the correct letter.

1. The probability that a newborn baby at a certain hospital is male is 50%. What is the probability that exactly 2 of 3 babies born in the hospital on any day are male?

   Ⓐ 37.5%   Ⓑ 50%   Ⓒ 66.7%   Ⓓ 75%

2. The probability that a newborn baby at the hospital is female is 50%. What is the probability that at least 2 babies of 3 children born on a certain day are female?

   Ⓕ 33.3%   Ⓖ 37.5%   Ⓗ 50%   Ⓘ 66.7%

3. What is the fifth term of the expansion of $(2x - y)^8$?

   Ⓐ $-1792x^5y^3$ Ⓑ $-448x^3y^5$ Ⓒ $256x^4y^4$ Ⓓ $1120x^4y^4$

4. A poll shows that 30% of voters favor an earlier curfew. Find the probability that all of five voters chosen at random favor an earlier curfew.

   Ⓕ 0.24%   Ⓖ 1.5%   Ⓗ 4.1%   Ⓘ 16.7%

5. The probability that a machine part is defective is 10%. Find the probability that no more than 2 out of 12 parts tested are defective.

   Ⓐ 28%   Ⓑ 66%   Ⓒ 89%   Ⓓ 98%

Short Response

6. A scientist runs an experiment 4 times. Each run has a 65% chance of success. Calculate and graph the distribution of binomial probabilities for the experiment.

Lesson 11-8

11-9 Think About a Plan

Normal Distributions

Agriculture To win a prize, a tomato must be greater than 4 in. in diameter. The diameters of a crop of tomatoes grown in a special soil are normally distributed, with a mean of 3.2 in. and a standard deviation of 0.4 in. What is the probability that a tomato grown in the special soil will be a winner?

Know

1. A tomato must have a diameter greater than [   ] to win a prize.

2. The mean diameter of the crop of tomatoes is [   ].

3. The standard deviation of the diameters of the crop of tomatoes is [   ].

Need

4. To solve the problem I need to find:

   _____

   _____.

Plan

5. Draw a normal curve. Label the mean and intervals that are multiples of the standard deviation from the mean.

6. What is the percent of the crop with diameters that are greater than the mean?

7. What is the percent of the crop with diameters that are greater than the mean and less than 4 in.? How do you know? _____

   _____.

8. How can you find the percent of the crop with diameters greater than 4 in.?

   _____

   _____.

9. What is the probability that a tomato grown in the special soil will be a winner?

11-9 Practice

Form K

Normal Distributions

Identify each of the following distributions as *positively skewed, negatively skewed,* or *normally distributed.*

1.
2.
3.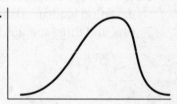

The bar graph below displays the heights of the students at a high school. Use the graph to answer the following questions.

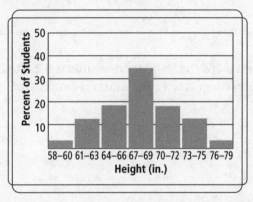

4. Approximately what percent of students are between 61 in. and 67 in. tall?

5. Approximately what percent of students are between 64 in. and 75 in. tall?

6. Approximately what percent of students are between 70 in. and 79 in. tall?

7. Reasoning Your mother has a rose garden. Every day, she sprays fertilizer on the roses in one section of the garden. Do you expect that the heights of the rose bushes in her garden are normally distributed? Explain why or why not.

11-9 Practice (continued)   Form K
Normal Distributions

Sketch a normal curve to represent each of the following normal distributions.

8. The average weight of a tomato in a tomato garden is 10 oz. The standard deviation is 1.6 oz. Sketch a normal curve showing the tomato weights at one, two, and three standard deviations from the mean.

9. The average score on a math test is 76. The standard deviation is 6.2. Sketch a normal curve showing the test scores at one, two, and three standard deviations from the mean.

Draw a normal curve to solve the following problems.

10. A local bakery makes chocolate chip cookies. The number of chocolate chips in the cookies is approximately normally distributed, with mean 11.4 and standard deviation 1.3. What percent of the cookies have between 8.8 and 14 chocolate chips?

11. The bakery described in Exercise 10 sold 200 chocolate chip cookies. How many of the cookies had less than 8.8 chocolate chips?

12. **Reasoning** One of the cookies sold by the bakery had 18 chocolate chips. Would this be considered an outlier? Explain why or why not.

11-9 Standardized Test Prep

Normal Distributions

Multiple Choice

For Exercises 1–5, choose the correct letter.

1. The mean number of pairs of shoes sold daily by a shoe store is 36, with a standard deviation of 3. On what percent of days would you expect the store to sell from 33 to 42 pairs of shoes?

   A 13.5%   B 50%   C 68%   D 81.5%

2. What is the standard deviation for the normal distribution shown at the right?

   F 60   H 120
   G 360   I 676

3. A normal distribution has a mean of 700 and a standard deviation of 35. What is the probability that a value selected at random is at most 630?

   A 0.0235   B 0.025   C 0.700   D 0.975

4. Scores on an exam are distributed normally with a mean of 76 and a standard deviation of 10. Out of 230 tests, about how many students score above 96?

   F 2   G 3   H 6   I 8

5. A hardware store sells bags of mixed nails. The number of nails of a given length is distributed normally with a mean length of 5 in. and a standard deviation of 0.03 in. About how many nails in a bag of 120 are between 4.97 in. and 5.03 in. long?

   A 34   B 41   C 68   D 82

Short Response

6. The heights of the girls in a school choir are distributed normally, with a mean of 64 and a standard deviation of 1.75. If 38 girls are between 60.5 in. and 67.5 in. tall, how many girls are in the choir? Show your work.

12-1 Think About a Plan

Adding and Subtracting Matrices

Data Analysis Refer to the table.
  a. Find the total number of people participating in each activity.
  b. Find the difference between the numbers of males and females in each activity.
  c. **Reasoning** In part (b), does the order of the matrices matter? Explain.

U.S. Participation in Selected Leisure Activities (millions)

Activity	Male	Female
Movies	59.2	65.4
Exercise Programs	54.3	59.0
Sports Events	40.5	31.1
Home Improvement	45.4	41.8

Source: U.S. National Endowment for the Arts

1. Write matrices to show the information from the table.

$M =$ ☐ $F =$ ☐

2. Write a matrix equation to find the number of people, in millions, participating in each activity.

3. Solve the matrix equation. How many million people participate in each activity?

   $T =$ ☐

   Movies ☐   Exercise Programs ☐

   Sports Events ☐   Home Improvement ☐

4. Write a matrix equation to find the difference, in millions, between the number of males and females in each activity.

5. Solve the matrix equation. What is the difference, in millions, between the number of males and females in each activity?

   $T =$ ☐

   Movies ☐   Exercise Programs ☐

   Sports Events ☐   Home Improvement ☐

6. Does the order of the matrices matter? Explain. _____

   _____

   _____

   _____.

12-1 Practice

Adding and Subtracting Matrices

Form K

Find each sum or difference.

To start, add or subtract corresponding elements.

1. $\begin{bmatrix} 2 & 4 \\ 5 & -7 \end{bmatrix} + \begin{bmatrix} -4 & -1 \\ 3 & 5 \end{bmatrix}$

2. $\begin{bmatrix} 5 & 3 \\ 8 & 2 \end{bmatrix} - \begin{bmatrix} 1 & 7 \\ 4 & -3 \end{bmatrix}$

3. $\begin{bmatrix} -3 & 7 & 1 \\ 4 & 3 & -2 \end{bmatrix} + \begin{bmatrix} 5 & 2 & -6 \\ -4 & 6 & 9 \end{bmatrix}$

$\begin{bmatrix} 2 + (-4) & 4 + (-1) \\ 5 + 3 & -7 + 5 \end{bmatrix}$

4. $\begin{bmatrix} 2 & -2 & 6 \\ -4 & 3 & 8 \end{bmatrix} - \begin{bmatrix} 5 & 3 & 1 \\ 2 & 7 & 4 \end{bmatrix}$

5. $\begin{bmatrix} 9 & -6 \\ -2 & 5 \\ 8 & -1 \end{bmatrix} + \begin{bmatrix} -4 & 7 \\ 5 & 3 \\ 1 & 6 \end{bmatrix}$

6. $\begin{bmatrix} 2 & 4 \\ 8 & 5 \end{bmatrix} - \begin{bmatrix} 6 & 9 \\ 3 & 2 \end{bmatrix}$

Solve each matrix equation.

To start, use the Addition Property of Equality to isolate the variable matrix.

7. $\begin{bmatrix} 7 & -1 \\ 3 & 5 \end{bmatrix} + X = \begin{bmatrix} 4 & 5 \\ 8 & 2 \end{bmatrix}$

8. $\begin{bmatrix} 2 & 7 \\ 9 & -3 \end{bmatrix} - X = \begin{bmatrix} -5 & 1 \\ 3 & 4 \end{bmatrix}$

9. $X - \begin{bmatrix} 2 & 8 \\ -1 & 5 \end{bmatrix} = \begin{bmatrix} 3 & -6 \\ 4 & 2 \end{bmatrix}$

$X = \begin{bmatrix} 4 - 7 & 5 - (-1) \\ 8 - 3 & 2 - 5 \end{bmatrix}$

10. **Error Analysis** Maria added $\begin{bmatrix} 5 & 9 \\ 1 & -3 \end{bmatrix} + \begin{bmatrix} -2 & -5 \\ 6 & 3 \end{bmatrix}$ and found a sum of $\begin{bmatrix} 0 & 7 \\ 4 & 3 \end{bmatrix}$. What error did Maria make, and what is the correct sum?

Lesson 12-1

12-1 Practice (continued)   Form K
Adding and Subtracting Matrices

Find each sum.

11. $\begin{bmatrix} 3 & -1 \\ -5 & 8 \end{bmatrix} + \begin{bmatrix} -3 & 1 \\ 5 & -8 \end{bmatrix}$ **12.** $\begin{bmatrix} -4 & 9 \\ -7 & 5 \end{bmatrix} + \begin{bmatrix} 0 & 0 \\ 0 & 0 \end{bmatrix}$ **13.** $\begin{bmatrix} 7 & 4 \\ 5 & -2 \end{bmatrix} + \begin{bmatrix} -7 & -4 \\ -5 & 2 \end{bmatrix}$

Find the value of each variable.

14. $\begin{bmatrix} 3 & 4 \\ -1 & 6 \end{bmatrix} + \begin{bmatrix} 5 & -5 \\ 7 & -3 \end{bmatrix} = \begin{bmatrix} 8 & x \\ y & z \end{bmatrix}$ **15.** $\begin{bmatrix} 2x & 7 \\ -4 & 3y - 1 \end{bmatrix} = \begin{bmatrix} 18 & 7 \\ -4 & 8 \end{bmatrix}$

$x = 4 + (-5) = \boxed{}$

$y = -1 + 7 = \boxed{}$

$z = 6 + (-3) = \boxed{}$

16. $\begin{bmatrix} -8 & 3 & -5 \\ 1 & -7 & -6 \end{bmatrix} = \begin{bmatrix} 5x + 2 & 3 & 2 - y \\ 1 & 2z + 1 & -6 \end{bmatrix}$ **17.** $\begin{bmatrix} 13 & 4b + 3 \\ -5a & -6 \end{bmatrix} = \begin{bmatrix} 3c + 1 & 11 \\ -25 & -2c + 2 \end{bmatrix}$

18. Writing Describe the Commutative and Associative Properties of Matrix Addition. How are these properties similar to the Commutative and Associative Properties of Real-Number Addition?

19. Reasoning Is it possible to find the value of x in the following equation? Why or why not?

$$\begin{bmatrix} 2x & -1 \\ 4 & -5 \end{bmatrix} = \begin{bmatrix} 5x - 4 & -1 \\ 4 & -5 \end{bmatrix}$$

12-1 Standardized Test Prep

Adding and Subtracting Matrices

Multiple Choice

For Exercises 1–4, choose the correct letter.

1. What matrix is equal to the difference $\begin{bmatrix} 5 & 9 & -3 \\ 6 & -2 & 1 \end{bmatrix} - \begin{bmatrix} 6 & 4 & 2 \\ 0 & 3 & 5 \end{bmatrix}$?

Ⓐ $\begin{bmatrix} -1 & -5 & -5 \\ -6 & -5 & -4 \end{bmatrix}$ Ⓑ $\begin{bmatrix} 1 & -5 & 5 \\ -6 & 5 & 4 \end{bmatrix}$ Ⓒ $\begin{bmatrix} -1 & 5 & -5 \\ 6 & -5 & -4 \end{bmatrix}$ Ⓓ $\begin{bmatrix} 1 & 5 & 5 \\ 6 & 5 & 4 \end{bmatrix}$

2. Which matrix is equivalent to X in the equation $\begin{bmatrix} 4 & 0 \\ 1 & -2 \end{bmatrix} + X = \begin{bmatrix} -2 & 0 \\ 1 & 4 \end{bmatrix}$

Ⓕ $\begin{bmatrix} -6 & 0 \\ 0 & 6 \end{bmatrix}$ Ⓖ $\begin{bmatrix} 2 & 0 \\ 0 & 2 \end{bmatrix}$ Ⓗ $\begin{bmatrix} 2 & 0 \\ 2 & 2 \end{bmatrix}$ Ⓘ $\begin{bmatrix} 6 & 0 \\ 0 & -6 \end{bmatrix}$

3. Which matrix is equivalent to P in the equation $\begin{bmatrix} 7 & 8 \\ 9 & 10 \\ 11 & 12 \end{bmatrix} - P = \begin{bmatrix} 0 & 0 \\ 0 & 0 \\ 0 & 0 \end{bmatrix}$

Ⓐ $\begin{bmatrix} 0 & 0 \\ 0 & 0 \\ 0 & 0 \end{bmatrix}$ Ⓑ $\begin{bmatrix} -1 & -1 \\ -1 & -1 \\ -1 & -1 \end{bmatrix}$ Ⓒ $\begin{bmatrix} -7 & -8 \\ -9 & -10 \\ -11 & -12 \end{bmatrix}$ Ⓓ $\begin{bmatrix} 7 & 8 \\ 9 & 10 \\ 11 & 12 \end{bmatrix}$

4. Let $R + S = \begin{bmatrix} 0 & 0 & 0 & 0 \\ 0 & 0 & 0 & 0 \end{bmatrix}$. If $R = \begin{bmatrix} -3 & 2 & 9 \\ 7 & 6 & -4 \end{bmatrix}$, which matrix is equivalent to S?

Ⓕ $\begin{bmatrix} -3 & 2 & 9 \\ 7 & 6 & -4 \end{bmatrix}$ Ⓖ $\begin{bmatrix} -1 & -1 & -1 \\ -1 & -1 & -1 \end{bmatrix}$ Ⓗ $\begin{bmatrix} 3 & -2 & -9 \\ -7 & -6 & 4 \end{bmatrix}$ Ⓘ $\begin{bmatrix} 0 & 0 & 0 \\ 0 & 0 & 0 \end{bmatrix}$

Short Response

5. If $\begin{bmatrix} 8 & 2x - 1 \\ 2y + 1 & 3 \end{bmatrix} = \begin{bmatrix} 8 & -7 \\ y & -x \end{bmatrix}$, what values of x and y make the equation true? Show your work.

12-2 Think About a Plan

Matrix Multiplication

Sport Two teams are competing in a track meet. Points for individual events are awarded as follows: 5 points for first place, 3 points for second place, and 1 point for third place. Points for team relays are awarded as follows: 5 points for first place and no points for second place.

a. Use matrix operations to determine the score in the track meet.

b. Who would win if the scoring was changed to 5 points for first place, 2 points for second place, and 1 point for third place in each individual event with relay scoring remaining 5 points for first place?

Team	Individual Events			Relays	
	First	Second	Third	First	Second
West River	8	5	2	8	5
River's Edge	6	9	12	6	9

Know

1. _____

Need

2. To solve the problem I need to: _____

_____ .

Plan

3. Write the number of wins as a 2 × 5 matrix and the original and alternate point values as 5 × 1 matrices.

4. Use matrix multiplication to find the original total team scores and the alternate total team scores for the track meet.

5. What was the score in the track meet? _____

6. Who would win if the scoring were changed? _____

12-2 **Practice**
Matrix Multiplication

Let $A = \begin{bmatrix} 2 & -7 \\ -5 & 3 \end{bmatrix}$ and $B = \begin{bmatrix} -6 & 4 \\ 1 & -11 \end{bmatrix}$. **Find each product and each sum.**

1. $2A$ **2.** $5B$ **3.** $3A + 4B$

$$2\begin{bmatrix} 2 & -7 \\ -5 & 3 \end{bmatrix} = \begin{bmatrix} 2(2) & 9(-7) \\ 2(-5) & 2(3) \end{bmatrix}$$

Solve each matrix equation.

To start, use the Subtraction Property of Equality to isolate the variable matrix.

4. $2X + \begin{bmatrix} 4 & -5 \\ 1 & -12 \end{bmatrix} = \begin{bmatrix} 10 & 1 \\ -7 & -2 \end{bmatrix}$ **5.** $4\begin{bmatrix} -2 & 4 \\ 3 & -1 \end{bmatrix} - \frac{1}{2}X = \begin{bmatrix} 3 & 9 \\ -2 & 6 \end{bmatrix}$

$\qquad 2X = \begin{bmatrix} 6 & 6 \\ -8 & 10 \end{bmatrix}$

6. $5\begin{bmatrix} 1 & 5 \\ 4 & 3 \end{bmatrix} + 3X = \begin{bmatrix} 14 & 22 \\ 8 & 18 \end{bmatrix}$ **7.** $\frac{1}{4}X + \begin{bmatrix} 3 & -1 \\ -5 & 7 \end{bmatrix} = \begin{bmatrix} 8 & 5 \\ -8 & 16 \end{bmatrix}$

8. Open-Ended Create an example to demonstrate that the Associative Property applies to scalar multiplication.

12-2 Practice (continued)   Form K
Matrix Multiplication

Find each product.

To start, find the element in the first row and first column of the product matrix.

9. $\begin{bmatrix} 4 & -2 \\ -3 & 7 \end{bmatrix}\begin{bmatrix} 3 & 6 \\ 1 & -5 \end{bmatrix}$

10. $\begin{bmatrix} 5 & 3 \\ -2 & 0 \end{bmatrix}\begin{bmatrix} 2 & -3 \\ -1 & 4 \end{bmatrix}$

$4(6) + (-2)(1) = 10 \rightarrow \begin{bmatrix} 10 & \\ & \end{bmatrix}$

$4(6) + (-2)(-5) = 34 \rightarrow \begin{bmatrix} 10 & 34 \\ & \end{bmatrix}$

$(-3)(3) + 7(1) = -2 \rightarrow \begin{bmatrix} 10 & 34 \\ -2 & \end{bmatrix}$

$(-3)(6) + 7(-5) = -53 \rightarrow \begin{bmatrix} \Box & \Box \\ \Box & \Box \end{bmatrix}$

11. $\begin{bmatrix} 2 & 5 \end{bmatrix}\begin{bmatrix} -1 & 3 \\ 4 & 7 \end{bmatrix}$

12. $\begin{bmatrix} 6 & -2 \\ -3 & 0 \end{bmatrix}\begin{bmatrix} 1 & 5 \\ 8 & 3 \end{bmatrix}$

Determine whether the product exists.

$A = \begin{bmatrix} 2 & 0 \\ -6 & 9 \end{bmatrix}$ $B = \begin{bmatrix} -2 \\ 6 \end{bmatrix}$ $C = \begin{bmatrix} 1 & -3 \\ 13 & -5 \end{bmatrix}$ $D = \begin{bmatrix} -7 & 5 \end{bmatrix}$

13. AC **14.** BA **15.** DC **16.** BD

17. The table below shows the number of small, medium, large, and extra-large drinks sold at two snack stands in an hour. The small drinks cost $1.00, the medium drinks cost $1.50, the large drinks cost $2.00, and the extra-large drinks cost $2.50. Using matrix multiplication, what was the sales total for each snack stand?

	Small	Medium	Large	Extra Large
Stand 1	16	8	10	9
Stand 2	6	12	9	18

12-2 Standardized Test Prep

Matrix Multiplication

Multiple Choice

For Exercises 1–3, choose the correct letter.

1. Which matrix is equivalent to $-2\begin{bmatrix} 1 & 5 & -3 \\ 0 & 2 & 4 \\ 7 & -2 & 0 \end{bmatrix}$?

   Ⓐ $\begin{bmatrix} -2 & -10 & 6 \\ 0 & -4 & -8 \\ -14 & 4 & 0 \end{bmatrix}$　　Ⓒ $\begin{bmatrix} -2 & -10 & 6 \\ 0 & 2 & 4 \\ 7 & -2 & 0 \end{bmatrix}$

   Ⓑ $\begin{bmatrix} 1 & 5 & -3 \\ 0 & -4 & -8 \\ 7 & -2 & 0 \end{bmatrix}$　　Ⓓ $\begin{bmatrix} -1 & 3 & -5 \\ -2 & 0 & 2 \\ 5 & -4 & -2 \end{bmatrix}$

2. What is the product $\begin{bmatrix} 6 & -1 \\ 3 & 9 \end{bmatrix}\begin{bmatrix} 3 \\ -6 \end{bmatrix}$?

   Ⓕ $\begin{bmatrix} 18 & -3 \\ -18 & -54 \end{bmatrix}$　　Ⓖ $\begin{bmatrix} 24 & -45 \end{bmatrix}$　　Ⓗ $\begin{bmatrix} 24 \\ -45 \end{bmatrix}$　　Ⓘ $\begin{bmatrix} 15 & 36 \\ -30 & -72 \end{bmatrix}$

3. Which matrix is the solution of $\begin{bmatrix} 1 & -1 & 2 \\ 2 & 0 & -1 \end{bmatrix} - 2X = \begin{bmatrix} 4 & 5 & 6 \\ 6 & 5 & 4 \end{bmatrix}$?

   Ⓐ $\begin{bmatrix} 3 & 6 & 4 \\ 4 & 5 & 5 \end{bmatrix}$　　Ⓒ $\begin{bmatrix} \frac{3}{2} & 3 & 2 \\ 2 & \frac{5}{2} & \frac{5}{2} \end{bmatrix}$

   Ⓑ $\begin{bmatrix} -6 & -12 & -8 \\ -8 & -10 & -10 \end{bmatrix}$　　Ⓓ $\begin{bmatrix} -\frac{3}{2} & -3 & -2 \\ -2 & -\frac{5}{2} & -\frac{5}{2} \end{bmatrix}$

Extended Response

4. The table shows the number of tiles used in a house. Blue tiles cost $1.20 each, white cost $1.50 each, and green cost $.80 each. Write and solve a matrix equation to find the total cost of the tile. Show your work.

Tiles Used

	Blue	White	Green
Bath #1	20	50	10
Bath #2	15	30	5
Kitchen	25	100	50

12-3

Think About a Plan

Determinants and Inverses

Geometry Find the area of the figure to the right.

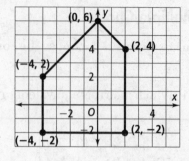

Understanding the Problem

1. You know how to find the area of what shape using matrices?

2. Can you divide the figure into these shapes? Explain.

_____
_____
_____.

3. What is the problem asking you to find?

_____
_____.

Planning the Solution

4. Divide the figure into these shapes. List the vertices of the shapes.

_____
_____.

5. Write an expression to find the area of the figure.

Getting an Answer

6. Simplify your expression to find the area of the figure.

7. Is your answer reasonable? Explain.

_____
_____.

12-3 Practice

Form K

Determinants and Inverses

Determine whether the following matrices are multiplicative inverses.

1. $\begin{bmatrix} 2 & 1 \\ 6 & 4 \end{bmatrix}$, $\begin{bmatrix} 2 & -0.5 \\ -3 & 1 \end{bmatrix}$

2. $\begin{bmatrix} 2 & -4 & 1 \\ 6 & -3 & -7 \\ 9 & 5 & -2 \end{bmatrix}$, $\begin{bmatrix} 8 & 3 & -3 \\ -9 & 2 & 7 \\ 4 & -1 & -6 \end{bmatrix}$

3. $\begin{bmatrix} 5 & 3 \\ 3 & 2 \end{bmatrix}$, $\begin{bmatrix} 2 & -3 \\ -3 & 5 \end{bmatrix}$

Evaluate the determinant of each matrix.

To start, write the formula for the determinant of a 2×2 matrix.

4. $\begin{bmatrix} 4 & 1 \\ -5 & 3 \end{bmatrix}$

5. $\begin{bmatrix} -1 & 3 & -4 \\ 6 & -2 & 8 \\ 5 & 7 & -3 \end{bmatrix}$

6. $\begin{bmatrix} 2 & 1 \\ 6 & 4 \end{bmatrix}$

7. $\begin{bmatrix} 2 & 0 & -4 \\ -1 & 3 & 2 \\ -2 & 1 & 4 \end{bmatrix}$

8. $\begin{bmatrix} -2 & -3 \\ 5 & 7 \end{bmatrix}$

9. $\begin{bmatrix} 3 & 4 & -1 \\ 1 & 8 & 3 \\ 5 & 2 & 2 \end{bmatrix}$

10. **Error Analysis** Your friend evaluated the determinant of the matrix $\begin{bmatrix} -6 & -7 \\ 3 & 2 \end{bmatrix}$ and got -9. What error did your friend make, and what is the correct determinant?

11. **Open-Ended** Write a 2×2 matrix with a determinant of zero.

12-3 Practice (continued)
Determinants and Inverses

Form K

Use matrices to find the areas of the following triangles. Express your answers in square units.

12.

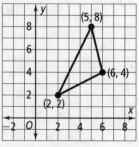

$\text{Area} = \frac{1}{2}|\det A|$

$\text{Area} = \frac{1}{2}\det\begin{bmatrix} 2 & 2 & 1 \\ 6 & 4 & 1 \\ 5 & 8 & 1 \end{bmatrix}$

$\text{Area} = \boxed{}$

13.

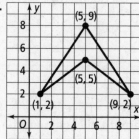

Find the inverse of each matrix, if one exists.

To start, find the determinant of the matrix.

14. $A = \begin{bmatrix} 6 & 2 \\ 2 & 1 \end{bmatrix}$

$\det A = 6(1) - 2(2) = 2$

$A^{-1} = \frac{1}{2}\begin{bmatrix} 1 & -2 \\ -2 & 6 \end{bmatrix}$

15. $A = \begin{bmatrix} 5 & 8 \\ 3 & 5 \end{bmatrix}$

16. $\begin{bmatrix} 10 & 5 \\ 4 & 2 \end{bmatrix}$

17. Your aunt's checking account number is 6143-0571-2943-3072. Use the coding

matrix $C = \begin{bmatrix} -2 & 1 \\ -1 & 3 \end{bmatrix}$ to encode the account number.

Name _____ Class _____ Date _____

12-3 Standardized Test Prep

Determinants and Inverses

Gridded Response

Solve each exercise and enter your answer in the grid provided.

1. What is the determinant of $\begin{bmatrix} 4 & -2 \\ 5 & -3 \end{bmatrix}$?

2. If $A = \begin{bmatrix} 2 & 1 \\ -9 & 3 \end{bmatrix}$, and the inverse of A is $x\begin{bmatrix} 3 & -1 \\ 9 & 2 \end{bmatrix}$, what is the value of x?

3. If $\begin{bmatrix} 6 & 2 \\ 4 & 1 \end{bmatrix}$, and $A^{-1} = \begin{bmatrix} x & 1 \\ 2 & -3 \end{bmatrix}$, what is the value of x?

4. What is the determinant of $\begin{bmatrix} 1 & 0 & 2 \\ -1 & 2 & 3 \\ 0 & 3 & 2 \end{bmatrix}$?

5. What is the area of a triangle with vertices at $(-5, 0)$, $(3, -1)$, and $(2, 6)$?

Answers

1. 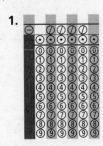 2. 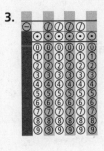 3. 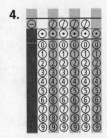 4. 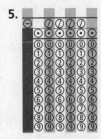 5.

12-4 Think About a Plan

Inverse Matrices and Systems

Nutrition Suppose you are making a trail mix for your friends and want to fill three 1-lb bags. Almonds cost $2.25/lb, peanuts cost $1.30/lb, and raisins cost $.90/lb. You want each bag to contain twice as much nuts as raisins by weight. If you spent $4.45, how much of each ingredient did you buy?

Know

1. I need [   ] of ingredients that cost a total of [   ].

2. _____ .

3. _____ .

Need

4. To solve the problem I need to: _____ .

Plan

5. Let x = the number of pounds of almonds, y = the number of pounds peanuts, and z = the number of pounds of raisins. Write a system of equations that solve the problem.

6. Write the system as a matrix equation.

7. Use a calculator. Solve for the variable matrix.

8. How much of each ingredient did you buy?

_____

9. How can you check your solution? Does your solution check?

_____

_____ .

12-4 Practice

Inverse Matrices and Systems

Form K

Solve each matrix equation.

To start, find the determinant of the coefficient matrix.

1. $\begin{bmatrix} 5 & 2 \\ 2 & 1 \end{bmatrix} X = \begin{bmatrix} 11 & 24 \\ 5 & 10 \end{bmatrix}$

$\det\begin{bmatrix} 5 & 2 \\ 2 & 1 \end{bmatrix} = 5(1) - 2(2) = 1$

$A^{-1} = 1\begin{bmatrix} 1 & -2 \\ -2 & 5 \end{bmatrix} = \begin{bmatrix} 1 & -2 \\ -2 & 5 \end{bmatrix}$

$\begin{bmatrix} 1 & -2 \\ -2 & 5 \end{bmatrix}\begin{bmatrix} 5 & 2 \\ 2 & 1 \end{bmatrix} = \begin{bmatrix} 1 & 0 \\ 0 & 1 \end{bmatrix}$

$X = \begin{bmatrix} 1 & -2 \\ -2 & 5 \end{bmatrix}\begin{bmatrix} 11 & 24 \\ 5 & 10 \end{bmatrix} = \boxed{}$

2. $\begin{bmatrix} 7 & 5 \\ 3 & 2 \end{bmatrix} X = \begin{bmatrix} 13 \\ 5 \end{bmatrix}$

Write each system as a matrix equation. Identify the coefficient matrix, the variable matrix, and the constant matrix.

3. $\begin{cases} 3x + y = 9 \\ 2x - 4y = -8 \end{cases}$

4. $\begin{cases} a + 4b = 13 \\ 3a + 2b = 19 \end{cases}$

5. $\begin{cases} 5x + 3y = 35 \\ 2x = 38 - 6y \end{cases}$

6. $\begin{cases} 3x + y = 9 \\ x - y + 4z = -5 \\ 3y + 2z = 7 \end{cases}$

7. $\begin{cases} 4x = 2 - 2y \\ 3y = -12 - x \end{cases}$

8. $\begin{cases} 2a - 2c = -6 - b \\ 4a = 10 + c \\ 3c = 8 - 5b \end{cases}$

315

12-4 Practice (continued)

Inverse Matrices and Systems

Solve each system of two equations using a matrix equation.

9. $\begin{cases} 3x - y = 16 \\ 5x - 9y = 12 \end{cases}$

$\begin{bmatrix} 3 & -1 \\ 5 & -9 \end{bmatrix} \begin{bmatrix} x \\ y \end{bmatrix} = \begin{bmatrix} 16 \\ 12 \end{bmatrix}$

$A^{-1} = -\dfrac{1}{22} \begin{bmatrix} -9 & 1 \\ -5 & 3 \end{bmatrix} = \begin{bmatrix} \frac{9}{22} & -\frac{1}{22} \\ \frac{5}{22} & -\frac{3}{22} \end{bmatrix}$

$\begin{bmatrix} x \\ y \end{bmatrix} = \begin{bmatrix} \frac{9}{22} & -\frac{1}{22} \\ \frac{5}{22} & -\frac{3}{22} \end{bmatrix} \begin{bmatrix} 16 \\ 12 \end{bmatrix} = \boxed{}$

10. $\begin{cases} y = 32 - 4x \\ -2x = -2 - 3y \end{cases}$

11. $\begin{cases} 3a + 4b = -3 \\ 2a + 3b = -1 \end{cases}$

12. $\begin{cases} 2b = 3a - 14 \\ 2b = -20 + 4a \end{cases}$

Solve each system of three equations using a matrix equation.

13. $\begin{cases} 3x + 5y = 19 \\ x + 3y - 4z = 1 \\ 6x + 8z = 12 \end{cases}$

14. $\begin{cases} 3b + 5c = 7 \\ 9 = a - 2c \\ 4a + 7c = 17 + b \end{cases}$

15. $\begin{cases} 6y = 8 - x \\ x + y + z = -8 \\ 7y - 3z = 32 \end{cases}$

12-4 Standardized Test Prep

Inverse Matrices and Systems

Multiple Choice

For Exercises 1–4, choose the correct letter.

1. Which matrix equation represents the system $\begin{cases} 2x - y = 11 \\ x + 3y = 2 \end{cases}$?

   A $\begin{bmatrix} x \\ y \end{bmatrix}\begin{bmatrix} 2 & -1 \\ 1 & 3 \end{bmatrix} = \begin{bmatrix} 11 \\ 2 \end{bmatrix}$ C $\begin{bmatrix} 2 & -1 \\ 1 & 3 \end{bmatrix}\begin{bmatrix} x \\ y \end{bmatrix} = \begin{bmatrix} 11 \\ 2 \end{bmatrix}$

   B $\begin{bmatrix} 2 & -1 & 11 \\ 1 & 3 & 2 \end{bmatrix} = \begin{bmatrix} x \\ y \end{bmatrix}$ D $\begin{bmatrix} 2 & -1 \\ 1 & 3 \end{bmatrix} = \begin{bmatrix} x \\ y \end{bmatrix}\begin{bmatrix} 11 \\ 2 \end{bmatrix}$

2. Let $\begin{bmatrix} 3 & 5 \\ -4 & -1 \end{bmatrix}\begin{bmatrix} x \\ y \end{bmatrix} = \begin{bmatrix} -4 \\ -6 \end{bmatrix}$. What values of x and y make the equation true?

   F $(-12, -1)$ G $(-4, -6)$ H $(-3, -20)$ I $(2, -2)$

3. Which system has a unique solution?

   A $\begin{cases} 3x - 2y = 43 \\ 9x - 6y = 40 \end{cases}$ B $\begin{cases} 6x + 8y = 16 \\ -3x - 4y = 12 \end{cases}$ C $\begin{cases} 2x - 5y = 6 \\ 4x + 7y = 12 \end{cases}$ D $\begin{cases} 4x + 2y = 10 \\ 8x + 4y = 18 \end{cases}$

4. Let $\begin{bmatrix} 5 & 1 \\ 2 & -1 \end{bmatrix}X = \begin{bmatrix} 0 \\ -14 \end{bmatrix}$. What value of X makes the equation true?

   F $\begin{bmatrix} -2 \\ 10 \end{bmatrix}$ G $\begin{bmatrix} -6 \\ -15 \end{bmatrix}$ H $\begin{bmatrix} 0 \\ 14 \end{bmatrix}$ I $\begin{bmatrix} -5 \\ 2 \end{bmatrix}$

Short Response

5. The Spirit Club sold buttons for $1, hats for $4, and t-shirts for $8. They sold 3 times as many buttons as hats. Together, the number of hats and t-shirts sold was equal to the number of buttons sold. They earned a total of $460. Write and solve a matrix equation to find how many buttons, hats, and t-shirts the club sold.

Lesson 12-4